JOHN BROWN'S
JOURNEY

ALBERT FRIED teaches history at the State University of New York at Purchase. He is widely published in magazines and journals. His books include

THE PRESCOTT CHRONICLES

A HISTORY OF THE MODERN AGE (as Julian K. Prescott)

THE JEFFERSONIAN & HAMILTONIAN TRADITIONS IN AMERICAN POLITICS

EXCEPT TO WALK FREE: Documents and Notes in the History of American Labor

SOCIALIST THOUGHT: A Documentary History (coedited by Ronald Sanders)

SOCIALISM IN AMERICA

CHARLES BOOTH'S LONDON (with Richard Elman)

Albert Fried

———◆———

JOHN BROWN'S JOURNEY

*Notes and Reflections on
His America and Mine*

———◆———

Anchor Press/Doubleday
Garden City, New York   1978

ISBN: 0-385-05511-0
Library of Congress Catalog Card Number 72–79388
Copyright © 1978 by Albert Fried
Printed in the United States of America
All Rights Reserved
First Edition

"God keep me from ever completing anything. This whole book is but a draught—nay, but the draught of a draught. Oh, Time, Strength, Cash, and Patience!"

Melville, *Moby Dick*

"You would not seek me if you had not already found me."

Augustine, *Confessions*

"The last thing we discover when writing a work is what we should put first."

Pascal, *Pensées*

FOR EDITH

Contents

List of Illustrations

Illustrations 1–7

1. John Brown, 1859
2. John Brown's birthplace
3. Owen Brown
4. Mary Ann Brown and children
5. John Brown in Kansas
6. House at North Elba
7. Hugh Forbes

Illustrations 8–17

8. William H. Leeman
9. Lewis Sheridan Leary
10. Gerrit Smith
11. Samuel Gridley Howe
12. George Luther Stearns
13. Theodore Parker
14. Thomas Wentworth Higginson
15. F. B. Sanborn
16. John A. Copeland
17. John E. Cook

Illustrations 18–24

18. Osborn P. Anderson
19. John Brown, 1858
20. Watson Brown
21. Oliver Brown
22. Owen Brown
23. Kennedy Farm
24. Harpers Ferry

Acknowledgments

My thanks to many friends for the kindnesses they showed, the help they provided in the years I spent with my vexing companion John Brown.

To Brandon Cole, Ralph Della Cava, B. J. Widick, Herbert Hill, Trudy Hayden, Palmer Singleton, Bell Chevigny, George Rawick, Steven Buttner, Judi Bloch, Derek Regin, Richard Elman, Solomon Resnik, Earl Fredericks, and Frank Randall for reading and of course criticizing the manuscript, or for conversations, however brief, which raised or settled (often both) questions of considerable moment.

To Loretta Barrett, special thanks for her extraordinary patience and understanding and for her wise suggestions, most of which I think I adopted.

Edith Fried, shrewdest of readers and critics, has some idea, I believe, of the depth of my gratitude to her.

My thanks also to institutions: to Columbia University and the New York Public Library, where I did the research, the compiling of a mammoth archive, and the writing; and to the West End Cafe on upper Broadway, whose hospitality and good cheer made a thousand discussions possible.

Foreword

This book recounts an experience that occurred in the tumultuous years of the 1960s, telling how and why I became interested in John Brown, what I learned about him and his world, what conclusions I tentatively reached about his famous adventure, his astonishing leap into history. I have attempted to chronicle an act of understanding—the making of a picture from the first sketch to the last, from the intimation of a portrait to the unfinished composition on canvas.

Part One
Portrait of the Man

Chapter One
Preliminary: A John Brown Reader

1

That day in late July began routinely enough—over coffee and the *Times* in Columbia University's John Jay cafeteria. The headline loudly announced what everyone already knew in dreadful detail: Thirty-six people were dead in the battle of Detroit, the black section a gutted province occupied by federal troops. Though large-scale violence and disorder had been our daily fare for years, the Detroit riot threw us badly. Detroit was our glowing exemplar of American plural democracy, the place where great institutions— the United Auto Workers, General Motors and Ford and Chrysler, the federal, state, and local governments—had collaborated to produce social peace, even solidarity, between blacks and whites, ethnic and native workers. We were proud of Detroit.

And so we recoiled in despair from yet another blow. We wondered how many more we could take before we ourselves reached the breaking point. The Cuban Missile Crisis had come and gone in a fury, leaving the stench of death in its wake. President Kennedy's assassination was a monstrous prevision of the violence that lay in store for us. Cruelest of all was the Vietnam War, unleashed by a liberal Democratic regime—*our* regime—only months after its leader and master strategist, President Lyndon B. Johnson, had won a smashing victory because he'd sworn on his honor and all he held sacred that he'd never plunge us into armed conflict in Southeast Asia, never "shoot from the hip." And now the anger of the black urban proletariat was bursting the last integuments of restraint. The ghetto uprisings of a few years before (especially in Watts and Harlem) had been trifles compared to what we were witnessing then in the summer of 1967. It was as though the terror we were inflicting abroad was being paid back to us in kind, in our own cities and neighborhoods. The apocalypse wasn't that far away.

While pondering this chronicle of recent horrors I overheard two black students at a nearby table.

"The only good white's a dead white," one of them said.

"Yeah," said the other, "except John Brown. He was the only good white this country's ever had."

"And they killed him pretty quick."

That kind of obscene talk, however, no longer shocked us. We dealt with it in the accustomed way, by passing it off as the manifestation of rage, as a psychological condition. White liberals had no other way of coming to terms with these apostles of black nationalism and separatism, with the Stokely Carmichaels and Malcolm X's of the world. By reducing their unpalatable statements or programs to an emotion, we could at once reject them as misguided and wrongheaded and still maintain our sympathy for them. We understood why they felt as they did. We could applaud Martin Luther King and patronize the militants.

But I thought about what the two students had said. Why John Brown alone? They must have known about Garrison and Sumner and Thaddeus Stevens and Thomas Wentworth Higginson, among other well-known radical abolitionists of the Civil War era, about the Quakers who fought against slavery when no one else did, about the whites who in our own day sat-in at Southern lunch counters and bus stations and were beaten and jailed side by side with their black comrades, who died in Mississippi and Alabama and Georgia at the hands of the Ku Klux Klan. So why John Brown? Was it because he was an armed avenger who had no compunction against taking the lives of others, no fear of losing his own? Did they see him as a harbinger (white at that) of the Armageddon that they, the blacks, would visit on America?

These thoughts were on my mind as I left the cafeteria for Burgess Library where I was researching the utopian communities of the nineteenth century as part of a broader study of socialism in America. It occurred to me that many of these utopians were John Brown's contemporaries and like him deviants from the conventional norm. But I knew little about him.

I therefore counted it providential to notice lying on a pile of books at the end of my library table *A John Brown Reader,* edited by Louis Ruchames, a scholar (as I subsequently learned) in the field of American abolitionism. I took it to my seat to sample it before getting on with my work-in-progress. (I couldn't afford to dally long in the Elysium of idle curiosity: A living had to be made for a family of three. The socialist project was itself an indulgence—I hadn't yet found a publisher for it—and I would soon have to return to hack writing, the chains of my thralldom.)

I opened *A John Brown Reader* to the frontispiece, a photograph or daguerreotype of Brown taken a few months before Harpers Ferry.* A well-known picture: I'd seen it often. Now I looked at it carefully for the first time. Another image suddenly came into focus. John Brown was standing with gun in hand, lean and gaunt and defiant, his white hair and beard in wild disarray, his eyes bent to heaven. Around him hung a pall of smoke, the aftermath of battle. At his feet lay his dead or wounded sons and a host of swaying, moaning, supplicating blacks. It was a terrifying image, sculpted on my memory like a frieze, all that remained of a movie I'd once seen about him (or did he merely figure in it?) when I was about eight or nine. It was my introduction to John Brown.

I didn't easily get over the chiliastic impression conveyed by the movie. As I grew up I learned how and where to place John Brown in the scheme of American history. I learned a morality tale. It went more or less as follows:

In the early 1830s a tiny band of abolitionists demanded the immediate and unconditional emancipation of the slaves. Like early Christian martyrs they were vilified, spat on, beaten, even murdered. But within ten years abolitionism was a crusade numbering thousands. It was forming parties, affecting national elections. Then, in the 1850s the antislavery Republican party arose, a mighty cataract that swept everything before it and under Lincoln took national power. Finally, the consummatory act: the holocaust of war, the emancipation of the slaves, the vindication of the abolitionists, the rebirth of America.

And this I learned too in the course of my education: Just as

* It is in fact a slightly touched up reproduction of the original, shown opposite page 80 of this book, made in New York City in early June 1859.

other great movements produced their aberrations, so abolitionism
produced John Brown. He disrupted the even, measured flow of
history, breaking the delicate balance between means and ends,
committing crimes for which he and his family paid dearly. In
sum, a fanatic who scrupled at nothing to advance his purpose,
laudable as it might be.

Studying the photograph in Burgess Library that morning, I
tried to suspend my judgments of Brown. I tried to bracket them
out, neutralize them. If I knew nothing about this man, I asked
myself, what impressions would I have of him? (I realized of
course that the very act of interrogating myself this way presup-
posed a set of prior assumptions. Why, after all, the interest in the
photograph? Why bother to pick up a *A John Brown Reader?*) I
saw before me not the John Brown I'd grown up with but a solid,
equable citizen of his time, well groomed and dressed, self-assured,
a businessman and church elder perhaps, certainly a dutiful paterfamilias and member of his community. A striking contrast between the historical personage I took for granted and the man
presented to me in the picture.

2

Borne along by my curiosity I spent part of that summer day
casually going through *A John Brown Reader,* stopping at random, occasionally pursuing a line of inquiry, absorbing such contents as I cared to. The book is an interesting potpourri: a generous representation of Brown's own writings, the testimony of
people who knew him, and comments on his work by famous men
—all in all amounting to an unabashed apologia, often hyperbolic
in the claims it makes for Brown. ("The purpose of this volume,"
Editor Ruchames writes, "is not . . . the examination of all that
has been written about John Brown, whether pro or con, or its
evaluation from the point of view of historical accuracy. It is intended, rather, to present the positive impact of John Brown upon
American thought, viewing his life and death as events which
evoked great idealism as well as some of the most memorable

writing in the history of American letters.") But I could abide this minor vice of overpraise.

In his brief biographical sketch Ruchames defends Brown from the charge of insanity, the entrails of his legacy. On the subject of slavery, he says, Brown differed scarcely at all from the likes of Garrison, Wendell Phillips, Lydia Maria Child, Theodore Parker, among other celebrated abolotionists. They also "devoted their lives to the anti-slavery cause, suffered hardships and privations for its sake, and at various times were also accused of being fanatic and insane on the subject on slavery." But hard as he tries Ruchames can't diminish the enormous fact that none of these respectable New Englanders did what Brown did: He organized and led an armed uprising, he died on the gallows, he became a legend. He, not they, was guilty of murderous deeds for the accomplishment of no clearly articulated objective. On the face of it the charge against Brown might just be valid.

Ruchames refers in passing to two famous historians—Allan Nevins and C. Vann Woodward—who most recently "have emphasized the case for John Brown's insanity." Taking up the lead, I promptly consulted the books in question: Nevins's multivolume *Ordeal of the Union* and *The Emergence of Lincoln* and *America in Crisis,* an anthology (edited by Daniel Aaron) which contains Woodward's essay "John Brown's Private War." I respected Nevins's and Woodward's work and believed their views on American history to be pretty close to mine. Could they both be wrong about Brown?

Years before, I'd read *Ordeal of the Union* and *The Emergence of Lincoln.* I remembered liking the rolling, cadenced narrative, the rich detail, the ripeness of judgment, the Republican, antislavery bias underlying the whole work. Here was history writing on a magisterial scale, a theme worthy of a master's skill; Nevins was the Macaulay of his profession. As to his appraisal of Brown —I recalled nothing. At the time, I'd found nothing objectionable in it.

The second volume of *Ordeal of the Union* beautifully describes the bloody conflict between the Free State and proslavery parties for control of the Kansas Territory. Kansas was where Brown first

made his name. Nevins holds him responsible for escalating a war
that would claim many lives—Brown and his guerrillas alone took
a fair number—before it ran its course. Here is Nevins's assess-
ment of Brown: "A taint of insanity had marked Brown's family
history; his mother and grandmother had died insane, while a maternal mother and three maternal uncles suffered from the same
malady. . . . John Brown, brought up with little education, for he
disliked school, followed his father in wandering widely, experi-
menting unsuccessfully with many vocations and begetting a large
family—by two wives he had twenty children."

A recitation follows of Brown's failures, lawsuits, bankruptcy,
incessant movement back and forth across the American landscape. And the ultimate reproach: "he could not even make a living." He was "a restless trader, always looking for new deals, and
with a missionary's belief that some spectacular transaction would
yet make his fortune." There was something demonstrably wrong
with Brown, something unstable and defective in his character.
This explains his conduct in Kansas. "He was ignorant, narrow-
minded, fanatically prejudiced on many issues, highly tenacious, a
thoroughly selfish egoist, ready to commit acts that others would
term unscrupulous and to justify them by devious psychological
processes, and a man with a vein of hard cruelty."

Three years later, in the second volume of *The Emergence of
Lincoln* (the chapter on the Harpers Ferry raid), Nevins finds
room for a more sympathetic portrayal. Brown, he admits, "was
no ordinary man. All who saw him, whether friends or foes, were
struck by his iron will, his consuming inner fire, and his intense
though erratic devotion to causes outside himself. Great as were
his faults, he united a certain elevation of character with the traits
of a born leader. His intimates—members of his family, em-
ployees, his picked Kansas band, the eastern conspirators soon to
befriend him in a desperate venture—regarded him with deferen-
tial admiration."

But then Nevins returns to the insanity theme, calling it this
time a tendency toward monomania. "Endowed with a narrow, intense, dogmatic mind, he fastened upon one subject with a fervor
which shut out all other considerations. But how early did this
tendency appear? Was it upon slavery alone that he was a
monomaniac? If so, we might doubt the analysis, for by 1860 the

country had a multitude of monomaniacs upon slavery. But evidence appears of inordinate preoccupation with one topic after another before he turned to slavery. He was subject to extravagant religious fixations. In 1852, worried because his son John did not exhibit piety, he spent an entire month writing a letter of pamphlet length to him, composed largely of scriptural quotations. We might question the sanity of a nearly penniless man with a large family who devotes a month to such an exhortation—which proved futile."

Nevins, a persuasive writer, builds a powerful case against Brown. How does he prove it? Where is his evidence for insanity in the family? For the "monomania?" According to Ruchames, the evidence is suspect to say the least. Nevins fails to say—one would expect such a scrupulous scholar at least to allude to it— that the information on insanity came either from affidavits written after Brown's conviction or from people who reminisced about him long after his death.† Nothing in Nevins's account indicates that any of Brown's contemporaries (before Harpers Ferry, that is) thought him insane or abnormal.‡

Ruchames also nicely disposes of Nevins's devastating example of Brown's "monomania"—the "pamphlet length" letter on religious piety, a careful reading of which "reveals the very opposite of what Prof. Nevins believes it to prove." Brown, it turns out, didn't spend a month writing it, as Nevins claims. The month in question refers to the interval between the time Brown started it and resumed it. To quote Brown himself: "It is now nearly a month since I began on another page. I did mean that my letter

† "Putting aside the basic question of whether one's insanity may be established by the presence or absence of insanity in one's family," Ruchames writes, "it may be noted that the affidavits were highly suspect as valid evidence. Their primary purpose was to save Brown from execution by showing him to be insane. They must, therefore, be regarded not as objective reports but as partisan statements made to achieve a certain purpose. . . . Moreover, their reliability as evidence is weakened still further by the fact that they include significant sections which are based, quite explicitly, not on direct knowledge but on hearsay and secondhand information."

‡ "Finally," Ruchames correctly points out, "perhaps the most important evidence as to the nature of John Brown's mind and character is to be found in the devotion to him of the twenty-one young men—intelligent, able and high-minded—who lived with him and knew him as a leader and friend, and who followed him even unto death."

should go off at once, but I have not become very stout, and I
have a great deal to look after, and have had many interruptions.
We have done part of our sowing, and expect to get all our corn
(of which we have a good crop) secure from frost this day." Etc.

As far as I was concerned the case for insanity or monomania
was unproved.*

I reflected for some time on what I'd just read. Gradually,
Nevins's approach to John Brown became clear to me. Implicitly
Nevins was saying that slavery was an institution toward which
one should *not* have been violently monomaniacal. In effect he
was asserting a value judgment, a moral position: that is, condemning Brown's acts as undesirable and wrong. But in doing so he
was shifting the discussion from the moral plane—where he and
Brown are equal, his judgment of slavery versus Brown's—to the
clinical plane, thereby reducing Brown to a victim of compulsions
and aberrations, lacking a grasp of reality. By indicting Brown's
whole personality, by tracing the alleged pattern of pathology
back to childhood and across generations, Nevins was explaining
away a significant historical event (on which by the by he spends
many pages), trivializing it, rendering it innocuous.

I read C. Vann Woodward's essay hoping for something better.
I thought highly of Woodward. I learned much from his books
(those I'd read: *Tom Watson, The Rise of the New South, The
Strange Career of Jim Crow*) and saw him as a Southern liberal in
the tradition of Frank Graham and Hugo Black and Estes
Kefauver and W. J. Cash, for whom the inveterate racism of the
region has always operated to the advantage of the Bourbon
classes and the detriment of the poor, white no less than black.
Woodward amply demonstrated (it had come as a revelation to
me years earlier) that a white-black lower-class alliance once
tenuously existed in the South and that its failure in the 1890s led
to the malignant forms of racism so characteristic of American life

* Nevins cites no particular evidence, only "testimony from many sources
relating to Brown's insanity." He also relies on two books in the field
(Charles Berg's *Clinical Psychology* and Edward H. Williams's *Doctor in
Court*), neither exactly authoritative, and on two doctors who privately advised him on psychopathological matters.

down to the 1960s. Could such an alliance arise again? He gave one reason to hope.

All the more disappointing then is his appraisal of Brown. It hardly differs from Nevins's. The allegation that Brown's family on his mother's side had a streak of insanity is elaborated at length, the evidence again consisting of affidavits submitted after Brown's trial for treason and accepted uncritically. And like Nevins, Woodward fails to note the time and circumstances of the evidence on which his judgments depend.† Insanity provides the explanatory motif for the rest of the essay, and much is made of Brown's instability, failures, litigations, etc. This is supposed to help us understand why Brown was a fanatic, an extremist, an incendiary, who exacerbated sectional differences already at the breaking point.

For Woodward assumes that slavery constituted a norm, legitimized and protected by the law of the land. To have sought its violent extirpation, as Brown did, meant taking the law into one's own hands. His "code of political methods and morals," Woodward writes, was "at odds with the Anglo-American tradition." Brown's solution was quite simple. "It is set forth in the preamble of his Provisional Constitution of the United States, which declares that in reality slavery is an 'unjustifiable War of one portion of its citizens upon another.' War, in which all is fair, amounted to a suspension of ethical restraints. This type of reasoning is identical with that of the revolutionaries who hold that the class struggle is in reality a class war. The assumption naturally facilitates the justification of deeds otherwise unjustifiable."

Woodward's statement surprised me. What objection could he

---

† "By accepting the affidavits at their face value," Ruchames writes, "Professor Vann Woodward, though a very careful historian, is led into committing serious errors. He states, for instance, that one of Brown's brothers was insane. This assertion is made in only one of the affidavits and is not substantiated by any evidence. The brother referred to was the editor of the New Orleans *Bee* and a prominent figure in New Orleans public affairs. All that we know of him indicates that he was quite sane. Prof. Vann Woodward also asserts that Brown's mother, grandmother, sister and sister's daughter were insane. Family letters and other records cast doubt upon that part of the assertion to refer to the grandmother and sister's daughter, while a careful reading of the affidavits themselves fail to reveal any reference to the insanity of Brown's mother. All available evidence affirms her sanity."

possibly have, I wondered, to Brown's contention that slavery is an "unjustifiable War of one portion of its citizens upon another"? And I also wondered how Woodward defined "the Anglo-American tradition" with which Brown was ostensibly at odds. To me that tradition rests solidly on the social contract theory (the product of three great Anglo-American revolutions) which categorically announced that slavery precisely was a state of unjustifiable warfare of the strong over the weak, a lawless state, the slave possessing the natural right to rebel. The framers of the Declaration and the Constitution were vigorous apostles of the social contract theory and loathed slavery and said so repeatedly, none more vehemently than the slaveholders themselves. Why they failed to act on their principles is another matter, part of the tragedy of America. But John Brown did act on them, and in that sense, far from being at odds with "the Anglo-American tradition"—applying Woodward's own criterion—he upheld and renewed it.

Woodward's main point is that Brown played into the hands of his Southern counterparts, the extremes inadvertently collaborating to destroy the vital center of American democracy, the fabric that held the country together. "Southern zealots had no better ally than John Brown. Rhett, Ruffin, and Yancey all rejoiced over the effect of Harper's Ferry." For among other things it "aroused Virginia from her hesitant neutrality and started her on the road to secession."

I thought Woodward's reasoning here pretty far off base. I'd learned to suspect any argument that ascribes great and terrible events, powerful historical movements, to the agitation of "extremists." And in fact that argument Woodward himself demolishes. Long before John Brown arrived on the scene, he explains, the ante-bellum South had been moving steadily toward isolation, separatism, conflict. "The South's insecurity was heightened by having to defend against counterattacks an institution it knew to be discredited throughout the civilized world and of which Southerners had once been among the severest critics. Its reaction was to withdraw increasingly from contact with the offending world, to retreat into an isolation of spirit, and to attempt by curtailing freedom of speech to avoid criticism. . . .

"One of the South's tensions sprang from a lack of internal security—the fear of servile insurrection. By the nature of things a slave uprising had to be secret, sudden, and extremely bloody, sparing neither men, women, nor children. The few occurrences of this kind had left a deep trauma in the mind of the people. The pathological character of this tension was manifested in periodic waves of panic based on rumor. It is significant that two of the most severe panics of this sort occurred in the years 1856 and 1860, and were accompanied by charges that abolitionists from the North were fomenting uprisings. Harper's Ferry was therefore a blow at the most sensitive area of Southern consciousness."

Fair enough. But then why the furor over John Brown? If the condition was so extreme, why the particular condemnation of *his* "extremism"? Why reprove him?

3

My interest sharply whetted, I returned to *A John Brown Reader*. I wanted to read Brown's own writings, few of which Nevins and Woodward quote except as foils for their criticisms. Here again, judging from his personal and business letters over a twenty-five-year period, I encountered a different person from the one depicted by the historians. Here was a rational, intelligent, responsible man who had few illusions about himself, who showed a keen understanding of his situation, who courageously swallowed the bitter draughts of suffering and pain that life measured out to him.

Most moving of all were his letters from the Charlestown, Virginia, jail where he awaited his end. He was able in these writings to articulate his hopes and compassions with scriptural eloquence, calling to mind the best of Lincoln's prose.

I had once or twice read Brown's last speech to the court, certainly his most famous piece of writing, but could hardly remember a thing about it, only my own guarded feelings of pity. I now read it with some emotion. "Had I interfered with slavery," he said, "in the manner which I admit and which I admit has been fairly proved (for I admire the truthfulness and candor of the greater portion of the witnesses who have testified in this case),— had I so interfered in behalf of the rich, the powerful, the intelligent, the so-called great, or in behalf of any of their friends,—

either father, mother, brother, sister, wife, or children, or any of
that class,—and suffered and sacrificed what I have in this interference, it would have been all right; and every man in this court
would have deemed it an act worthy of reward rather than punishment.

"This court acknowledges, as I suppose, the validity of the laws
of God. I see a book here which I suppose to be the Bible, or at
least the New Testament. That teaches us that all things whatsoever I would that men should do unto me, I should do even so to
them. It teaches me, further, to 'remember them that are in bonds,
as bound with them.' I endeavored to act up to that instruction. I
say, I am yet too young to understand that God is any respecter of
persons. I believe that to have interfered as I have done—as I
have always freely admitted I have done—in behalf of His
despised poor, was not wrong, but right. Now, if it is deemed necessary that I should forfeit my life for the furtherance of the ends
of justice, and mingle my blood further with the blood of my children and with the blood of millions in this slave country whose
rights are disregarded by wicked, cruel, and unjust enactments,—I
submit; so let it be done!"‡

He wrote to his family soon after: "Remember, dear wife and
children all, that Jesus of Nazareth suffered a most excruciating
death on the cross as a felon, under the most aggravating circumstances. Think also of the prophets and apostles and Christians of
former days, who went through greater tribulations than you or I,
and try to be reconciled. May God Almighty comfort all your
hearts, and soon wipe away all tears from your eyes! To Him be
endless praise! Think, too, of the crushed millions who 'have no
comforter.' I charge you all never in your trials to forget the grief
'of the poor that cry, and of those that have none to help them.' "

And to a friend four days before his death: "The great bulk of
mankind estimate each other's actions *and motives* by the measure
of success or *otherwise* that attends them through life. By that rule
I have been one of the *worst* and one of the *best* of men. I *do* not
claim to have been one of the *latter;* and I leave it to an impartial
tribunal to decide whether the world has been the *worse* or the
better of my *living* and *dying* in it. My present great anxiety is to

‡ I have taken the liberty of editing Brown's writings where necessary for
punctuation and spelling. Nothing else has been changed, added, or omitted.

get as near in readiness for a different field of action as I well can. . . . I have enjoyed *remarkable cheerfulness and composure of mind* ever since my confinement; and it is a greater comfort to *feel assured* that *I am permitted* to die (for a cause) not *merely* to pay a debt of nature (as all must). I feel myself to be *most* unworthy of so *great* distinction."

He asked Virginia officials to spare him "from having any *mock or hypocritical prayers made over me* when I am publicly *murdered:* and that my only *religious attendants* be poor *little, dirty, ragged, bare headed,* and *barefooted* slave boys and girls, led by some old *grey headed Slave Mother.*"

And his final prophetic message, the day of his hanging: "I John Brown am now quite *certain* that the crimes of this *guilty* land will never be purged away but with blood. I had *as I now think vainly* flattered myself that without *very much* bloodshed it might be done."

Now, Nevins and Woodward concede Brown's heroism but are hardly carried away by the pathos of his condition, the poignancy of his words. They see him acting out the martyr's role for all it was worth, wringing from a credulous, inflamed public as much pity and sympathy as he could get, while artfully concealing the violence of *his* past, the crimes *he* committed. Woodward calls him "a genius of self-justification." His "letters and his famous speech at the trial constructed for the hero a new set of motives and plans a new role. For Brown had changed roles." And Nevins writes: "John Brown, no doubt partly self-deluded, was striking the pose of a blameless as well as heroic figure for the benefit of his unseen audience of Northern millions. If he could not be the Spartacus of a new freedmen's state, he could be the martyred Stephen of a new gospel."

It seemed to me, however, that even if the historians were correct, even if Brown, lying wounded in Charlestown prison, was striking a pose, justifying himself to the world—what of it? He *was* a martyr, whatever else he might have been, and he had a right—nay, an obligation—to exploit the circumstances of his impending death, the drama, the passion, the tension it evoked, to advance the cause of militant abolitionism just as Christ and his votaries (to carry the comparison no further) exploited *his* death for Christianity.

By now *A John Brown Reader* had served its purpose. My curiosity assuaged (or so I believed), I left Burgess Library for home expecting to return the next day to my work-in-progress.

4

The next day came, so did the day after, but socialism in America lay moribund on my desk. I couldn't yoke my thoughts to their assigned task. They kept returning to John Brown. I even found myself going over passages of the *Reader* and resurrecting the controversies I'd had with the historians, a minor tempest to be sure.

At length, a decision crystallized: I would devote two or three weeks, no longer, to a study of John Brown's life, a reading of the available literature. Would this be a waste of precious substance? A flight from dull commitments? Further procrastination? No matter. The project would, after all, take no more than a few weeks, and by then I'd be done with John Brown once and for all.

Chapter Two
Reacquaintance

1

Before embarking on the project I thought I would do well to go over Ruchames's *Reader* again, this time very carefully, very intensively, nailing down the essential biographical facts, taking notes as I went along. (For future reference? A book in the making? Perhaps. No doubt intentions were lurking beneath intentions.) I wanted to become acquainted with John Brown directly, without intermediaries, through his own writings and those of his contemporaries. The *Reader* would serve my purpose well enough.

———◆———

The first document is an extraordinary autobiographical memoir, the only source we have for Brown's early years. He wrote it at the age of fifty-seven, during a pause in his guerrilla campaign, from a place called Red Rock, Iowa, across the border from the Nebraska Territory. Some months before, he had promised a twelve-year-old admirer of his, Henry Luther Stearns, son of a wealthy Boston abolitionist who was supporting Brown's efforts in Kansas, that he would tell about his own youth when he had the chance.

(Young Stearns later remembered the scene: "On Sunday, January 4th, 1857 John Brown came to our house to consult with my father and mother about the troubles in Kansas. . . . I was touched by what he said about the sufferings of the little children there. When he was about to take his leave, I went to my father and in a whisper asked him if I could give what pocket money I had to Captain Brown. . . . I took it to John Brown and said, 'Will you please buy something with this for some poor little boys in Kansas?' He patted me on the head and replied: 'I will, my son, and God bless you for your kind heart.' Then I said: 'Captain Brown, will you sometime write me a letter and tell me what sort of little boy you were?' He smiled and said that he would when he could spare the time.")

The letter is John Brown's version of his Pilgrim's Progress, his struggle to become a Christian. He hopes it will help Henry Luther Stearns avoid the "follies and errors" of "a certain boy of my acquaintance" named John.

Brown quickly disposes of the vital details of his birth and genealogy. He was born on May 9, 1800, in Terrington, Connecticut, of "poor but respectable" parents, a descendant, he claims, of *Mayflower* stock (this Ruchames questions). Both grandfathers served in the Revolution; one, his namesake, gave his life to it.

From his earliest memories, he's at some pains to point out, John was locked in mortal combat with one temptation after another. There was the temptation of the forests surrounding the frontier township of Hudson, Ohio, to which his family had come in 1805. He "used to hang about" with the local Indians "quite as much as was consistent with good manners, and learned a trifle of their talk." He was also "quite a rambler in the wild new country, finding birds and squirrels and sometimes a wild turkey's nest." From his father he learned how to dress skins, "so that he could at any time dress his own leather such as squirrel, raccoon, cat, wolf, or dog skin." But he had to suppress these pleasures. He could no longer lose his self "in the wilderness filled with wild beasts and Indians." He had to be trained "in the school of adversity."

Then there was the temptation of things, possessions, the desire for "earthly treasure." "When John was in his sixth year a poor Indian boy gave him a yellow marble, the first he had ever seen. This he thought a great deal of and kept it a good while, but at last he lost it beyond recovery. It took years to heal the wound." Soon after he found and tamed a wild bobtail squirrel. Yet this pet, which he "almost idolized," was lost too, and "for a year or

two John was in mourning and looking at all squirrels he could
see to try and discover bobtail if possible." John owned a little
ewe lamb which suddenly died when nearly grown; "this brought
another protracted mourning season . . . so strong and earnest
were his attachments." All the more reason why he required a
"much needed course of discipline," why he had to learn the hard
way "that the Heavenly Father sees it best to take all the little
things out of his hands which he has ever placed in them."

These "sore trials" were necessary and right, especially since he
acquired the habit of telling lies to "screen himself," as he puts it,
"from blame or punishment"; he "could not well endure to be
reproached."

We have a faint idea from his letter of how severely his parents
did punish him for his transgressions: One day he stole some
brass pins belonging to a girl who was staying with the Browns;
his mother found out and, "after having a full day to think of the
wrong received from her a thorough whipping." Here then was
double punishment: the whipping and the anticipation of it.
Reassessing matters in his old age, Brown is forced to admit that
the beatings and the fear of them were ineffective in driving the
devil out of him and that if he had been "oftener encouraged to be
entirely frank, by making frankness a kind of atonement for some
of his faults he would not have been so often guilty of this fault,
nor have been obliged to struggle so long in after life with so
mean a habit." (This truism Brown didn't learn until after he'd
reared his own children and had meted out *his* share of punishment, establishing through pain and suffering his bond of solidarity with generations past.)

John was becoming disciplined in the ways of Christianity, and
like the hero of Bunyan's epic he was going to test himself at the
earliest moment out in the world, where wickedness and redemption competed for mastery. He always disliked the "confinements
and restraints of school" (preferring rather "to wrestle and snow
ball and run and jump and knock off old seely wool hats"), and
by the age of twelve he was working for his father, driving cattle
through the forests. And while he "did not become much of a
scholar," he did enjoy reading history and other subjects. The
Bible he knew backward and forward, memorizing every word, its

literal truth burned into his soul. Self-education was what the
remorseless school of adversity demanded of its pupils.

John was winning out in his war against lowly pleasures and
false hopes. He "never attemped to dance in his life; nor did he
ever learn to know one of a pack of cards from another." At an
early age he was drawn not to other youths but to "the company
and conversation of old and intelligent persons." Brown makes
much of his maturity, his attraction for adults with whom he
talked about serious subjects, particularly about the "lives of
great, wise, and good men."

Brown returns to one theme repeatedly, insistently: his calling.
When he was quite young, he asserts, "he became ambitious to
excel in . . . anything he undertook to perform." John "followed
up with tenacity whatever he set about so long as it answered his
general purpose, and hence he rarely failed in some degree to
effect the thing he undertook." There may be some posturing and
exaggeration here. He in fact failed in every one of his numerous
business ventures and was still heavily in debt when he penned the
letter. But then again he may have regarded those failures as
unimportant: They weren't undertakings in the sense that he
means them. For he goes on to advise Henry Stearns that one
should avoid drifting or responding to chance and contingency,
that one should commit oneself to "some definite plan" in life.
"Many seem to have none, and others never stick to any that they
do form." Brown's words convey the impression that he is carrying out such a commitment. He's doing battle with the slave empire.

Now, that commitment, he says, germinated in his mind when
he was about twelve. During the War of 1812, he recalls, while
leading his father's cattle through the forests he stayed briefly at
the home "of a very gentlemanly landlord." This landlord happened to own a slave boy whom Brown describes as "very active,
intelligent and good feeling" and to whom he owed much "for
numerous little acts of kindness." The contrast between his lot
and the slave's disturbed him. The landlord admired John's
precocity and "made a great pet of him." But the slave boy, "who
was fully if not more than his equal," was "badly clothed, poorly
fed, and lodged in cold weather." And he was "beaten before his
eyes with iron shovels or any other thing that came first to hand."

And so in his youth, as a result of this experience, Brown reflected "on the wretched, hopeless condition of fatherless and motherless slave children" and asked himself, "Is God their father?"

This incident, he says, was etched on his conscience. It converted him to "a most determined abolitionist" and "led him to declare or swear eternal war with slavery."

We might be skeptical. Brown was at war with slavery when he wrote about the incident, and he could have imagined making such a vow in his youth, forty-five years earlier. His own word is the only proof we have.

But if the incident did have this transforming effect on him, it would have been consistent with his character as he portrays it in his memoir. Can we doubt that John had internalized the values of his parents and community? He was already an exemplary Calvinist: His transcendent self, his superego (except for lapses here and there), was decidedly in charge of him, and we can assume that he responded indignantly to a crime against the divine order of things whenever he encountered it. (He tells us, for example, how the War of 1812 left its impress on him. What he witnessed "was so far to disgust him with military affairs that he would neither train or drill but paid fines and got along like a Quaker until his age finally cleared him of military duty." Only "the sum of all iniquities" would cause him to abandon his self-imposed injunction against ever bearing arms.)

By the age of fifteen John was ready "to perform the full labor of a man." He was a tanner and currier now, the trade he learned from his father. He was so dutiful and conscientious his father appointed him foreman of the family establishment and keeper and cook of its bachelor quarters (learning virtues by the way that would stand him in good stead later on). But as always the serpent was busy. Precisely Brown's success cultivated the sin of pride, "and he came forward to manhood full of self-conceit. . . . The habit so early formed of being obeyed rendered him in after life too much disposed to speak in an imperious or dictatory way."

We would expect an adolescent like Brown to have been shy and uncomfortable in society, especially with girls—and he was. His "extreme bashfulness" has continued to bother him, he admits, the more so since he's been so "naturally fond" of women.

In an interesting passage he attributes his difficulties with them to the death of his mother when he was eight. It was a devastating blow. His "loss was complete and permanent," and he "pined after" her for many years. And though he admired his stepmother as a "sensible, intelligent," and "estimable woman" he "never adopted her in feeling." The substitute of another woman for his mother "operated very unfavorably upon him," somehow depriving him "of a suitable connecting link between the different senses, the want of which might under some circumstances have proved his ruin." What circumstance is he referring to? He doesn't tell us, and given the scant information about his early life it would be foolhardly to speculate on what he means. Yet this much can be inferred. His mother's death inflicted a deep psychic wound on him, and he's aware of it. If she'd lived, he seems to say, he might have been less rigid, less driven, less obsessive, than he was; he might have been more at peace with himself and the world.

John needed to take one final step if he was to win his manhood and independence. Shortly after turning twenty he married Dianthe Lusk, a "remarkably plain" woman, in his words, "but neat, industrious and economical," of "excellent character, earnest piety, and good practical common sense." Brown appreciated her most for her help in mollifying his disposition, her ability to tame him and correct his more egregious faults. Her "kind admonitions," he writes, "generally had the right effect, without arousing his haughty, obstinate temper." John had incorporated his wife into his superego; she was the soft, fragile reproach of his better angel, an invaluable helpmeet in the great contest between his hostile selves.

Brown abruptly breaks off his letter, promising Henry Luther Stearns that he might be "tempted" someday to write more on his "after life or manhood." But if the temptation ever moved him, he never acted on it. Posterity's misfortune.

———◆———

I couldn't help wondering as I read John Brown's memoir if he typified his time and place and community. Or if he reflected his neighbor's values *in extremis,* exaggerating a common type. Or

again if he was unique, idiosyncratic, anomalous, a *tertium quid*.
To answer these questions I would, of course, need to know more
about northern Ohio, Hudson Township, his family, the particular
influences on his life. Ruchames has next to nothing on Brown's
father and mother and the milieu he grew up in. His biographers,
I thought, would fill in the interstices of my ignorance.

(Of this much I was certain: Young John Brown was no one I
could have recognized on the landscape of my past, my youth.
Had I grown up in white Protestant America rather than Ben-
sonhurst, Brooklyn, I might have understood him better than I
did. Yes, I've come to know white Protestants, many of them,
some quite well, but they seem to bear no resemblance to him.
They were either intellectuals and professionals who'd broken
with the style of their distant forebears [if not their parents] or
desiccated ministerial types or working-class stiffs [encountered
mostly in the Army]. The world that had shaped Brown's youth
more than a century ago was now a cracked and weathered arti-
fact found only in the museum of antiquities. Could my impressions of him, then, be necessarily shallower than anyone else's,
however privileged their backgrounds or ethnic credentials?)

2

A litany of suffering, the travails of Job. This was my reading of
Brown's family and business life as described and documented in
the *Reader*. The school of adversity inflicts excruciating pain. But
Brown absorbs it all and perseveres—a remarkable feat, a miracle
of character.

At first he does fairly well. He sets up a tannery in Hudson and
has three healthy boys. Then, in 1826, for no apparent reason, he
moves to a town in northwestern Pennsylvania, Randolph (today
New Richmond). He builds a house, a barn (with a room for runaway slaves), and a tannery on land he has cleared himself. Soon
he becomes a prominent member of the community: a church and
school official, a postmaster, a respected employer. He's on the
verge of worldly success.

Twice serious misfortune strikes during the Browns' stay in

Randolph. In 1831 the fourth of his children, Frederick, dies at
the age of four. The following year his wife dies along with an infant son born a few days before. "We are again smarting under
the rod of our Heavenly Father," he writes. "Last night, about
eleven o'clock, my affectionate, dutiful and faithful Dianthe (to
use her own words) bade 'farewell to earth.' "

And so like his mother Brown's wife succumbed to the rigors of
pioneer life. The American myth celebrates frontier women for
their strength and resourcefulness, models of quiet heroism. But
it's a self-reinforcing myth: Only the strong and resourceful and
heroic among them survived. Natural selection, ruthlessly applied,
governed the American wilderness. Brown's experience, losing his
mother in his youth and his wife in early manhood, couldn't have
been uncommon. And that question too I thought worth exploring
someday. Maybe Dickens's unforgettable description of the frontier in *Martin Chuzzlewit* isn't as far-fetched as it appears. A
charnel house disguised as nature.

Brown, naturally, doesn't remain a widower for long, not with
five young children on his hands. A year after burying Dianthe he
marries a blacksmith's daughter, Mary Ann Day. It's she who fits
the stereotype of the indestructible pioneer woman. While raising
five stepchildren (four boys) she will bear thirteen of her own in
the next twenty-one years. Seven of these will die natural deaths
and two will die at their father's side in the holocaust of Harpers
Ferry. In that time too she will travel back and forth across the
country like a shuttlecock (no simple matter then), setting up new
homes only to abandon them after a couple of years, repeating
the ordeal over and over until Brown embarks at last on his life's
work.

(In his introduction Ruchames devotes two short lines to Mary
Day Brown, getting her out of the way pronto for more important
matters. I wished he could have discussed her in more abundant
detail. Something else to look forward to in Brown's biographies.)

After ten years in Randolph Brown returns to Ohio, settling in
a place not far from Hudson called Franklin Mills. Ruchames
writes that Brown is "attracted by new business opportunities"—a
euphemism for land speculation in which he uses other people's
money. He's caught up in the get-rich mania of the 1830s and

stakes everything he has, including his debts, on the prospect of imminent success.

But the great crash comes in 1837, and like thousands of others in the country John Brown is wiped out, condemned to remain at the mercy of his creditors for the rest of his life.

As he struggles to right himself, his letters (those included in the *Reader*) grow more pathetic. Circumstances are beating him down. In late 1838 (while driving cattle herds from Ohio to New England he asks his wife and children to "forgive the many faults and foibles you have seen in me, and try to profit by anything good in either my example or my counsel." Six months later (from New Hartford) he writes: "I hope God who is rich in mercy will grant us grace to conform to our circumstances with cheerfulness and true resignation." He expects little to change, though, for God is chastising him.

The chastisements become more severe. In Connecticut he makes a deal with the New England Woolen Company. It places $2,800 in his account for the purchase of wool. He spends the money instead to redeem other debts. Plainly, Brown has committed fraud, and unable to make good the $2,800 throws himself on the compassion of the company. It decides not to prosecute. It extracts a written promise from him (signed and witnessed on October 17, 1842): "I hereby agree in consideration of the great kindness and tenderness of said company toward me in my calamity, and more particularly of the sworn obligation I am under to render all their due, to pay the same and the interest thereon, from time to time, as Divine Providence shall enable me to do." At his death in 1859 (as specified in his last will and testament) he will still be paying off the New England Woolen Company.

(How to explain this weird act of peculation, this blatant bit of thievery? Brown, I conjectured, believed that prosperity lay just ahead; it was bound to come shortly; if he could only hold off his creditors until then. The New England Woolen Company advance arrived at exactly the right moment. He could see the turn in his fortunes, his freedom, the restoration of what he'd once been. So he took the awful chance, committed the peculative deed.)

Actually the company has little choice (beyond putting Brown in jail). He has the month before been officially certified a bankrupt, meaning that he owns absolutely nothing except a few personal effects, the rest having been attached and auctioned. Among the propertied class, which once honored him as a member in good standing, he's now a cipher, a disgrace, a hopeless failure.

His situation must have been intolerably cruel. There he was in his sparse Ohio cabin with an enormous family to support (though by now the oldest children could fend for themselves), forty-two years old, an age when most men would have been securely if not comfortably circumstanced. (Or so I assumed.) That he blames himself goes without saying. He's brought this "calamity" down on himself, his family, those who trusted him. Ultimately, to be sure, God is the author of his condition. He's done something to offend God. His punishment is deserved. If so the pain could not have been as enormous as we with our humanistic and secular values might believe. We turn our guilt in on ourselves. We hold ourselves responsible not only for our acts but for the standards by which we judge them. We have no excuse, no poultice, for our moral wounds. If Brown's faith in providential justice intensifies his feelings of guilt for the wrongs he's committed, it also serves to neutralize them. Christianity has given him a way out.

None of his suffering prepares us for what follows. A "pestilence" strikes northern Ohio in the late summer of 1843. The Brown family comes down with fever and dysentery. On September 11 his son Charles, aged six, dies. Ten days later Peter, who was not quite three, dies. The next day Austin, the youngest of the children, expires; he was just under one. And the day after that Sarah, nine, goes too. The last three Brown buries together "in a little row."

His response is characteristic of the man. If I experienced anything like it (so I imagine) I would be driven to lunacy. It is in fact beyond the limits of what I could imagine, a heavy veil closing off any thoughts I might have on the death of my children. (Mahler's *Kindertotenlieder* isn't easy to take.) Consider how John Brown dealt with it. In a letter to his son, John, Jr., the day after he buried three of his children, he writes: "This has been to us all a bitter cup indeed, and we have drunk deeply, but still the Lord reigneth, and blessed be his great and holy name forever."

An occasion, then, to bless the Lord's name—the same Lord who has just taken four innocent souls.

This requires some understanding. One has the sense that Brown welcomes their death, that as he suffers so he's drawn so much closer to God. At such moments he feels God more intensely, the passion of Christ being the source of exquisite pain and pleasure. Brown appears to envy little Sarah as she lay dying. She "discovered great composure of mind, and patience," he says, "together with strong assurance at times of meeting God in paradise. She seemed to have no idea of recovering from the first, nor did she ever express the least desire that she might, but rather the reverse. We fondly hope that she is not disappointed."

Providence works in mysterious ways. Shortly after the death of his children, Brown's economic situation improves for the first time in six years. In May 1844 a wealthy Akron businessman, Simon Perkins, Jr., takes him on as a partner in a sheep concern, Perkins to supply food and shelter, Brown to give all the "care and attention" which "the good of the flock may require, wash the sheep, shear the wool, sack and ship the same for market in the neatest and best manner," and so forth. Perkins also lets Brown have the use of a house just outside Akron. Brown exults to his oldest son: "I think this is the most comfortable and the most favorable arrangement of my worldly concerns that I ever had, and calculated to afford us more leisure for improvement, by day and by night, than any other." And though like Job he is prepared for anything, he hopes—we can imagine how fervently—that God would not "send leanness into our souls."

(Why, I mused, would a rich and presumably shrewd businessman like Simon Perkins, Jr. become John Brown's partner, furnishing the capital and assuming the risks, unless he had reason to trust Brown, regard him highly? This despite Brown's bankruptcy, his succession of failures, the aura of defeat that enveloped him. He must have struck his neighbors as eminently normal and responsible. They at least—in contrast to recent historians—didn't indict his character because he'd failed.)

Brown appears to have found his métier: shepherd. He tells us in his memoir that he "began early in life to discover a great liking" for horses, sheep, swine, and cattle and developed "a kind of enthusiastic longing" to be a shepherd. His children attest to his love of sheep and his uncanny ability to understand them, each of them, no matter how large the flock. "His kindness toward dumb animals was proverbial," his son Salmon writes. "He was like the Israelite of old, sheltering the ninety-and-nine, but refusing shelter for himself till the straying hundredth was safely folded." He spared no energy on "a chilled and dying lamb . . . till it either died or stood solidly upon its crooked legs."

In June 1846 Brown moves to Springfield, Massachusetts, as the agent not only of Perkins and Brown but of wool growers in general from several states who are co-operating to get the best possible prices from eastern manufacturers. His job is to receive, store, sort, and sell the wool by grade. Further testimony to his talents and the regard in which he's held.

But right from the start he encounters a problem. The Democratic-controlled congress passes a new tariff. The wool market collapses. Another cataclysm.

(I consulted the *Encyclopedia of American History,* edited by Richard B. Morris, an invaluable reference, and under the "Commerce and the Tariff" section found that the Walker Tariff, passed on July 30, 1846, was essentially a revenue rather than a protective tariff and was based on a more open trade principle, the eventual object being to allow most commodities to enter the United States duty-free. I already knew that the Democrats, centered in the South and West, regions which depended on the export of agricultural commodities, favored free trade and that the Whigs, representing nascent manufacturers and woolen interests, favored protection. So the Walker Tariff was a devastating blow to Brown and Perkins and the other people for whom Brown acted as agent. I recalled how Nevins had come down very hard on Brown as a businessman, especially as a wool merchant in Springfield, proof of his instability, etc., etc. But Nevins had said nothing about the effects of the Walker Tariff on Brown's business, placing the whole burden of the disaster on his head. Hardly cricket.)

One day in November 1846 Brown receives "dreadful news" from Akron (where his family is still staying; it won't be until the following July that they rejoin him in Springfield): His youngest child, Amelia, one and a half, has been accidentally scalded to death by her sister Ruth. The news is more than even he can take. "I seem to be struck almost dumb," he writes his wife and children. He regrets that he wasn't there when it happened, that he couldn't spend the final moments with Amelia and shepherd the family through yet another trial. "One more dear little feeble child I am to meet no more," he laments, "till the dead, small and great, shall stand before God." He apologizes for his absence, beating his breast in guilt: "If I had a right sense of my habitual neglect of my family's eternal interests I should probably go crazy."

He admonishes his wife and children to avoid blaming Ruth, who is being punished enough. Then he sets the whole episode in its proper perspective. It reveals to him, as all afflictions do, the mysterious ineffable wisdom of God who weaves around man a seamless web of deeds and effects. "I humbly hope this dreadful afflictive Providence will lead us all more properly to appreciate the amazing, unforeseen, untold consequences that hang upon the right or wrong doing of things seemingly of trifling account. Who can tell or comprehend the vast results for good or evil that are to follow the saying of one little word." Again he asks that God be blessed, "for a brighter day shall dawn, and let us not sorrow as those that have no hope."

Brown tries to recoup the firm's losses and even goes to Europe in the fall of 1849 to sell wool there. To no avail. Business continues to deteriorate. Perkins finally gives up in 1850. But the partnership isn't dissolved. Brown, groaning under the weight of yet more lawsuits (his creditors are still pressing down on him) has to continue working for Perkins as a shepherd in Ohio.

Meanwhile he's been laying plans to settle elsewhere permanently. A few years earlier Gerrit Smith, the extremely rich abolitionist from upstate New York, offered 140,000 acres of land in the North Country to blacks who wanted to become self-sufficient yeomen farmers. Brown bought 244 acres from Smith near the Adirondack village of North Elba, where a tiny colony of black farmers has been planted. "I can think of no place where I think I would sooner go," Brown writes, "than to live with those poor despised Africans to try and encourage them and show them a little, so far as I am capable, how to manage."

Year after year passes, but Brown can't see his way clear to
leave Akron. Like Jacob he must toil until his obligation is paid.
At last, in 1854, Perkins releases him, and he and his family go to
North Elba. By now a son-in-law who's been there for some time
has built a modest cabin for them on Brown's property. Here's
where he will remain while he takes care of his other business, the
consummation of his life's work.

His most despotic personal worries are over. Almost all his children are grown; some are married and have families. He's free,
unburdened, for the first time since his marriage to Dianthe Lusk
in 1820. He's been borne through, saved for a larger destiny.

3

But I was unsure about John Brown. I needed to flesh out in
more exact detail the portrait I'd already formed. I needed to
know about his conduct at home, about his relations with his wife
and children. And so I examined the part of *A John Brown
Reader* entitled, "In the Words of Those Who Knew Him," with
the same close attention I'd been giving to *his* words.

There are few inconsistencies in John Brown's life; it's all of a
piece. He ran his household as though it were a family church organized according to the strictest canons of the Calvinist dispen-
sation. Every day on rising and retiring he and the family and occasional guests prayed and read Scripture and sang hymns. (His
favorite: "Blow Ye the Trumpet Blow.") Sometimes he would
deliver a sermon or a catechism. He allowed nothing of course to
disturb the Sabbath peace, a day of reflection and rest.

His children, visitors, acquaintances—all testify to the regimen
that prevailed. When Brown was home, his son Salmon remembers, no one dared break the heavy silence. The meals,
served on a long table (to accommodate the large number) and
"never without a white tablecloth," consisted of "coarse, hearty
farmer's food, always in abundance and always well served." (A
favorite dish was "corn-meal mush cooked the whole afternoon
long in a huge iron cauldron and served with rich milk or cream."
How appetizing still!) Everyone had his or her assigned task. The

moment the Brown children learned to walk "the world of work opened to them. There was no pampering, little petting. The boys could turn a steak or brown a loaf as well as their mother." And by the age of seven or so they were being treated as young adults, citizens of the household.

At the same time Brown enforced the most rigorous discipline to rein-in the incalculable passions of youth. And rein them in he did (or sought to do) by "terribly severe" physical punishment. The children knew what to expect. There was nothing indeterminate or ambiguous or capricious in his responses. He might be unfailingly severe; he was also scrupulously fair. They recognized, even in their pain, that he was punishing them out of Christian duty (the legitimacy of which they accepted), not out of personal weakness, not out of the desire to prove something to himself.

(I suddenly remembered tall, gaunt Mr. Fried [no relation], my Hebrew schoolteacher, who whacked the daylights out of us, usually for good reason. I can still see the calloused hand poised for assault, I can still hear the ringing in my ear. Fear of him kept me in line, and I always came back for more, until one day I was rid of him and Hebrew school, effacing from my mind the whole experience, all those years, those thousands of lessons memorized but unlearned. From time to time I recalled Mr. Fried, a John Brown in black gabardine and skullcap, like Brown God's vicegerent, a man consecrated to the faith who had suffered much too, and wore his sadness with dignity.)

Brown's oldest son, John, Jr., gives us a remarkable description of how the old man dealt with his children's infractions, how he attempted, in true Christian fashion—with a mingling of blood and self-sacrifice—to internalize their guilt and so get them to feel deep in their souls the wrongs they committed.

Brown owned an "account book" of transgressions: for example, eight lashes "for disobeying mother," three lashes for "unfaithfulness at work," eight for telling a lie, etc. "This account," John, Jr., writes, "he showed to me from time to time. On a certain Sunday morning he invited me to accompany him from the house to the tannery, saying that he had concluded it was time for a settlement. We went into the upper or finishing room, and after a long and tearful talk over my faults, he again showed me

my account, which exhibited a fearful footing up of *debits*. I had
no credits or off-sets, and was of course bankrupt. I then paid
about one-third of the debt, reckoned in strokes from a nicely-pre-
pared blue-beech switch, laid on 'masterly.' Then, to my utter
astonishment, father stripped off his shirt, and seating himself on
a block, gave me the whip and bade me 'lay it on' to his bare back.
I dared not refuse to obey, but at first I did not strike hard.
'Harder!' he said; 'harder! harder!' until he *received* the balance of
the *account*. Small drops of blood showed on his back where the
tip end of the tingling beech cut through. Thus ended the account
and settlement, which was also my first practical illustration of the
Doctrine of Atonement."

John, Jr. concludes with a touch of acerbic irony: "I was then
too obtuse to perceive how Justice could be satisfied by inflicting
penalty upon the innocent instead of the guilty; but at the time I
had not read the ponderous volume of Jonathan Edwards' sermons which father owned."

If in fact Brown had tyrannized over his children, if they'd felt
enthralled to his terror, it's extremely unlikely they would have
remained so close to him long after they became adults and family
men, that they would have joined him in his crusade against the
slavocracy, three of them falling in battle.

It should also be noted that when his wife and children needed
him he was always there. His devotion to the family is attested to
over and over by his children. "He sometimes seemed very stern
and strict with me," his daughter Ruth Brown Thompson writes,
"yet his tenderness made me forget that he was stern." And Salmon Brown brings out "the John Brown little known to history,"
the John Brown "who sat around the great open fireplace at night
with his children in his arms and sang them to sleep; who rose in
the coldest nights and paced the floor with a collicky child, while
his wife, worn by child-bearing and child-rearing, lay in bed
asleep; and who was ever the nurse in sickness, watchful, tireless,
tender, allowing no one to lift the burden of the night watch from
him."

In one respect John Brown failed. To be more accurate, his
children failed him. They broke the thread of continuity that had
stretched back across the generations from him to the first Peter

Brown, circa 1650. For they rejected the faith, at least in its Calvinist-Hebraic form, turned their backs on the God of terror and retribution (who after all had taken so many of their brothers and sisters), and denied the absolute authority, the literal truth, of Scripture. Again and again in his later years he complained of their lapse and pleaded with them to return to the fold. A typical lament to John, Jr., some time in August 1853: "In choosing my texts and in quoting from the Bible I perhaps select the very portions which another portion of my family hold are not to be wholly received as *true*. I forgot to say that my younger sons (as is common in this 'progressive age') appear to be a little in advance of my older, and have thrown off the old shackle entirely. And through a candid investigation they have discovered the Bible to be ALL a fiction! Shall I add that a letter received from *you* some time since gave me a little less than pain and sorrow? 'The righteous shall hold on his way.' 'By and by he is offended.' "

But his sons had strayed too far and apostates they remained to the very end.

On Brown's wife, or wives, I found precious little in the *Reader*. Though Mary Day Brown survived him by twenty-five years, she said hardly anything in public about him, avoiding even the ordinary pieties. He simply treated her (and Dianthe too, of course) —so much the evidence does suggest—as his helpmeet in the great travails of their lives. And she accepted as given the role laid down for her and sanctioned by the heavenly order of things, defined in the tenets of seventeenth-century Calvinism. She understood what lay in store for her when she married him.

The evidence also indicates that Brown's attitude toward her mellowed, that he learned to prize her for manifesting the good qualities he lacked (conversely, for lacking the bad qualities he manifested), that he came to feel a kind of compassion and pity for her. This is strikingly borne out in a letter he wrote to her on March 7, 1847, from Sprinfield. He hadn't seen her and the family for almost nine months (during which time infant Amelia had died in that horrible accident) and he was full of contrition and guilt. "I do not forget the firm attachment of her who has remained my fast and faithful affectionate friend, when others said

of me: now that he lieth he shall rise up no more. When I reflect
on these things together with the very considerable difference in
our age, as well as the follies and faults with which I am justly
chargeable, I really admire at [*sic*] your constancy and really feel,
notwithstanding I sometimes chide you severely, that you ar[e]
really my better half." He goes on to detail some of his faults and
asks her to treat the children with a kindness and understanding
they could not expect from him. "I feel considerable regret by
turns that I have lived so many years and have in reality done so
very little to increase the amount of human happiness. I often
regret that my manner is no more kind and affectionate to those I
really love and esteem, but I trust my friends will overlook my
harsh, rough ways when I cease to be in their way. . . . If the
large boys do wrong call them into your room and expostulate
with them kindly, and see if you cannot reach them by a kind but
powerful appeal to their honor. I do not claim that such a theory
accords very much with my practices. I frankly confess it does
not. But I want your face to shine even if my own should be dark
and cloudy."

————◆————

These facets of his personal life, intriguing in themselves (and
all too cursorily presented in Ruchames), interested me because
they helped me better understand the character of the abolitionist,
the John Brown of the history books, the John Brown who was
the subject of my inquiry. I wanted to know as precisely as possible the genesis and development of his abolitionism. What did he
think a Christian could do against an evil so enormous, so deeply
rooted, so distant from the humble pathways of his life? When
and why did he take up arms against slavery? What was his strategy or intention? What did he accomplish?

While pursuing the answers (so far as I could obtain them from
the *Reader,* my *vade mecum*), I tried to isolate such knowledge
and preconceptions as I had, to wipe the slate clean. And what I'd
learn afresh from the documents on his abolitionism and armed
struggle I'd assimilate to the image of the man (his personal and

family life, etc.) that was becoming fixed in my mind and objectified in the countless pages of my notes.

4

Brown was always an abolitionist. He grew up in an abolitionist home, his father having been one long before abolitionism was a movement, a crusade, a term of reproach and provocation. John Brown was taught to hate slavery as a matter of course. When he encountered it in the flesh for the first time at the age of twelve (when his friend the slave boy was mercilessly beaten), the abolitionist hatred hardened into a concrete passion and he swore then and there "eternal war" against slavery.

As citizen and family man Brown's antislave sentiments are buried deep and out of sight. He never goes in for a public profession of his faith. He is no conspicuous part of the crusade, led by Garrison, Birney, Weld, the Tappans, the Grimkés, and others that arose in the 1830s and that has caused such a furor. Brown's abolitionism hardly gets beyond the confines of his family and locality. His house is a station on the Underground Railroad, and he seeks to help local blacks wherever possible. Beyond these more or less private measures he doesn't go. His is a solitary vigil of righteousness.

In 1834 he writes one of his brothers, telling of a scheme he's hatched to undermine the citadel of slavery. He wishes "to get at least one negro boy, a youth, and bring him up as we do our own —viz., give him a good English education, learn him what we can about the history of the world, about business, about general subjects, and, above all, try to teach him the fear of God." More generally, Brown proposes to set up a school for blacks. The example of what can be done will spread wider and wider. Similar schools will proliferate. Slavery will crumble.

On the face of it the scheme is harebrained. How does Brown make the leap across the chasm of reality from schools (assuming even those to be possible) to the extinction of human bondage in America? For Brown it's no leap at all. He's certain "God is about to bring them all out of bondage." He fails to explain, however, why he thinks God is about to do this. Maybe Brown is swept along by the spirit of reform that is abroad in the land and throughout the world: by the rise of democracy, the revolutions in Europe, the Chartist agitation in England, the emancipation of the slaves in the British Empire, the various humanitarian crusades at home. Whatever it is Brown believes the time for manumission has come, and the slaveholders themselves will recognize the fact. Brown's letter continues: "I do think such advantages ought to be afforded the young blacks, whether they are all to be immediately set free or not. Perhaps we might, under God, in that way do more toward breaking their yoke effectually than in any other. If the young blacks of our country could once become enlightened, it would most assuredly operate on slavery like firing powder confined in rock, and all slaveholders know it well. Witness the heaven-daring laws against teaching blacks. If once the Christians in the free states would set to work in earnest in teaching the blacks, the people of the slaveholding states would find themselves constitutionally driven to set about the work of emancipation immediately."

Such was Brown's early sanguine hope of abolition. It came to naught. At least there's no further word of it.

Brown's abolitionism grows more and more militant. Exactly why we don't know. Nor apparently does Ruchames (who never speculates). Brown discloses not a word of what he's thinking, what effect the evils of the day have on him. The slave empire, far from yielding its ground, has continued to expand, so that even the moderates and the liberals, previously reluctant to discuss the slavery issue, are becoming alarmed and begin to mobilize their forces. Brown gives up expecting that God will bring about a miracle. The evil of slavery, he becomes convinced, demands a human remedy. Or rather a violent remedy administered by God through human means. Brown regards himself as the vehicle of God's wrath, the agent of his purpose.

His anger lacks "healthy" outlets. He belongs to no community of like-minded people. His passion, feeding on itself, turns more profoundly inward, more obsessive. He must do something himself. Unperceived by others he gradually forms his own plan to bring down the slave empire.

The best evidence we have that Brown has been working out such a plan comes from Frederick Douglass, the great black leader, who, according to his own stately account (for which I consulted his autobiography), learned of it during a visit to Brown's Springfield home in 1847. He made the call because he'd heard about this unusual white man from some "colored men" in the area. In Brown's sparsely furnished home ("no sofas, no cushions, no curtains, no carpets, no easy rocking chairs inviting to enervation or rest or repose"—a replica of the frontier cabin), after a meal of potatoes and cabbage and beef soup, the two men discuss the slavery question.

Brown is cautious, wary at first. He seems to "apprehend opposition to his views." Douglass's position in fact is known to nearly everyone through his countless speeches and articles; he's a celebrated figure in the North. He favors the peaceful, legal emancipation of the slaves. The Constitution, he maintains, is "in its letter and spirit an anti-slavery instrument, demanding the abolition of slavery as a condition of its own existence as the supreme law of the land."

Brown takes exception and denies "that moral suasion could ever liberate the slaves, or that political action would abolish the system." Slaveholders, he says, have "forfeited their right to live"; slaves have "the right to gain their liberty in any way they could." Brown then reveals his plan for forcibly abolishing slavery. A plan, he's quick to emphasize, that contemplates no large-scale insurrection, no mass Jacquerie against the slaveholders, with its attendant horrors (of which the Nat Turner rebellion gives frightening testimony). No, what he proposes is the formation of a guerrilla unit, a sort of Gideon's army operating "in the very heart of the South."

Brown shows Douglass a map of the United States and points to the Alleghenies, extending in a continuous line from Canada to the Deep South. "These mountains," he says, "are the basis of my plan. God has given the strength of the hills to freedom; they were placed here for the emancipation of the negro race; they are full of natural forts, where one man for defense will be equal to a hundred for attack; they are full also of good hiding places, where large numbers of brave men could be concealed, and baffle and elude pursuit for a long time." "I know these mountains well, and could take a body of men into them there despite of all the efforts of Virginia to dislodge them. . . . My plan, then, is to take at first about 25 picked men, and begin on a small scale; supply them with arms and ammunition and put them in squads of five on a line of 25 miles." How would this harm the slave empire? "The most persuasive and judicious of them will go down to the hills from time to time, as opportunity offers, and induce the slaves to join them, seeking and selecting the most restless and daring." In time the guerrilla force will grow into a biracial army, ranging more and more widely, picking up new recruits all the time.

Douglass interrupts Brown with a sensible question: How will the men live? Brown answers: Off the enemy, by confiscating the slaveholders' property. But, Douglass asks, "suppose you succeed in running off a few slaves, and thus impress the Virginia slaveholders with a sense of insecurity in their slaves, the effect will be only to make them sell their slaves further south." That, says Brown, is part of the plan. "If we could drive slavery out of *one county* it would be a great gain; it would weaken the system throughout the State." "But they would employ bloodhounds to hunt you out of the mountains!" "That they might attempt, but the chances are we should whip them, and where we should have whipped one squad, they would be careful how they pursued." Douglass persists: Suppose Brown and his men are completely cut off from food supplies, trapped. He's prepared to die, Brown replies without a trace of heroics. He personally has "no better use for his life than to lay it down in the cause of the slave."

And so the argument goes on into the night.

Douglass's account is (retrospectively) the first indication we have that Brown is going to wage war on the slavocracy. How, when, where, with whom—these are questions for the future, and he will deal with them in the fullness of time, when, moved by Providence, he crosses over from intention to action.

Shortly after his meeting with Frederick Douglass, Brown takes time out from his labors as a Springfield wool merchant to do something that's quite out of character: He composes an article for a black abolitionist journal, *The Ram's Horn,* the title of which, "Sambo's Mistakes," suggests its content. It's a black man's confession of a feckless and misspent life. Brown's irony in posing as a black moralist, a black Ben Franklin, is blunt, artless, heavy-handed. "Sambo" repeatedly asserts that his "peculiar quick-sightedness" enables him to "see in a wink" where he went astray. But it's too late; the past is irrecoverable.

The chief problem, Sambo discovers, is that he's always wanted to be "but little inferior to some of the whites" and has adopted their peccant habits. Instead of reading "sacred and profane history," thereby learning "the true course for individuals, societies and nations to pursue" and accumulating "an endless variety of rational and practical ideas," profiting from "the experience of others of all ages," training himself "for the most important stations in life"—instead of these worthy ends Sambo spent all his time "devouring silly novels and other miserable trash," acquiring "a taste for nonsense of low wit" and neglecting "sober truth, useful or practical wisdom." And so Sambo has "passed through life without profit" to himself or others. He's become a "mere blank on which nothing worth perusing is written," a cipher. "The money I spent," Sambo complains, "would with the interest of it have enabled me to have relieved a great many sufferers, supplied me with a well-selected, interesting library, and paid for a good farm . . . whereas I have now neither books, clothing, the satisfaction of having benefited others nor where to lay my hoary head. But I can see in a moment where I missed it."

Reading "Sambo's Mistakes" reminds us of Brown's autobiographical memoir, the chronicle of his pilgrimage from temptation and weakness to manly self-reliance. "Sambo" is John Brown himself as a child, wild and unconquered, loving possessions, roaming the forests, consorting with Indians. But unlike young Brown "Sambo" has stayed where he was. He never sought out "the company of intelligent, wise and good men," never pursued "some respectable calling," never practiced "any present self-denial." ("For instance," Sambo admits, "I have bought expensive gay clothing, nice canes, watches, safety chains, finger rings, breast pins and many other things of like nature, thinking I might by that means distinguish myself from the vulgar, as some of the better class of whites do.") Brown here echoes a familiar criticism of the black man's alleged improvidence and self-indulgence, criticism that has come from diverse quarters: white bigots along with high-minded abolitionists and black leaders who affirm the Protestant ethic as strongly as Brown did. What differentiates Brown from the others is his ulterior purpose. For him the moral or characterological reformation of blacks is not enough. He wants blacks to depend no longer on whites—even the best among them, the "really benevolent" ones like Garrison—for their deliverance. Sambo's message is this: If we blacks fail to deliver ourselves, by our own efforts, no one will and we will always be "Sambos."

Brown accordingly offers his black readers two pieces of advice. First, they must learn to organize, to act in concert. They must overcome their pride, individuality, hypersensitivity, disputatiousness, above all their religious sectarianism. "Another error of my riper years," Sambo says, "has been that when any meeting of colored people has been called in order to consider of any important matter of general interest I have been so eager to display my sprouting talents and so tenacious of some trifling theory or other that I have adopted that I have generally lost all sight of the business in hand. . . . Another small error of my life (for I never committed great blunders) has been that I never would (for the sake of union in furtherance of the most vital interests of our race) yield any minor point of difference. In this way I have always had to act with but a few, or more frequently alone and could accomplish nothing worth living for. . . . Another little blunder which I made is that while I have always been a most zealous Abolitionist I have been constantly at war with my friends about certain religious tenets. I was first a Presbyterian, but I could never think of acting with my Quaker friends for they were the rankest heretics and the Baptists would be in the water and the Methodists denied the doctrine of Election, etc."

The second piece of advice follows directly. Only when they have organized as a collective force will the blacks be able to defy the whites. Sambo admits he "always expected to secure the favors of the whites by tamely submitting to every species of indignity, contempt and wrong." But he promises now that he will "nobly" resist "their brutal aggression from principle." He will take his "place as a man" and assume "the responsibilities of a man, a citizen, a husband, a brother, a neighbor, a friend. . . ." What, after all, has humility brought him? "I find that I get for all my submission about the same reward that the Southern Slavocrats render to the Dough-faced statesmen of the North for being bribed and browbeat and fooled and cheated, as the Whigs and Democrats love to be, and think themselves highly honored if they be allowed to lick up the spittle of a Southerner."

Speaking as Sambo, then, Brown calls upon the free blacks—as Moses called upon the Israelites—to throw off their fetishisms and idolatries, seek nothing from their oppressors, and defend their dignity, their self-respect, their rights, as they would their lives.

Now, what I didn't know and what I would have liked Ruchames to bring out in his *Reader* was whether any other white abolitionist favored the mobilization of the black community. Garrison was a militant pacifist. The anti-Garrison abolitionists believed with Douglass in lawful, evolutionary change under constitutional auspices. Did anyone of note take Brown's position, clandestinely if not openly? This whole matter of abolitionism and the Northern blacks, I felt, needed further exploration. The abyss of my ignorance was opening wider and wider.

A few years later, in response to the outrageous Fugitive Slave Act of 1850, Brown goes a step beyond offering advice to blacks; the time for moral injunctions is over. He establishes a black self-protection group in Springfield called the League of Gileadites. "I have improved my leisure hours quite busily with colored people here," he informs his wife, "in advising them how to act, and in giving them all the encouragement in my power."

(We learn from Brown's letter how the Fugitive Slave Act must have terrified blacks, even in a presumably secure place like Springfield. "They very much need encouragement and advice," he writes, "and some of them are so alarmed that they tell me they cannot sleep on account of either them or their wives and children. I can only say I think I have been enabled to do something to revive their broken spirits. I want all my family to imagine themselves in the same dreadful condition.")

Under the motto "Union Is Strength" John Brown draws up the League of Gileadites' statement of purpose, dated January 15, 1851. The first sentence reads: "Nothing so charms the American people as personal bravery." The rest follows logically. Blacks must arm and defend themselves against anyone seeking to take them away. They must unite, prepare to act collectively, and, when the battle is joined, make "clean work" of their enemies. They must, obviously, be willing to die.

Brown has an extraordinary recommendation for the Gileadites. The moment their enemies have regrouped (following the initial surprise assault) the Gileadites must repair, fall back as it were, to "the houses of your most prominent and influential white friends with their wives; and that will effectually fasten upon them the suspicion of being connected with you, and will compel them to make common cause with you, whether they would otherwise live up to their professions or not. This would leave them no choice in the matter." In other words, use the occasion to broaden the conflict, divide the white community, make it their struggle as well. Brown's advice is the admonition of a guerrilla leader trying to bring the uncommitted, the neutral, the fence-sitting multitude into the war.

Brown has a final bit of advice for the Gileadites: "Hold on to your weapons and never be persuaded to leave them, part with them, or have them taken away from you. Stand by one another and by your friends while a drop of blood remains; and be hanged if you must but tell no tales out of school. Make no confession."

A premonition of Harpers Ferry: his very words in Charlestown prison.

Brown organizes the Gileadites in the belief that they would swell and become an army, with branches in various communities, the officers to be chosen from "those who shall have rendered the most important services."

But the Gileadites disappear entirely from view. At any rate there's no further reference to them anywhere else in the *Reader*.

(I had several questions: What would have happened to the Gileadites if circumstances had compelled them to carry out their pledge? How many whites would have joined them in a showdown? What would have been the fate of blacks in general, especially those [like Douglass] who openly espoused abolitionism? The very thought made me shudder. John Brown, I readily admitted, was made of sterner stuff.)

The League of Gileadites, then, tells us very pointedly what is going on in John Brown's head. Clearly he's already fighting the slaveholders and their Northern surrogates. He's nurturing the right temperament, priming himself psychologically, long before he's ready to gird his loins.

5

God is bringing the struggle to a head, a final resolution. This is how John Brown must have interpreted events in 1854, as he's tending his sheep and farming his land outside of Akron, keeping his creditors at bay, waiting to return to his property in the North Country hills of New York State. From his viewpoint the apocalyptic moment is near at hand. The slavocracy is on the march, more audacious and truculent than ever. In May 1854 Congress passes the Kansas-Nebraska Act, permitting the introduction of slavery into a part of the Louisiana Territory from which it's hitherto been excluded under the Missouri Compromise of 1820, now defunct. Again the slavery issue is opened.

The Kansas-Nebraska Act electrifies the North. It's as though an invading army threatens its very borders, ready to destroy its free institutions, its way of life. Northerners wonder again where the line between slavery and freedom will be drawn. Will the slavocrats rest at anything less than the imposition of slavery throughout the country, in the Free States as well as the territories? Overnight an "anti-Nebraska" movement—that is, anti-Southern, antislavery, antiadministration—springs up in the North, forming the nucleus of the Republican party. War clouds gather in the distance.

To John Brown it's all inexorable, fated, preordained. Nothing can have surprised him. He's never doubted that the Democrats, who run Congress, the administration, and the federal courts, are "dough-faced" servitors of the Southern oligarchs, that the American political system, despite its rhetoric of equality, its professed belief in the rights of man, is really rigged in favor of the slave power. But now the cloak of deception has been torn away. The contest between the children of light and the children of darkness is no longer concealed. All Americans have come to realize that the country cannot endure as a house divided, half slave and half free, that it will have to be one or the other.

A mini-civil war is shaping up as settlers from the Northern states and from adjacent Missouri converge on the Territory of Kansas. And though the federal government under President Franklin Pierce (a doughface's doughface) supports the principle of popular sovereignty, according to which the settlers alone would opt for or against slavery, it's in fact committed to making Kansas a fit habitation for slaveholders. So that even popular sovereignty, intended by its advocates as a concession to the South, is exposed as a snare and a delusion. So the Kansas Free Staters and their Republican friends maintain. To them it's obvious beyond question that the Missouri "Border Ruffians," with the help of the proslave governor, are stealing the territory, committing every crime—fraud and pillage and murder—with perfect impunity. The Free Staters refuse to acquiesce and deny the legitimacy of the "bogus" proslave legislature voted into office in 1855 through the intervention of the Border Ruffians.

Exciting times for John Brown. Every day brings news of the impending battle between good and evil. But he remains only a witness from afar. God hasn't yet called him to his task. The ravaging of Kansas provokes no active response from him. Organizing a guerrilla outfit is furthest from his mind. He broods over his Virginia plan, the cynosure of his life. He keeps his own counsel as usual, sharing his thoughts with no one, waiting for providential signs and portents.

By the spring of 1855 five of his sons have settled in Kansas, at a place called Osawatomie in the southeast part of the Territory. They ask him to join them. He refuses, saying that while he sympathizes with their desire "to help defeat Satan and his legions in that direction" he's "committed to operate in another part of the field." He wants no radical disruption of his plan.

But events overtake his calculations, his more distant hopes. He concludes that he's needed in Kansas, that he must lay aside the plan until Satan is defeated in "that direction." A momentous decision. He will abandon the peaceful pursuits of a lifetime (regardless of what's been going on in his head, the contained rage). He will cease to be a law-abiding citizen. He will fight the slaveholders and their allies to the death and will observe few of the legal scruples and authorizations that hedge them about on every side. In the summer of 1855 he says good-bye to his family (what remains of it) at North Elba and with a son and son-in-law heads West, stopping along the way to collect money for arms at abolitionist meetings.

At fifty-five a new John Brown is born. He has struck off the attachments of the past. The doubts and hesitations and constraints and petty tyrannies are gone. He's free at last to embark on the final and greatest test of his faith.

And no one who knows him doubts that the old man can sustain his transfiguration, that his flesh will be equal to the demands of his spirit. Physically, he is (according to Frederick Douglass) "lean and sinewy, of the best New England mold, built for times of trouble, fitted to grapple with the flintiest hardships." And Salmon Brown describes him as being "five feet ten inches in height, slightly stoop-shouldered after middle life, with eyes sky blue, hair dark brown till tinged with grey, nose hawked and thin, skin florid, spare but muscular in build. . . . So far as I know he was never sick a day and never missed a meal on account of his own illness." A shining product of the school of adversity, John Brown has retained at fifty-five the resiliency and vigor of his youth. In every respect he's held himself ready.

Brown arrives at the family compound, Osawatomie, in October 1855. Conditions are poor. Food and shelter are hardly adequate. Everyone is sick. ("I felt very much disappointed at finding all my children here in such uncomfortable circumstances," he writes his aging father.) They struggle through the worst of the winter: "it is now nearly six weeks that the snow has been constantly driven (like dry sand) by the fierce winds of Kansas"—this in a letter to his wife on February 1, 1856; yet no one dies. He wishes more than anything that he could be back at North Elba, but he has his God-appointed mission. "The idea of again visiting those of my dear family at North Elba is so calculated to unman me that I seldom allow my thoughts to dwell on it."

Spring comes and the conflict between Free State and proslave settlers flares up. John Brown and his children are at the center of it. He's one of the leaders of the militant Free Staters, the chief apostle of aggressive action. Among the Free Staters, however, the "moderates" are in control despite the depredations, murders, rampant fraud. They believe in the ballot and obedience to law and due process. But the situation is fluid. Differences are growing more intractable, more violent. Determined not to yield their advantage, especially since the Free Staters will soon have numbers on their side, the proslavers rely heavily on Missouri thugs and desperadoes. Willy-nilly the Free Staters defend themselves by arms. They welcome John Brown's presence, then, though they hardly care for his ideology: He's an abolitionist; they emphatically are not. Only he's a fighter and that's what they need for the nonce.

(Brown's function is a familiar one in history—one that radicals or "extremists" often assume. They take the pressure off others, do the dirty work, act as catalysts, receive the brunt of opposition and punishment. "Moderates" have "extremists" to thank for appearing reasonable, open, pragmatic—and for whatever benefits are eventually to be derived from the restoration of order. I won't forget what one ex-radical recently told me: "The chief beneficiary of revolutions is always the class above the one that makes it." The observation holds true even when the "extremists" take power: the Jacobins, Bolsheviks, etc. Who in the end reaped the reward of their power? Not the people who sacrificed everything, an endless list of the faithful. Out in Kansas in 1856 John Brown is one of the faithful.)

It isn't long before Brown forms his own band of guerrillas, his own version of New Model Covenanters on the western frontier of America. He's Cromwell redivivus, a man thrilled by the discovery of his gifts, who imparts that discovery to others, drawing them into the ambit of his divinely inspired self-confidence. He fights a number of remarkable skirmishes. Heavily outnumbered, he inflicts stinging defeats on his enemies. On one occasion (the "Battle of Black Jack") he captures 23 men led by a captain of the Missouri militia. On another he and his covenanters, no more than 30 or 40 men, confound a force of 250 proslavers who have destroyed the Osawatomie settlement, escaping in a brilliantly executed maneuver. But not before one of his sons has been killed. (Earlier, two others were captured; one of them, John, Jr., suffered a mental breakdown.) By now Brown is feared far and wide for his daring and ruthlessness as a guerrilla chieftain. He's the notorious Captain Brown of Osawatomie.

The moderates owe him an enormous debt of gratitude. They

know it and their sentiment is fulsomely summed up in a letter from their leader, Charles Robinson (later the first elected governor of Kansas), to Brown, dated September 15, 1856. "Your course," Robinson writes, "so far as I have been informed, has been such as to merit the highest praise from every patriot and I cheerfully accord to you my heartfelt thanks for your prompt, efficient and timely actions against the invaders of our rights and the murder of our citizens. History will give your name a proud place on her pages, and posterity will pay homage to your heroism in the cause of God and humanity."

During these months of combat and notoriety Brown commits the most controversial, the most heavily condemned deed of his public life, a godsend to the enemies of his name. Now I was familiar with the "Pottawatomie massacre," Allan Nevins for one having described it in all its incarnadine brutality, while letting us know what he thinks of it and what effect it's had in exacerbating the conditions of "Bleeding Kansas." And so I read the documents in Ruchames pertaining to the massacre with special care and made sure I would get down the facts as clearly as possible. To tell the truth I was hoping to find proof of extenuation.

On May 22, 1856, John Brown and his party of irregulars are headed for Lawrence, headquarters of the Free State faction. They're going to help defend the town from the proslave forces that have been preparing to attack it. Too late. They learn that Lawrence has been sacked (by a "swearing, whiskey-drinking, ruffianly horde"), its newspaper destroyed, its hotel fired, Charles Robinson's house leveled, and so forth. Shortly before, two Free State men have been killed. Brown blames the inhabitants of Lawrence and the other Free Staters for trusting the authorities instead of their arms. He decides to avenge the crime. For the loss of a tooth he will break many bones.

Two days later, in the thick of night, he and seven accomplices —his sons Owen, Frederick, Salmon, and Oliver, his son-in-law, Henry Thompson, one James Townsley, and one Theodore Weiner (Weiner, Ruchames informs us, is an Austrian Jew who owns a store in the vicinity)—go to a proslavery settlement in nearby Pottawatomie. Salmon Brown many years later tells what follows:

"We went to Doyle's first and encountered a number of savage dogs. Old Man Tousley [Townsley] went after the dogs with a broadsword and he and my brother Fred soon had them all laid out. Tousley then went in without being asked. . . . The three Doyles were taken out of the house to a point a half mile or so away and were slain with broadswords. Owen Brown cut down one of them and another of the Browns cut down the old man and the other. Old man Doyle's wife gave the Doyles a terrible scoring as they were being taken from the house. She said, 'I told you you would get into trouble for all your devilment, and now you see it has come.'

"Henry Sherman was killed by Henry Thompson, and also Wilkinson, at about the same time the Doyles were. Our party divided, Thompson and Winer [Weiner] in one party and Owen Brown, Fred Brown, Salmon Brown, Oliver Brown and old man Tousley in the other, father running back and forth between the two parties. Father never raised a hand in slaying the men. He shot a bullet into the head of old man Doyle about a half hour after he was dead, but what for I do not know."

(I wondered, as I read about these sickeningly cruel killings, did any of the Doyles witness the murder of the others? Was there an interval, and if so how long, between the time the victims realized they would die and their death? How much was sadism part of the deed?)

In his introduction Ruchames attempts to minimize the enormity of the massacre by placing it in its historical context. The "killings and reprisals," he maintains, "were a hopeful sign of resistance to the pro-slave terror." They nerved the Free State people to fight back and so marked a turn in the Kansas struggle. Ruchames cites a document published for the first time in his *Reader*, a letter written shortly after Pottawatomie by the Reverend Samuel Adair (Brown's brother-in-law, "as mild and decent a person as one could find in the Territory"). "The excitement produced has been most tremendous," Adair writes. "Some proslavery men took the alarm and fled. . . . Runners were sent to Missouri for help—and proslavery men in different localities gathered together or stood in fear of their lives. Missouri troops have not come and it is thought they will not come in large numbers, and it is well for them not to. . . . As many pro-slavery men must die as free state men are killed by them, and they will not be particular who he is. . . . 'Eye for eye, tooth for tooth'—dollar for dollar and compound interest in some cases may be demanded."

Now, I wished Ruchames could have persuaded me. I wanted to believe in John Brown. But I wouldn't accept justification by historical context. What deed, even the most heinous, couldn't be explained away by circumstances, conditions, crises, the whole matrix of reality from which it springs, and so forth? Having examined the context of Pottawatomie (within the limits of the available material) I concluded that Brown had *no* such justification. He was bent on revenge and selected those five men as his tribute. The selection was arbitrary: They happened to be there. They owned no slaves. Nor were they Ruffians or interlopers. They were proslave settlers, undoubtedly partisan ones. Nothing worse than that.

Pottawatomie was political and ideological murder, the cracking of eggs necessary to make the omelet. John Brown was prepared to serve up the innocent to a remorseless destiny. (A destiny, of course, that denies innocence. To Brown Satan and God were at war, and he who refused to join God sided with Satan. More recent millenarians change the terms of the conflict, but their controlling assumptions are the same: To be indifferent to the revolution is to fail humanity and the inexpugnable laws of history.) What I couldn't understand, however, was where the omelet lay. For on further reflection I found it hard to imagine that Brown's *sole* or even primary motive was revenge. If it was (given his personality, his predictable responses), he would have gone after the proslave leaders, or the culprits who sacked Lawrence, waiting as long as he had to for the propitious occasion to strike. Impulsiveness, insensate desire, was no part of his character. He must have had compelling political or ideological reasons— compelling to him—for butchering relatively harmless and obscure men. What were they?

By the fall of 1856 there's little more for John Brown to do in Kansas. A new governor brings an armed truce. The hopes of the Free Staters rise; their numbers grow relentlessly. Two of Brown's sons and his son-in-law have already left Kansas; they've had their fill of violence and murder. With his three other sons Brown heads East, too.

He can now return to his original plan, the assault on the South. He has proved his mettle as a guerrilla fighter. He has a better idea of how to conduct clandestine warfare, how he should lead men, what kind of men he should recruit.

Kansas has served his purposes excellently in another respect, this one wholly unanticipated. His exploits have made him famous, and nowhere more than in the East where abolitionist feelings run strong and people are willing to give material support to activists like him. "Osawatomie Brown" or Old Brown or Captain Brown is a romantic figure, a legend. He visits Boston, Concord, Hartford, and other cities and solicits funds from philanthropists and concerned citizens in general, leading them to believe that he will return to Kansas to resume the struggle there.

The New England Brahmin set are especially taken with him. They lionize him, claim him as their own, a son of common parentage, flesh of their flesh, avatar of past glories. He's a favorite of the salons. He dresses like a frontiersman. He carries weapons. They know he's an outlaw: A federal warrant is out for his arrest. He has to spend some of his time hiding out among his new-found Brahmin friends, evading the marshals. His presence brings home the awful tempest of the war. It's all quite thrilling to them.

(One of them, Mrs. Thomas Russell, wife of the prominent Boston judge, vividly remembers the week John Brown stayed in their house, barricaded in his room, refusing to see any outsider, even the servants. He told Mrs. Russell, apparently with a straight face, "I shall never be taken alive, you know. And I should hate to spoil your carpet." She goes on:

("One evening he and I alone were sitting together in the parlor. Suddenly he drew from one boot a long, evil-looking knife. Then, from the other boot, he extracted two smaller knives. Then he produced a big pistol, and a smaller one. He looked at me doubtfully: I think he had a third concealed about him, but felt it inadvisable to resort, in my presence, to the measures necessary to get at it. Then he drew all the charges from the barrels and solemnly deposited them in the palms of my hands, filling both with cartridges. I was paralyzed with fear of the things.

("'Now, don't be awk'ard,' said he, 'don't trouble, or they will all fire off!'

("I sat stiff with fright, while he solemnly blew down the barrels, looked at the locks, examined the blades of the knives, and finally reloaded the firearms. I think he really, seriously, wished to make sure that his defenses were in good condition; also, it amused him to see the effect on me.

("'You haven't had this in your parlor before, have you?' he remarked at last.")

Brown pulls every stop in exploiting Brahmin guilt. Disappointed in the contributions he's received (for he wants to equip an army and has hired a professional soldier, Hugh Forbes by name, to train the men and write a special manual for the purpose —a costly arrangement), Brown composes for general distribution a sentimental farewell to "The Plymouth Rocks, Bunker Hill Monument, Charter Oaks, and Uncle Tom's Cabin"—an unabashed appeal in short to the hearts of his New England kinfolk. He's returning to Kansas, he writes, "with a feeling of deepest sadness." He "and his brave men" have "suffered hunger, cold, nakedness, and some of them sickness, wounds, imprisonment in irons, with extreme cruel treatment, and others death," "hunted like wolves" in an empty forest. They have gladly borne such suffering "for a cause which every citizen of this 'glorious republic' is under equal moral obligation to do and for the neglect of which he will be held accountable by God." Yet he and his men cannot secure from the children of Plymouth Rock and Bunker Hill "even the necessary supplies of the common soldier," despite "all the wealth, luxury and extravagances of this Heaven exalted people." Brown must report the melancholy truth: "How are the mighty fallen."

Such appeals to the conscience of New England bring some relief. Hardly enough. Brown is galled continually by insufficient funds. He worries especially about his wife and children. Who would look after them should he die? He complains to one wealthy supporter: "The parting with my wife and young uneducated children, without income, supplies of clothing, provisions, or even a comfortable house to live in, or money to provide such things, with at least a fair chance that it was to be a last and final separation, had lain heavily on me." But he receives some assurances from his friends that his family will be taken care of in the event of his death. The whole thing—the pleading and cajoling and sly deception and self-abasement—is deeply humiliating to him. One more sacrifice God demands of him.

He does secure the active support of some rich and well-known radical abolitionists—Gerrit Smith, Thomas Wentworth Higginson, Theodore Parker, Dr. Samuel Gridley Howe, George L. Stearns, and Franklin B. Sanborn—who want to see the Kansas war continued and widened. Brown manifestly is their man, and they promise to do what they can to help him. They constitute themselves an informal committee of support for him. They know nothing—not yet—of his more ambitious plan to bring down the slavocracy.

Brown returns to Kansas late in 1857 for a brief stay—long enough to enlist a cadre of seasoned abolitionist guerrillas willing to participate in operations elsewhere. He wishes to get started as quickly as possible. Events in the nation are gathering for a denouement. The South's pugnacity is growing by leaps (its leaders now insist on resuming the slave trade along with federal *guarantees* of slavery in the territories). The Republican party, which stands for resistance to the South, is growing too. And with the 1860 presidential election only a few years away, talk of disunion is heard more and more frequently in the land.

John Brown can't afford to procrastinate. His first order of business is to establish his New Model Army. At a minimum the nucleus of one. He sends a remarkable letter (January 30, 1858) to his wife and children. After going through the obsequies and lamentations (the "cries of my poor sorrow-stricken despairing children whose 'tears on their cheeks' are ever in my eyes and whose sighs are ever in my ears") he begs his daughter Ruth to let her husband, Henry Thompson, join him once again. He promises that "some way can be devised so that you and your children could be with him, and be quite happy even." He cannot, he says, ask his wife to prevail on his own sons (thereby asking her to do just that of course) because he has "kept her trembling here and there over a stormy and tempestuous sea for so many years," even though he needs Salmon and Oliver and Watson and the others quite badly. "But courage, courage, courage. The great work of my life (the unseen hand that 'guided me, and who has indeed holden my right hand, may hold it still,' though I have not known him at all as I ought) I may yet see accomplished (God helping) and be permitted to return and 'rest at evening.'"

(The upshot: Brown recruits three of his sons, Owen, Oliver, and Watson, and two of Henry Thompson's brothers, not Henry.)

Finally, Brown reveals his plan to his distinguished committee of six supporters. He can't keep it from them any longer (though it wasn't clear to me from Ruchames why he can't). "I now have a measure afoot," he informs Thomas Wentworth Higginson on February 12, 1858, "that I feel sure would awaken in you something more than a common interest if you could understand it." They all give their stamp of approval to the plan and agree to raise as much of the money he requires as they can.

Extraordinary, then, are the lengths to which these notable men, Smith, Howe, Higginson, Parker, Stearns, and Sanborn, are willing to go. For in supporting his proposed military venture they have become coconspirators, participants in a treasonous act if caught, whether or not Brown executes the plan. Why are they driven to this extremity? Why have they broken with the other abolitionists and allowed themselves to be convinced by John Brown? (Incidentally, they have no doubts of his sanity. In fact he meets their most exacting standard of responsibility, earns their fullest trust.) These seemed very important questions to me, for they pointed up the more comprehensive issue of the nature, effectiveness, viability of the abolitionist movement, and for that matter of the Republican party. Why, if the North was mobilizing to resist the slavocracy, did six prominent citizens, otherwise practical and worldly-wise, throw their weight behind an armed rebel, an avowed insurrectionist?

Here's an answer: an excerpt (included in Ruchames's *Reader*) from John Jay Chapman's fine piece on Dr. Samuel Gridley Howe. Chapman, himself a descendant of New England abolitionists, was a great essayist. (I'd once read some of his essays in an Anchor paperback edition, among them a beautiful one on Garrison.) "The natural power and goodness of the man cast a

spell over many who met him," Chapman writes. "It was more
than a spell, it was the presence and shadow of martyrdom. And
it fell upon the imagination of enthusiasts who had spent years of
their lives in romantic, sacrificial law-breaking. More than this:
John Brown was the living embodiment of an idea with which the
anti-slavery mind was always darkly battling—the idea of atonement, of vicarious suffering. Howe and his associates somehow
felt that they would be untrue to themselves—false to God—if
they did not help John Brown, even if they were going to do
something that would not bear the telling. John Brown thus ful-
filled the dreams of the abolitionists; he was their man. He portended bloodshed—salvation through bloodshed. It was to come.
Brown himself hardly knew his own significance or he would have
demanded personal service, not money, from his patrons. Suppose
John Brown had said to Gerrit Smith and to Sanborn and Howe
and Higginson and Stearns: "I do not want your money, but come
with me. And if you will not come now, yet next year you will
come—and the year after—you and your sons by the thousand.
You will follow me and you will not return, as I shall not return."

Yes, this made sense to me. I didn't doubt for a moment that
guilt, atonement by blood, moved Brown's supporters profoundly,
that they saw in him a kindred soul, one moreover who enabled
them to do their moral ablutions without further consequences to
themselves. True enough. And Chapman puts it beautifully.

But the larger question remained. Why did so few abolitionists
go even this far? There were many, many abolitionists who felt
quite as guilty, who felt the need for atonement, as insistently as
the committee of six. Perhaps it's not Brown and the committee
who should be interrogated but the other abolitionists—Garrison,
Phillips, et al.—who opposed violence. I wished to know how one
could go on being an abolitionist of that sort, a Garrisonian or
constitutional abolitionist, in a society with millions of slaves, with
a vast structure of laws and institutions to protect their owners,
with no prospect in sight on emancipating them.

Now I could see the point of the counterargument, too: If slavery was so powerful, so immense, how could a tiny army of irregulars, led by an amateur, touch it even at its periphery? Sitting in
Columbia's Burgess Library, I had no reply to that counterargument. My intention—as I debated with myself in the endless

pages of my notes—was simply to call into question peaceable or constitutional abolitionism as an alternative to John Brown's affirmation of violence. Both may have been equally futile. I really didn't know.

Brown is moving ahead on his plan. Early in 1858, after another swing through New York State (spending considerable time with Frederick Douglass, whom he untiringly attempts to win over) and through Boston and environs (drawing the net of conspiracy tighter and tighter), he travels to southern Canada in search of more recruits. There are thousands of blacks up there, whole communities of them, who have fled the oppression of the United States and among whom Brown sees a fertile opportunity.

To drum up publicity and assert the seriousness of his enterprise, he holds a convention in Chatham, Canada, from May 8 to 10. A total of forty-six people attend: he and eleven of his soldiers, the rest local blacks. What are they to make of this strange old man? Are they willing to join him in some *ignis fatuus* of his own devising? To what end? The great black historian W. E. B. Du Bois, in his study of John Brown (a snippet of which appears in the *Reader*), deals with these questions. John Brown "touched their warm loving hearts but not their hard heads. The Canadian Negroes, for instance, were men who knew what slavery meant. They had suffered its degradation, its repression and its still more fatal license. They knew the slave system. . . . Most of them said no, as most of their fellows, black and white, ever answer to their voices without reply. They said it reluctantly, slowly, even hesitantly, but they said it even as their leader Douglass said it. And why not they argued? Was not their whole life already a sacrifice? Were they called by any right of God or man to give more than they had already given? What more did they owe the world? Did not the world owe them an unpayable amount?

"Then, too, the sacrifice demanded of black men in this raid was far more than that demanded of whites. In 1859 it was a crime for a free black man even to set foot on Virginia soil, and it was slavery or death for a fugitive to return. If worse came to worst, the Negro stood the least chance of escape and the least consideration on capture."

But Brown presses ahead. He draws up, and the convention approves, his "Provisional Constitution and Ordinance for the People of the United States." Here, it seems, Brown has entered cloud cuckoo land. He and his guerrilla band are offering the American people—or rather the people of the land they liberate—a new body of laws. (No wonder sharp-eyed critics like C. Vann Woodward can depict Brown as a revolutionary fanatic, the Chatham constitution being perfect grist for their mills.) The Preamble, to be sure, nicely conveys Brown's eloquence and egalitarian passion (some of it previously encountered in Woodward's essay). In full it reads:

"Whereas slavery, throughout its entire existence in the United States, is more than a most barbarous, unprovoked, and unjustified war of one portion of its citizens upon another portion —the only condition of which are perpetual imprisonment and hopeless servitude or absolute extermination—in utter disregard and violation of those eternal and self-evident truths set forth in our Declaration of Independence:

"Therefore we, citizens of the United States, and the oppressed people who, by a recent decision of the Supreme Court [i.e., Dred Scott, handed down in 1857], are declared to have no rights which the white man is bound to respect, together with all other people degraded by the laws thereof, do, for the time being, ordain and establish the following. . . ."

And what follows (Ruchames includes only seven of the forty-eight articles) is a parody of the United States Constitution. It sets up a three-branch government: a House, elected for three years, consisting of no more than five and no fewer than two members; a President and Vice-president, chosen by the majority, to serve for three years; and a five-man Supreme Court, voted in by the citizenry, with jurisdiction over civil and criminal affairs, not "breaches of the rules of war." Article Seven introduces a novel feature. It defines the authority of the Commander in Chief of the Army, the President, Vice-president, and a majority of both Congress and the Supreme Court having the power to appoint and remove him. Thus John Brown's rather fantastic constitution for the people of America. I would have liked to see the rest of it.

While the Chatham convention is going on he learns to his dismay that his chief associate, Hugh Forbes (who's being paid to train the men in guerrilla tactics), has not only broken with him;

he has disclosed the plan to several politicians. The Brahmin committee of six (intrepid Higginson and Howe excepted) fear the worst (arrest, disgrace, etc.) and insist that Brown give up the plan, certainly for the present. Reluctantly, Brown agrees. In any case, now that Forbes is gone, a dangerous tergiversator, Brown has to re-evaluate everything.

He assumes a new identity: He grows a long white beard (the John Brown of my youth, of the history books) and calls himself Shubel Morgan. With his squad of irregulars he returns to Kansas, now at relative peace, the Free Staters having just about won control. Why does he go back? Ruchames doesn't say. I had to assume that it was to keep himself and his men in action, perferably in combat, while waiting for reports of his plan to die down.

They carry out an audacious attack (about which there's precious little in the *Reader* beyond the barest detail). Stealing into Missouri around Christmas 1858, they liberate eleven slaves and in the remaining months of winter safely transport them to Canada, a trek of eleven hundred miles in eighty-two days, a spectacular feat. It earns Brown fresh notoriety.

It also reassures his finicky supporters back East. He has proved to them that their original faith in him wasn't misplaced, that he's a wonder-worker capable of pulling off anything he sets his mind to. He's destiny's instrument.

During his march up the American heartland Brown writes a piece for the New York *Tribune* justifying his raid into Missouri and abduction of the slaves. "Old Brown's Parallels," as he titles it, compares the wrongs committed by the proslave forces and his own and the response each evokes. A year earlier, he notes, five Free State men were killed and five wounded in Kansas. "Now, I inquire, what action has ever, since the occurrence in May last, been taken by either the President of the United States, the governor of Missouri, the governor of Kansas, or any of their tools, or by any pro-slavery or administration men, to ferret out and punish the perpetrators of this crime?" Brown draws the appropriate "parallels": "Eleven persons are forcibly returned to their 'natural and inalienable rights,' with but one man killed and all 'hell' is stirred from beneath. . . . All pro-slavery, conservative Free State, and doughface men, and administration tools, are filled with holy horror." For the law must be enforced, and the law protects the slavocracy.

(We had our own "parallels" in 1967. On the one hand certain punishment to those violating the law: those refusing to serve in Vietnam, burning draft cards, etc. On the other hand the impunity and legitimacy enjoyed by President Johnson, his advisers and assistants, as they prosecuted a war [to me] so clearly, so indisputably criminal. The bond of unity between myself and John Brown then lay in our attitude toward *institutional* wrongs or illegalities. A staggeringly difficult problem.)

By the early spring of 1859 Brown is ready to commence his operations in Virginia. The Hugh Forbes affair is over and forgotten. Brown reclaims the support of his committee of six. Resting at North Elba he ponders the tactics he will employ when he meets Satan face to face.

6

The moment has come. In early July 1859, Brown—now Isaac Smith—rents a large farmhouse in Maryland. It serves as the base of operation. His army of twenty-one men stealthily move in; they must be circumspect, arouse no suspicion. Two women, one of Brown's daughters and a daughter-in-law, help out with the cooking and housekeeping. For months they all remain holed up in the farmhouse.

Their daily routine is described by a member of the insurgent army, Osborn Perry Anderson (a short selection of whose memoir, *A Voice from Harper's Ferry,* is presented in the *Reader*), one of the handful who will survive to tell about it. Every morning Brown reads from the Bible and prays for the deliverance of the slaves. The rest of the day the men spend reading Hugh Forbes's Manual, drilling quietly in the loft, and burnishing their weapons. But, Anderson writes, "when our resources became pretty well exhausted, the *ennui* from confinement, imposed silence, etc. could make the men almost desperate." Relief comes at night: "we sallied for a ramble, or to breathe fresh air and enjoy the beautiful solitude of the mountain scenery around, by moonlight." Brown also encouraged the freest discussion and debate. "Frequently his views were severely criticized, and no one would be in better spirits than himself. He often remarked that it was gratifying to see young men grapple with moral and other important questions and express them independently; it was evidence of self-sustaining power."

(This must have been so. How else under such straitened circumstances, for such a length of time, could the group have stayed together? They had to be independent and self-sustaining. They acted out of inner compulsion, no other. A New Model Army in the best sense. More's the pity that Ruchames's data about them is so sparse. Who were these young men? Why did they join Brown? What did they think they were going to achieve? The *Reader* is a real disappointment here.)

In mid-August 1859 Brown leaves the farm for a meeting with Frederick Douglass in an old rock quarry outside Chambersburg, Pennsylvania. Douglass shows up with his assistant, Shields Green ("a poor, unlettered fugitive," writes Du Bois, "ignorant by the laws of the land, stricken in life and homely in body"). Brown asks Douglass's help in the impending assault, the details of which are laid bare. Douglass refuses. To attack the federal government, he asserts, would be a catastrophic mistake. "Our talk was long and earnest," he continues, "we spent the most of Saturday and part of Sunday in this debate—Brown for Harper's Ferry, and I against it; he for striking a blow which should instantly rouse the country, and me for the policy of gradually and unaccountably drawing off the slaves to the mountains, as at first suggested and proposed by him."

A poignant exchange follows: "In parting he put his arms around me in a manner more than friendly, and said: 'Come with me, Douglass; I will defend you with my life. I want you for a special purpose. When I strike the bees will begin to swarm, and I shall want you to help hive them.' But my discretion or my cowardice made me proof of the dear old Man's eloquence—perhaps it was something of both which determined my course."

As Douglass is about to leave he asks his friend Shields Green, " 'Now Shields, you have heard our discussion. If in view of it you do not wish to stay, you have but to say so and you can go back with me.' " Green replies: " 'I b'lieve I'll go wid de old man.' " Douglass will never see him again.

On the evening of October 16, 1859, Brown gives his men their final charge. "And now, gentlemen," Osborn Anderson quotes him, "let me impress this thing upon your minds. You all know how dear life is to your friends. And in considering that, consider that the lives of others are as dear to them as yours are to you. Do not, therefore, take the life of anyone if you can possibly avoid it; but if it is necessary to take life in order to save your own, make sure work of it."

Three remain at the farm to guard the weapons and ammunition. The others, Brown at their head, move out and head for Harpers Ferry, well known for the large federal arsenal it houses.

Brown's plan, according to Ruchames, is to seize the arms and distribute them to "the numerous slaves" who will "flock to Brown's standard." Then, presumably, the attackers and the slaves will repair to the nearby Alleghenies, there to carry on guerrilla warfare, swooping down on plantations, releasing and arming more slaves, and so on until the South is an inferno of revolt.

But Ruchames's attempt to explain the rationale behind the raid left me confused. The logic seemed faulty, a clue that the facts themselves might be erroneous, despite their appearance of veracity. I knew this much: that Harpers Ferry was situated in a part of Virginia comparatively void of slaves—compared, that is, to the densely populated plantations of the coastal plain farther east. If, then, Harpers Ferry was a good place to start a guerilla campaign, it was a bad place to organize a slave insurrection. And if insurrection was not (or might not have been) the heart of the plan, why bother to conduct a guerrilla campaign? I had the feeling that there was more to Harpers Ferry than met the eye, than is obvious to the retrospective reader. I just didn't know what John Brown intended to achieve.

The attack takes place early in the morning of October 17. Here *A John Brown Reader* goes blank, passing over the entire incident in a couple of sentences. All we learn is that Brown has miscalculated dreadfully (how? why?), thereby allowing such advantages as he may have initially enjoyed (to do what?) slip by, that he and some of his men and his hostages are trapped in the enginehouse, his children dead or dying beside him. The end comes the next morning, when a contingent of U. S. Marines under Col. Robert E. Lee breaks through and captures Brown, wounding him, superficially as it turns out.

John Brown's failure is total. The slaves of Harpers Ferry and

environs do not rise or visibly respond to their self-proclaimed lib-
erators, ten of whom have been killed, including two of Brown's
sons and Henry Thompson's brothers, and seven taken prisoner
and later executed. (Two who participated in the raid have gotten
away, as have the three at the farm.) Seven others have died in
the fighting: two slaves, one free black, a Marine, and three white
civilians. The battle has lasted one day.

Right after his capture Brown is interviewed at considerable
length by important Democratic politicians of the North and
South, among them Virginia Senator James Murray Mason and
Governor Henry Alexander Wise, and Congressman Clement
Vallandigham of Ohio. Present, too, are Robert E. Lee and Lt.
J. E. B. Stuart. A reporter describes Brown as he lay on the floor
of the armory's office "upon miserable shake-down, covered with
coarse old bedding." He has "keen and restless gray eyes, and a
grizzly beard and hair. He is a wiry, active man, and should the
slightest chance for an escape be afforded, there is no doubt that
he will yet give his captors much trouble. His hair is matted and
tangled, and his face, hands and clothes all smouched and
smeared with blood."

His interrogators want to find out who is really behind Brown's
attack. They would like nothing more than to pin it on the Republican party. He talks lucidly (a harbinger of his prison eloquence)
and tells them nothing of substance. "I will answer freely and
faithfully what concerns myself—I will answer anything I can with
honor—but not about others." They ask why he came. He says
vaguely that "we came to free the slaves, and only that." He
denies emphatically that he sought to incite a slave rebellion, even
that he sought to carry them off. (Causing me to wonder again
what he did seek to do. If the apparent purpose of the raid was so
contradictory, was there an underlying purpose, one hidden from
view, far, far below the level of appearance?)

They assume he's a mercenary, impelled by some tangible reward or interest. They can conceive of no other reason for his
coming. "I want you to understand," he says, "that I respect the
rights of the poorest and weakest of the colored people, oppressed
by the slave system, just as much as I do those of the most
wealthy and powerful. This is the idea that has moved us, and that

alone. We expected no reward except the satisfaction of endeavoring to do for those in distress and greatly oppressed as we would be done by."

These reasons are beyond their comprehensions. They cannot believe he and his white accomplices would give up their lives in behalf of black people. ("Q: Brown, suppose you had every nigger in the United States, what should you do with them? A: Set them free.") That possibility they dismiss out of hand.

Brown would have his interviewers understand one more thing: that he failed only because of his humanity, his wish to bring no harm to his prisoners. "I allowed myself to be surrounded by a force by being too tardy. I should have gone away; but I had thirty odd prisoners, whose wives and daughters were in tears for their safety, and I felt for them. Besides, I wanted to allay the fears of those who believed we came here to burn and kill . . . . You overrate your strength in supposing I could have been taken if I had not allowed it."

(Something more for me to mull over. How correct was Brown? Did he lose for the reason stated? And if he did, if he showed such exemplary compassion for his prisoners, how did it comport with the brutality he showed at Pottawatomie? Among his prisoners in the enginehouse were slaveholders. Why didn't he kill them? Perhaps, I thought, his behavior at Harpers Ferry could cast light on Pottawatomie. To be explored later.)

But in the end he doesn't fail. Fortune or Providence conspires with him to work his destiny to completion. The fact that he's been spared is itself a miracle. It's as though a scenario is being acted out. In the six weeks between his capture and his hanging (October 18–December 2), he's permitted to make his electrifying speech to the court (the trial being a pro forma exercise, the merest gesture of legality*) and send out to the world scores of

---

* And a poor one at that. According to historian Richard B. Morris, in his book *Fair Trial* (as quoted by Ruchames), Brown was brought to trial the day he was indicted, an obvious violation of due process right there. His lawyers, moreover, were given "no time to familiarize themselves with the case against their client." Morris also asks how the state of Virginia could have tried Brown for treason "when he was neither a citizen nor a resident of that state and owed it no allegiance." In sum, "Objectivity and reason gave way to hysteria and vigilantism. This was no time for technicalities. It

letters, quoted and repeated extensively, which reveal the full dimension of the man and the destiny he has been called on to consummate. (The tranquillity and grace of his prose suggest the imminence of his transfiguration; he's conquered death; the noose holds no terror for him.) And the world learns about the appalling sacrifice he and his family have made to the cause of abolition, about the simplicity and poverty of their lives and their commitment to the virtues of the Covenant; about his bravery as a soldier; about the eloquence of his words, his joyous acceptance of martyrdom. To him, then, has been granted the spectacular honor of duplicating the drama of Christ and the saints. He and his captors play their assigned roles perfectly.

And his audience, however much they may differ among themselves on the slavery and black issues (precisely *because* they differ on them so profoundly), sense that he's sounding their knell too, experiencing a martyrdom that they will sooner or later repeat on a vast anonymous scale. They sense this in their bones, "shuddering," as John Jay Chapman writes, "not only with horror, but with awe." No one defines John Brown's "portent" better than Melville, commemorating the execution in Charlestown prison with a tremendous prophecy of his own:

> Hanging from the beam,
>   Slowly swaying (such is the law),
> Gaunt the shadow on your green,
>   Shenandoah!
> The cut is on the crown
> (Lo, John Brown),
> And the stabs shall heal no more.
>
> Hidden in the cap
>   Is the anguish none can draw;
> So your future veils its face,
>   Shenandoah!
> But the streaming beard is shown
> (Weird John Brown)
> The meteor of the war.

---

was enough that John Brown be convicted of a crime carrying the capital penalty and that the sentences of the court be carried out with expedition."
    But from the South's point of view it was hardly expeditious enough, for a month elapsed between the sentence and the execution.

I then turned to Brown's own prophecy on the morning of his execution ("I, John Brown, am now quite certain that the crimes of this guilty land will never be purged away but with blood") and recalled those awful sentiments echoing in Lincoln's Second Inaugural five years later, after a half million American boys lay dead, the greatest bloodletting in the country's history, with the end still to come. "The Almighty has his own purposes. 'Woe unto the world because of offenses! for it must needs be that offenses come, but woe to that man by whom the offense cometh.' If we shall suppose that American slavery is one of those offenses which, in the providence of God, must needs come, but which, having continued through his appointed time, he now wills to remove, and that he gives to both North and South this terrible war, as the woe due to those by whom the offense came, shall we discern therein any departure from those divine attributes which the believers in a living God always ascribe to him? Fondly do we hope—fervently do we pray—that this mighty scourge of war may speedily pass away. Yet, if God wills that it continue until all the wealth piled by the bondsmen's 250 years of unrequited toil shall be sunk, and until every drop of blood drawn with the lash shall be paid by another drawn with the sword, as was said three thousand years ago, so still it must be said, 'the judgments of the Lord are true and righteous altogether.'"

Lincoln's Second Inaugural is John Brown's valedictory.†

7

A few days had passed, spent mostly note-taking. I was confident now that I knew John Brown well enough to read the

---

† This may strike some as blasphemous. We were taught that morally, temperamentally, intellectually, Lincoln was the opposite of John Brown. And so we were as children taught the other, more familiar part of the great Second Inaugural: "With malice toward none; with charity for all; with firmness in the right, as God gives us to see the right, let us strive on to finish the work we are in; to bind up the nation's wounds; to care for him who shall have borne the battle, and for his widow, and his orphan—to do all which may achieve and cherish a just and lasting peace among ourselves, and with all nations." But the magnificent theme of charity and healing *follows* the Brownian theme that defines the struggle heretofore waged and still to be concluded.

critical literature on him with fair acuity. I'd formed a conception of the man which I was willing to test against other conceptions, hoping that mine would grow subtler, more refined, more complex. And certainly this would happen, I thought, if I could resolve the questions I kept asking myself, if I could receive fuller explanations of issues and events inadequately treated or blithely overlooked in Ruchames's book, otherwise so helpful to me and so valuable in itself. Above all else I failed to comprehend John Brown's plan as so far presented. Could so many of his contemporaries have been taken in by a scheme so blatantly wrong-headed and suicidal? Were they simply coparticipants in a gigantic tableau of martyrdom?

And so my project was more interesting to me than before. It was a puzzle and a mystery and a curiosity—and, yes, a flight as well.

Chapter Three
Assays and Confrontations

1

August 1967 wasn't a happy time for us (family, friends, community). We shared an ineffable sense of apocalypse, differing in this from John Brown for whom the apocalypse was an everyday lived experience, as palpable as the Bible he'd memorized. For us it was new and unsettling. Liberalism had definitely not prepared us for it. There was President Johnson sending yet more troops to Vietnam (adding to the half million already there, an open-ended commitment), letting us know, moreover, that he would prevail, win the war—that is, preserve the military dictatorship—whatever the cost, that all the protests and demonstrations in Armageddon wouldn't bend him from his purpose. And meanwhile there was the next ghetto uprising which we fearfully awaited, wondering where it would strike (Milwaukee? Chicago? Philadelphia? right here in New York where Mayor Lindsay walked the ghetto streets with conspicuous [all too conspicuous?] intrepidity?), what trivial incident would set it off, what dimensions it would assume. And as our fears mounted so the administration mocked us by promising more and more extravagant expenditures for domestic needs—this despite the war, or rather thanks to the war, such being the miracle of American production, such being the humanitarian resolve of the "Great Society" and the President of the United States.

In this setting I carried on my daily routine, the terms of the strange contract I'd struck with myself. Each day, Sunday excepted, I'd squeeze into the streaming, thickly packed Seventh Avenue subway, arriving by 9:15 at my seat in one of the cavernous reading rooms of the New York Public Library. There I'd stay (with long and frequent breaks) until four, then head straight home before the rush hour resumed.

The white marble fortress on Fifth and Forty-second was my refuge from the swarm of rhetoric and mendacity that assailed me every morning in the pages of the *Times,* my messenger of ill-tidings. For a brief season the library was my lonely solace.

An imperfect solace, I should add. The library had changed astonishingly since I was last there a few years before. The staff wore a cheerless aspect, as though impatient, beleaguered, put upon. I could understand why: They were serving a different clientele now. The institution was becoming lumpenized. There were more voyeurs than I'd ever seen, more thieves and vandals (to judge from the elaborate security arrangements, the number of books mutilated and missing), more derelicts, largely black now, angry and aggressive (they gave you baleful looks, muttered imprecations, demanded money), a new breed encountered in the New York Public Library of all places. The urban decay had penetrated the walls of Arcadia.

But this was a minor distraction. The primary fact was that the library did have every biography or study of John Brown, sixteen in all (as I learned by checking the exhaustive Library of Congress Catalog), these apart from the plethora of novels, plays, poems, sermons, songs, etc. I imposed a method on my reading. I began with the first book published on Brown and worked my way through the rest in chronological sequence, keeping a careful journal of every step of my progress. I wanted to see how the literature had evolved over the years, how successive generations had interpreted John Brown, how my own conception of him would fare, vague and deliquescent though it was.

2

I began at the beginning: with James Redpath's *The Public Life of Captain John Brown,* a four-hundred-page opus, complete with letters and other documents, that came out within a year of Harpers Ferry—a prodigious feat of industry. Or rather act of piety and reverence. For what Redpath presents is pure hagiography, the story of a martyr and saint whose whole life, from birth to death, was ordained, the fulfillment of a specific mission.

(Redpath informs us that he met Brown in Kansas in 1856, where he was serving as a reporter for the New York *Tribune*. He immediately went over to Brown's cause, becoming an avowed apostle of "servile insurrection" and civil conflict. Then after traveling through the South and interviewing slaves, Redpath wrote a book, *The Roving Editor,* which he dedicated to his then obscure friend John Brown of Kansas, "for first showing how and how alone the gigantic crime of our age and nation can be effectually blotted out.")

Redpath holds nothing back from his biography. "God," he writes, "was raising him up as a deliverer of captives and a teacher of righteousness to a nation; as the conservor of the light of true Christianity, when it was threatened with extinction, under the rubbish of creeds and constitutions and iniquities enacted into law." (One's never sure when Redpath is telling the truth. Not that he deliberately lies. It's that the truth *is* John Brown, unsullied, beyond criticism or objurgation. Which is why he dismisses the Pottawatomie killings out of hand as a "false charge" disseminated by "his enemies, who feared him.")

As we'd expect, John Brown is beatified at the end of the book. His soul rises from the Charlestown gallows. We could almost hear Gounod's chords in the background, the sound of dripping treacle. "There was another procession at that moment—unseen by the Virginians—a procession of earth's holiest martyrs before the Throne of God: and from among them a voice which said: 'Come ye blessed of my Father, inherit the kingdom prepared for you from the foundation of the world. . . . Inasmuch as ye have done it unto one of the least of these my brethren, ye have done it unto me.'

"The soul of John Brown stood at the right hand of the Eternal. He fought the good fight and now wore the crown of victory."

Redpath's book would be ludicrous if it weren't for the fact that it sets the tone and furnishes the raw material for so many of the biographies (hagiographies really) that followed over the next forty years or so—eight of them to be exact. And they follow Redpath in one other respect: Most were written by men who were John Brown's friends or accomplices in one or another of his campaigns; this they are eager to point out, for it's a matter of some pride to them. In justifying him, therefore, they are justifying themselves, calling attention to their own roles as activists in the antislavery crusade. Nothing necessarily objectionable in that. Apologetics occupy an honored place in the stream of history-writing: witness Thucydides, Trotsky, Grant, Churchill, De Gaulle, et al. But John Brown's apologists demanded of me something I couldn't do: suspend my critical faculties and visualize not so much the man as the aureole that enveloped him. The icon they drew scarcely resembled the John Brown now firmly ensconced in my imagination.

One work, though, stands out in the desolate landscape, towering above the others like a cathedral. This is F. B. Sanborn's *Life and Letters of John Brown* (first published in 1885), subtitled "Liberator of Kansas, and Martyr of Virginia," a documentary source of enormous value, Sanborn having spared no effort over a period of twenty-five years to gather everything he could lay his hands on, a task he accomplished with the help of the Brown family and compared to which Ruchames's *Reader* is the merest appetizer. I realized at once, however, that Sanborn has to be read with some caution: He corrects Brown's punctuation, spelling, grammar, and other gaucheries without informing you of it; mercifully he refrains from putting words in Brown's mouth.

Sanborn makes no pretense to objectivity. His adulation is unqualified. "The story of John Brown will mean little to those who do not believe that God governs the world, and that He makes His will known in advance to certain chosen men and women who perform it, consciously or unconsciously. Of such prophetic, Heaven-appointed men John Brown was the most conspicuous in our time." (The obvious question: Are we who may not believe that God governs the world incapable then of understanding the meaning of John Brown?) Sanborn was very close to Brown, having been a member of the secret committee which sponsored the assault on Harpers Ferry. And as he tells us in his dull prolix two-volume memoir, *Reminiscences,* he continued to associate with radical heroes and causes for the rest of his days, which spanned the remainder of the nineteenth century and nearly two decades of the twentieth. This child of the romantic age kept searching for epiphanies and men of destiny. John Brown was the first and most cherished of his idols.

Sanborn takes us on a long voyage through the labrynthine complexities of John Brown's life. We emerge from it more knowledgeable than before, surer of the facts, less intimidated by our ignorance.

We learn first of all something about Brown's forebears, the hard-working, penurious Browns of frontier Connecticut, especially about his father, Owen, a few of whose autobiographical letters (written in very old age) we're permitted to read. Owen is unmistakably John's father, a Calvinist divine, a humble tanner and farmer (and abolitionist as well) whom God has seen fit to keep alive through three wives and sixteen children and numerous habitations from the foothills of the Berkshires to the forests of Ohio. He recounts a life of hardship and suffering and struggle without showing a trace of self-pity. "Job left us a good example," Owen Brown writes. "I look upon my life with but little satisfaction, but must pray, 'Lord forgive us for Christ's sake, or I must perish.'" Words that have a familiar ring, for we hear in them the voice of his son.

Sanborn leads us methodically through Brown's youth and early manhood to his role as paterfamilias and his career as a businessman, the amplitude of documents adding a touch here and there to our portrait. We have, for example, the testimony of Milton Lusk, the brother of Brown's first wife, Dianthe. Lusk remembers when his sister and mother worked for Brown in Hudson, before Brown and Dianthe were married. Sunday was the only day he, Lusk, could visit his family. But Brown "didn't like that" and told him, "'Milton, I wish you would not make your visits here on the Sabbath.' I said, 'John, I won't come Sunday, nor any other day,' and I stayed away a long time. When Dianthe was married, I would not go to the wedding."

An example of Brown's obtuseness as a businessman (one that Nevins relies on for his devastating characterization): The incident took place during Brown's ill-starred career as a wool merchant in Springfield and is recalled by a friendly eyewitness, E. C. Leonard by name. A manufacturer, it seems, had offered Brown sixty cents a pound for his choice Saxony fleeces. Brown refused, saying he could do better sending them to London. He sent them to London for a price he refused to divulge. Months later the manufacturer reappeared and asked Brown to go with him to the local warehouse to look at the wool he'd just bought from England. "One glance at the bags was enough," says Leonard. They were exactly the same bags of wool the manufacturer had offered to buy from Brown three months earlier for eight cents more a pound. "Uncle John wheeled, and I can see him now . . . , his brown coat-tails floating behind him, and the nervous strides fairly devouring the way."

(But on reflection what does this prove? The three-month interval is the crucial desideratum. How could Brown have known that the market would go against him? That's like saying someone is stupid or incompetent for holding on to a particular stock while it keeps falling, then is forced to unload at a heavy loss. We always know what we should have done after the fact. Had the wool market risen, Brown would have been hailed for his shrewdness and perspicaciousness. Too much is made of this side of his life, particularly by his critics.)

Next, an excerpt from Richard H. Dana's fascinating account of his brief stay with the Brown family at North Elba (Dana and some companions have stumbled on the Brown cabin one day in the summer of 1849 while hiking through the Adirondack woods). "He came forward and received us with kindness," Dana writes, "a grave, serious man he seemed, with a marked countenance and a natural dignity of manner. . . . At table he said a solemn grace. I observed that he called the two negroes by their surnames, with the prefixes of Mr. and Mrs. He introduced us to them in due form,—'Mr. Dana, Mr. Jefferson,' etc. We found him well informed on most subjects, especially in the natural sciences. He had books, and evidently made a diligent use of them. He had confessedly the best cattle and best farming utensils for miles around. He seemed to have an unlimited family of children, from a cheerful, wise, healthy woman of twenty or so, and a full-sized,

red-haired son through every grade of boy and girl, to a couple
that could hardly speak plain."

The preliminaries are disposed of. John Brown's first fifty-five
years, obscure and private, have brought him to the threshold of
his destiny. We can now accompany Sanborn in his reconstruction
of Brown's unique pilgrimage, "the fore-ordained and chosen task
of his life—the overthrow of American slavery."

We observe how the plan gestates in Brown's soul, though we're
given no precise evidence on how it's conceived and will be
carried out, for Brown never discusses it in his letters, those
collected by Sanborn at any rate. Frederick Douglass is the only
authoritative witness, and his remarks are of course quoted at
length. Nonetheless, from his own conversations with Brown,
from his own participation in the conspiracy and knowledge of its
purpose, Sanborn is able to disclose a great deal. "Although," he
informs us, "John Brown would have justified a slave insurrection,
or indeed almost any means of destroying slavery, he did not seek
to incite general insurrection among the Southern slaves. The venture in which he lost his life was not an *insurrection* in any sense
of the word, but an invasion or foray, similar in its character, to
that which Garibaldi was to make six months later in Sicily. . . ."

Why an invasion or foray? What was the point of it? In what
ways was it similar to Garibaldi's landing? Sanborn puts off detailed discussion of the plan for the moment. The time isn't ripe
yet.

For the Kansas war has flared up, and Brown, following his
sons, must go out there first. Sanborn gives us some idea of the
character of the proslave forces with whom Brown will contend
when he takes up arms. He quotes sections of the slave code
enacted by the "bogus" territorial legislature in 1855, a frightening document. According to Section 3 (Chapter 151) any person
could "suffer death" if, "by speaking, writing, or printing, advise,
persuade, or induce, any slaves to rebel, conspire against, or
murder any citizen of this Territory, or shall bring into, print,
write, publish, or circulate, or cause to be brought into, printed,
written, published, or circulated . . . in this territory, any book,
pamphlet, paper, magazine, or circular for the purpose of exciting
insurrection, rebellion, revolt, or conspiracy on the part of the

slaves, free negroes, or mulattoes, against the citizens of the Territory or any part of them." And Section 11 makes it a felony (five years at hard labor) for anyone to introduce "any statements, arguments, opinions, sentiments, doctrine, advice, or innuendo calculated to produce a disorderly, dangerous, or rebellious disaffection among the slaves of this Territory, or to induce such slaves to escape from the service of their masters, or resist their authority. . . ." That's the sort of law the people of Kansas must obey.

Can we be surprised that Brown and his children become as ruthless as circumstances require? "The cause here," Sanborn explains, "was a public one; the crisis was momentous, and yet invisible to all but the eyes divinely appointed to see it and to foresee its consequences." Brown's foresight—this is Sanborn's logic—leads him to kill the five men at Pottawatomie. Pottawatomie saves Kansas. Kansas saves America. "Had Kansas in the death struggle of 1856 fallen a prey to the slaveholders, slaveholding would today be the law of our imperial democracy; the sanction of the Union and the Constitution would now be on the side of human slavery, as they were from 1840 to 1860." This logic (Pottawatomie equals Kansas equals America) is of course pure speculation, incontestable, unfalsifiable, a logic that can justify any deed. Sanborn enfolds murder in the nacre of righteousness.

And as if to settle any doubts that may linger in the sentimental reader's mind, he tells us how brutish and uncouth the victims were, that fact alone (what else can we infer?) forfeiting their right to live. "Dutch Bill" Sherman, it's alleged, once pulled a knife on a young woman and said: "The day is soon coming when all the damned Abolitionists will be driven out and hanged . . . and as for you, Miss, you shall either marry me or I'll drive this knife to the hilt until I find your life." Allen Wilkinson was supposed to be "harsh and cruel to his wife," a "delicate, sickly woman"; and "he was a bad man in other respects." Accounts of the Doyle family remind us of the Snopeses. And so on and on.

Sanborn is unsparing in his description of the slayings, each of them coolly and systematically executed, John Brown presiding as his sons, son-in-law, and cohorts hack to death first the Doyles, then Wilkinson, then Sherman. Sanborn waits for the gory details to end ("it is not pleasant to read them or relate them") before clinching his argument. Pottawatomie, he claims, should be judged by the standards of war. If we condemn Brown for the killing of five men, how much more should we condemn "Grant and Sherman and Hancock and the other Union generals" for doing "on a grand scale what he did on a small scale"?

The argument is specious, forced, transparent. Even if there is war in Kansas (though no one has declared it), rules should prevail. Since when in war are unarmed "prisoners" taken out and slain by their captors? Did any Union general ever condone, much less order, such a crime?

No, Pottawatomie is no act committed in the heat of war. It's a political act, deliberately planned. Its purpose—so I tentatively concluded before reading Sanborn, so I was convinced after—is to *provoke* a war, produce a conflict that cannot be reconciled. John Brown selects the five men less for what they did than for what they represent, symbolize, for the consequences their death will elicit. He could have selected anyone in the neighborhood known to be proslave.

But Pottawatomie and subsequent engagements (the battles of Black Jack and Osawatomie) do make John Brown supremely notorious in Kansas, an avenging abolitionist who fears nothing (and is therefore invincibly brave), who may commit any atrocity. His notoriety is certainly borne out by the documents Sanborn has amassed: for example, the leader of the Border Ruffians, General Atchison, appealing for help to the people of Missouri on August 17, 1856: "On the 6th of August the notorious Brown, with a party of three hundred abolitionists, made an attack upon a colony of Georgians, murdering about two hundred and twenty-five souls, one hundred and seventy-five of whom were women, children, and slaves. Their houses were burned to the ground, all their property stolen,—horses, cattle, clothing, money, provisions, all taken away from them, and their plows burned to ashes. August 12th, at night, three hundred abolitionists, under this same Brown, attacked the town of Franklin, robbed, plundered and burned, took all the arms in town, broke open and destroyed the post-office, captured the old cannon, 'Sacramento,' which our gallant Missourians captured in Mexico, and are turning its mouth against our friends."

It's apocryphal of course. The proslave people by now are willing to believe anything about John Brown. He's here, there, everywhere, murdering or pillaging every opponent in sight. Part of his success against his more numerous foe in the field can be attributed to his fearful reputation.

From the August 5, 1967, New York Times, *a story on William Styron, whose book* The Confessions of Nat Turner, *which he'd been working on for five years, was soon to be published. Styron, a Southerner himself, was interviewed on Martha's Vineyard.*

Especially interesting were his comments on American blacks, on why they were turning "in agony and frustration" to violence. Styron sees the violence as a form of "purification," something outside the frame of morality and "a psychological necessity." The cost will be immense, he says, the tragedy and self-destruction rampant. No matter. "The Negro is animated by a desire to break through and assert himself."

Then Styron makes a telling point. Whites must get to know more about "Negro history and psychology," because, he contends, "the Negro is the chief factor in American history."

Yes, I could agree with that. The Negro, after all, made John Brown possible; also Abe Lincoln, etc. etc.

With a sure hand Sanborn demonstrates how John Brown, his fame established, takes the militant abolitionists by storm on his visit to the Northeast early in 1857. Sanborn's treatment of Brown's relation to his New York and New England supporters is the best and most informative portion of the book.

Brown's game we perceive very clearly. He manipulates his persona beautifully: He's an ancient New Englander, *Mayflower* stock at that, he claims, engaged in a struggle *à outrance* against the slavocrats in the wilderness of Kansas; he's New England's surrogate, continuing on the Kansas frontier what his forebears began on the coast in 1620. He receives the official backing of the prestigious Massachusetts Kansas Committee which, after some deliberation, proposes "to organize a secret force, well armed, and under control of the famous John Brown, to repel Border-Ruffian outrage and defend the Free-State men from all alleged impositions," the secret force to be a strictly "defensive one." A feather in Brown's cap, a personal tribute to him.

While Brown is exploiting the gullibility of the Brahmin set, leading them to believe Kansas is the theater of his revenge, he's surreptitiously going ahead with his master plan, using the money they've given him to begin putting it into effect. Sanborn brings out Brown's ploy in nice detail. He includes a copy of the contract that Brown signs with a Connecticut manufacturer (Charles Blair) for a thousand spears or pikes, these obviously to be distributed to slaves when they join him. He needs the spears, he assures Blair, because his "friends in Kansas are without arms or money. . . . A resolute woman with such a pike could defend her cabin against man or beast." Brown of course has no intention of removing them to Kansas. He will keep them in Connecticut until the propitious occasion arises, until he can put his plan into effect.

Unbeknownst to his backers, Brown at the same time has hired "Colonel" Hugh Forbes, the English adventurer who fought in the '48 revolutions, notably with Garibaldi. Sanborn neglects to say how Brown has discovered Forbes. At any rate, without checking him out Brown agrees to pay him thousands of dollars (at the rate of one hundred a month, six months' pay in advance) for teaching Brown's cadre the techniques of guerrilla warfare. Forbes never has enough money, thinks Brown is underpaying him, and grows more and more exasperated with the old man.

The two men fall out and Brown as a result is compelled to reveal his plan to his New England supporters. Here Sanborn relates the story firsthand. In December 1857 Sanborn, Charles Sumner, and Dr. Howe receive letters from Forbes "which greatly puzzled us all. Brown's Massachusetts friends, either from inadvertence, or because he was not yet ready to disclose his ultimate purpose, had not been informed by him who Forbes was. . . . They had never been consulted by Brown in regard to paying Forbes, nor of course had Brown given Forbes any assurances that they would pay him the salary stipulated for his services; of which, in fact, they knew nothing whatsoever." And so Brown must now tell the whole truth. He must confess that his intention is not to be the Miles Standish of the Kansas Territory but to be the servant of Providence in delivering the nation from slavery. His hopes depend on his ability to convince his friends that that is his calling, that that is the task for which he's elected. Without them his plan is nothing.

Sanborn describes the decisive meeting at Gerrit Smith's home in late February 1858. "Here, in the long winter evening which followed, the whole outline of Brown's campaign in Virginia was laid bare before our little council, to the astonishment and almost dismay of those present." What comes through in Sanborn's report is the thoroughness of Brown's strategy. He details no carefully reticulated blueprint, complete with maps, assault points, chain of command, etc.; only a conception of what Brown wants to achieve. He presents his "methods of organization and fortification; of settlement in the South, if that were possible, and of retreat through the North, if necessary; and his theory of the way in which such an invasion would be received in the country at large."

The council hears Brown out and argues with him, "proposing objections and raising difficulties," until early the next morning. Nothing can shake him. "Every difficulty had been foreseen and provided against in some manner," Sanborn says, and "the grand difficulty of all,—the manifest hopelessness of undertaking anything so vast with such slender means,—was met with the text of Scripture: 'If God be for us, who can be against us?' " And indeed Brown assures them that nearly everything is in readiness: the men, the supplies, a constitution "of such territory as they might occupy." He could move by the middle of May. All he needs is more money.

By the next day, after further discussion, Smith and Sanborn have come around. Like it or not, Brown, they realize, will attack Virginia as planned. "We cannot give him up to die alone," Smith asserts, "we must support him." Their support, though is less hesitant, less grudging than that. They've concluded that the plan has a good deal of merit to it, that it might indeed work, one thing leading to another in the infinite progression of God's universe.

In what sense do they consider it meritorious, workable? I spent many hours at the library that afternoon mulling over the question, trying to analyze Brown's plan. Again: Was he thinking of inciting slave rebellions? Perhaps. But then his band of guerrillas would have to hold out against all the forces the South would bring to bear (not to speak of the U. S. Army), and in hostile country at that. This could only be a one-shot suicide mission. But there was nothing in Brown's career as a fighter to suggest suicidal audacity. His model, his own nature and character, suggests Cromwell, methodical, relentless, persevering Old Ironsides. Brown, after all, had a *plan,* thought through, elaborated, refined, his private obsession for so many years. Nor were the men who decided to back him so many Hotspurs, carried away by insurmountable enthusiasm. If they were extreme abolitionists, they were also cautious and forbearing men. No, something in Brown's plan appealed to them beyond (or in spite of) the military assault he promised to make on the slavocracy. That *something* was what bothered me.

Two statements in Sanborn kept reverberating through my head: Brown spoke of his "methods of . . . retreat through the North, if necessary." Also "his theory of the way in which such an invasion would be received in the country at large." For reasons I couldn't explain to myself at the time these statements I regarded as immensely important, as points of entry into the deepening mystery of John Brown's plan.

A day after the meeting at Gerrit Smith's, Brown thanks Sanborn for his help. "Certainly the cause is enough to *live* for, if not to —— for," Brown says, bringing to mind the prison letters of the future. "I have had this one opportunity in a life of nearly sixty years, and could I be continued ten times as long again I might not again have another equal opportunity. God has honored but comparatively a small part of mankind with any possible chance for such mighty and soul-satisfying rewards. But, my dear friend, if you should make up your mind to do so I trust it will be wholly from the promptings of your own spirit, after having thoroughly counted the cost. I would flatter no man into such a measure, if I could do it ever so easily.

"I expect nothing but to 'endure hardness,' but I expect to effect a mighty conquest, even though it be like the last victory of Sampson. I felt for a number of years, in earlier life, a steady, strong desire to die; but since I saw my prospect of becoming a 'reaper' in the great harvest I have not only felt quite willing to live but have enjoyed life much, and am now anxious to live for a few years more."

Soon Brown also gets the backing of the remaining four: Higginson, Parker, Howe, and Stearns. The conspiracy is set. They all know what he's up to and are willing to go along with him. They're desperate for results, victory in Kansas being for them, as for Brown, a tiny, halting step in the war against slavery. They wish to bring about mighty leaps, seismic catastrophies, the apoca-

lyptic event that will change everything. Brown embodies for them
that vision of possibilities.

A misfortune however: We cannot know the full truth about
the plan. After Harpers Ferry Sanborn will destroy many of the
letters that have passed between the conspirators. We must therefore repair to our own wits, form our own conjectures, substitute
as best we can inference for the available evidence.

Col. Hugh Forbes, steaming with anger and resentment,
threatens now to expose *all* of them. Sanborn shows us how
greatly this perturbs them, how they prevailed on Brown to delay
execution of the plan, how he returns posthaste to Kansas (after
the Chatham convention), where he spends nearly a year as
Shubel Morgan, bearded patriarch of slave-running guerrilla outlaws.

The fear of exposure having dissipated in the meantime, the Secret Six regain their courage and hasten to renew their support for
John Brown. Gerrit Smith, who on May 7, 1858, told Sanborn,
"It seems to me that in the circumstances Brown must go no further, and so I write him. I never was convinced of the wisdom of
the scheme," tells him two months later: "I have great faith in the
wisdom, integrity, and bravery of Captain Brown. For several
years I have frequently given him money toward sustaining him in
his contests with the slave-power. Whenever he shall embark on
another of these contests I shall again stand ready to help him;
and I shall begin with giving him a hundred dollars. I do not
wish to know Captain Brown's plans; I hope he will keep them to
himself." None of the six persons on the committee, Sanborn adds,
wants Brown "to report progress except by action."

In short: They're off the hook, and as long as he doesn't
implicate them he can go ahead with his plan and count, as before, on their financial help.

An incident in the New York Public Library as the day—
August 6—was drawing to a close. I was sedulously note-taking
when I heard a scream, with it the cacophony of chairs scraping
and feet shuffling, the sounds of fragile order in dissolution. I
jumped up and saw a man running down the center isle, followed
by others shouting after him. I joined the chase, in the vanguard
of the posse. The man wasn't that fast, and I managed to get
within a few feet of him. Then, just as he turned into the reference

*room (the astonished guard cordially making way for him), he
tripped and fell. We were on top of him in a trice, men, women,
old and young, a community of vigilantes. One coward, a scholar
I'd seen around for years, his mark of distinction being a black
gabardine suit, high collar, and steel-rimmed glasses, came from
nowhere and began kicking the guy beneath us, now subdued beyond hope. If I could have gotten free, I would have punched the
coward-scholar in the face. Within a minute the cops had come.
The story was that the guy had stolen a purse, which he dropped
in the chase. He was young, black, respectably dressed. As they
led him off, his hands tightly cuffed, he gave us all a plaintive look
—no rage or defiance, just quietly sad.*

*I called it quits for the day and went home feeling not too he-
roic. The absurdity of New York life right there in the blessed
sanctuary of the Public Library.*

Before taking leave of Sanborn I paused to remark on and enu-
merate some of the other interesting material he presents.

1. The "Articles of Agreement" that Brown, posing as Shubel
Morgan, draws up for his Kansas irregulars in the summer of
1858. They specify that "a gentlemanly and respectful deportment
shall at all times and places be maintained toward all persons; and
all profane or indecent language shall be avoided in all cases";
that no "intoxicating beverages" ever be drunk "or suffered in
"camp"; that all captured property be equally distributed; that
"all prisoners who shall properly demean themselves shall be
treated with kindness and respect"; and so forth. They are typical
of the Christian virtues, codified as rules, John Brown always
demands of his army of covenanters.

2. Thoreau's impression of Brown, recorded in his diary two
years before Harpers Ferry:

"He is by descent and birth a New England farmer, a man of
great common sense, deliberate and practical as that class is, and
tenfold more so,—like the best of those that stood at Concord
Bridge once, in Lexington Common, and at Bunker Hill; only he
was firmer and higher-principled. . . . It was no Abolition lecture
that converted him. Ethan Allen and Stark, with whom in some
respects he may be compared, were rangers in a lower and less

1. John Brown in 1859. *(Compliments of the Library of Congress)*

2. John Brown was born here in Torrington, Connecticut, on May 9, 1800. He was the second of Owen Brown's sixteen children. *(Compliments of the Library of Congress)*

3. Owen Brown, John Brown's father, wa[s] an old, respected patrician of Hudson, Ohi[o.] He was born four years before the Revolu[u-] tion and died three years before his ow[n] son was killed in the opening skirmish [of] the Civil War. A lifelong radical abolition[n-] ist, he no doubt would have approved [of] John's enterprise. *(Compliments of th[e] Library of Congress)*

4. Mary Ann Brown, flanked by her daughters Annie (left) and Sarah, posed for this photograph around 1851, probably in Akron. She was then, thirty-five (sixteen years younger than her husband). She'd already borne eleven children, of whom five survived; and of these, two—her sons Watson and Oliver—would perish at Harpers Ferry. Her thirteenth and last child was born in 1854. *(Compliments of the Library of Congress)*

5. This picture is the only one extant of Brown in Kansas; it was taken in 1856, probably in Lawrence. *(Compliments of Columbia University Manuscript Collection)*

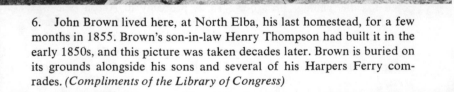

6. John Brown lived here, at North Elba, his last homestead, for a few months in 1855. Brown's son-in-law Henry Thompson had built it in the early 1850s, and this picture was taken decades later. Brown is buried on its grounds alongside his sons and several of his Harpers Ferry comrades. *(Compliments of the Library of Congress)*

7.   No photograph can be found of "Colonel" Hugh Forbes, self-styled hero of uprisings against tyranny, champion of oppressed peoples. When Brown discovered him in 1857, he was earning his living as a fencing instructor and translator in New York City. Forbes wasn't one to hide his talents under a bushel—and Brown hired him straightaway at a hundred dollars a month to train his incipient guerrilla army in the techniques of guerrilla warfare. *(Compliments of the Library of Congress)*

important field. They could bravely face their country's foes, but he had the courage to face his country herself when she was wrong."

3. Also Bronson Alcott's impression of Brown (from his diary):

"Concord, May 8, 1859. This evening I hear Captain Brown speak at the town hall on Kansas affairs, and the part taken by him in the late troubles there. He tells his story with surpassing simplicity and sense impressing us all deeply by his courage and religious earnestness. Our best people listen to his words,—Emerson, Thoreau, Judge Hoar, my wife; and some of them contribute something in aid of his plans without asking particulars, such confidence does he inspire in his integrity and ability. . . ."

Alcott's diary furthermore contains the best description of Brown I came across:

"Nature obviously was deeply interested in the making of him. He is of imposing appearance, personally,—tall, with square shoulders and standing; eyes of deep gray, and couchant, as if ready to spring at the least rustling, dauntless yet kindly; his hair shooting backward from low down on his forehead, nose trenchant and Romanesque; set lips, his voice suppressed yet metallic, suggesting deep reserves; decided mouth; the countenance and frame charged with power throughout. Since here last he has added a flowing beard, which gives the soldierly air and the port of an apostle. Though sixty years old, he is agile and alert, and ready for any audacity, in any crisis. I think him about the manliest man I have ever seen,—the type and synonym of the Just. I wished to see and speak with him under circumstances permitting of large discourse. I am curious concerning his natural opinions on the great questions,—as of personal independence, the citizen's relation to the State, the right of resistance, slavery, the higher law, temperance, the pleas and reasons for freedom, the ideas generally. Houses and hospitalities were invented for the entertainment of such questions,—for the great quest of manliness and nobility thus entering and speaking face to face:—

> Man is his own star; and the soul that can
> Render an honest and a perfect man
> Commands all light, all influence, all fate.

Nothing to him falls easily or too late:
Our acts our angels are,—or good or ill,
Our fatal shadows, that walk by us still."

4. Further notice from Sanborn that Brown's six Brahmin supporters destroy their correspondence with and about him the instant they learn of his capture. And of course they've kept no records. Also his family buries most of the letters he wrote them in 1859 for fear "they would compromise his friends." Posterity is on its own.

5. Finally, Virginia Governor Wise's generous and respectful judgment following his conversation with Brown. "They are mistaken who take Brown to be a madman. He is a bundle of the best nerves I ever saw; cut and thrust and bleeding, and in bonds. He is a man of clear head, of courage, fortitude, and simple ingenuousness. He is cool, collected, and indomitable, and it is but just to him to say that he was humane to his prisoners, and he inspired me with great trust to his integrity as a man of truth. . . . Colonel Washington [one of Brown's prisoners in the enginehouse] says that he was the coolest and firmest man he ever saw in defying danger and death. With one son dead by his side and another shot through, he felt the pulse of his dying son with one hand, held his rifle with the other, and commanded his men with the utmost composure, encouraging them to be firm, and to sell their lives as dearly as they could."

So much, then, for F. B. Sanborn, John Brown's faithful amanuensis and recording angel. If his collection leaves something to be desired, it is, alas, all we have.*

————◆————

Worth acknowledging as a documentary supplement to Sanborn is one other book in the hagiographical canon: *John Brown and His Men,* by Richard J. Hinton (published in 1894), a fiercely

* Which is to say that a good edition of the complete writings of John Brown is very much in order, a natural for some university press.

polemical defense of the Old Hero, whom Hinton is proud to have once called comrade and leader. It's an unembarrassed labor of reverence.

Hinton's prose tends to reach realms of high euphoria at the slightest provocation, especially when he's justifying Brown's idealism and self-sacrifice. Here, for example, is how Hinton deals with the Pottawatomie massacre: "There are many worse things in human history than the taking of human life. It may be that in days of millennial joy, if they ever come, that the race can put behind it all darkness of strife, all shadows of conflict, all the lurid scarlet in whose deep currents we now see the great forces that have often made life worth living. Even altruistic halos may gain reflected luster from the blood of atonement. The currents of life are not made of perfumes. War is a stern teacher; a sterner master. When its wrath is righteous, may it not be most just?"

But Hinton does provide new material on John Brown's plan: testimony by one of Brown's closest companions before a Senate committee investigating the Harpers Ferry raid. This man, Richard Realf, describes how the plan "arose spontaneously in Brown's mind" and germinated there for decades; how Brown "had read all the books upon insurrectionary warfare which he could lay his hands upon"; how these examples were to serve him when he launched his attack on the South; how the slaves would increasingly flock to his side as he drew closer to the plantation belt adjoining the lower Appalachian mountain range, from Virginia to Alabama; how he would first take on the local militias, defeat them, then the troops of the United States; how in the meantime he would organize the liberated blacks in their own territory under the "Provisional Constitution" he'd drafted at Chatham, Canada, and see to it that they were taught "the useful and mechanical arts" and "instructed in all the business of life"; and how in the end the black people of the North and Canada would join his swelling army in a grand diapason of victory, the redemption of a guilty land.

Realf's explanation of the plan omits nothing; it's plethoric, total. It seems, though, to be the product largely of his imagination. He claims to have learned of it from Brown's own mouth during the Chatham convention. But as Hinton informs us, no one else who attended the convention knew, except in the most general, undefined terms, what Brown was up to. Agreeing with Hinton, I thought it highly unlikely Brown would freely discuss his plan in detail before so many people—and just as he was about to embark on his invasion. No, Richard Realf, I suspected, was casting the plan in the mold of his own intelligibility, investing himself with an importance (as though *he* were privy to Brown's innermost secrets) he obviously didn't have.

August 7, 1967: a gray fetid day. Some early morning animadversions called forth by the Times, *or more specifically by the announcement that the United States would shortly have more than half a million men in South Vietnam. Maybe, it occurred to me, we needed a John Brown, a martyr to the military-industrial complex, an evil almost as malignant as slavery, and all the worse for being so ubiquitous, for the extensity of its power, embracing as it did labor, universities, scientists, as well as corporations. But then again it took decades to build up an abolitionist movement, at the very least to develop a healthy fear of slavery in the North. Were we at the beginning of a similar movement, this one against the militarization of American life (fed by our imperial role, our self-asserted responsibility to police the universe against communism)?*

Hinton's work is very informative on Brown's Provisional Constitution, a document which even Sanborn is hard put to defend and which he (like Ruchames) largely omits.

One can see why. Apart from establishing an instrument of government (Commander in Chief, President, Congress, Supreme Court) and deciding how captured property shall be used and distributed, the Constitution regulates behavior down to the smallest personal detail, calling to mind Deuteronomy and Leviticus and the codes of colonial New England. It outlaws "profane swearing, filthy conversation, indecent behavior, or indecent exposure of the person, or intoxication, or quarreling," or "unlawful intercourse of the sexes." It requires strict observance of the Sabbath, maintenance of "the marriage relation," creation of schools and churches, and insists that all, regardless of position and station, must "labor in the same way for the general good." For major crimes—desertion, violations of "parole of honor," the rape of female prisoners—the death penalty is prescribed. In short, a rather ferocious set of laws designed for an army in the field operating on Calvinist principles and an occupied territory under its control.

From one of the major functionaries at the Chatham convention, the American black leader Martin R. Delany, we learn that Brown at first drafted a constitution for a separate state government within the Union. This, Delany asserts, brought an objection from the members of the convention, nearly all of them black, for "according to American jurisprudence, negroes, having no rights respected by white men, consequently could have no right to petition, and none to sovereignty." Brown then redrafted the Constitution for an "independent community . . . within and under the government of the United States . . . similar to the cherokee nation of Indians, or the Mormons." Brown's Provisional Constitution, in a word, orders the existence of a black and white *nation,* sovereign within its sphere. Hence Article 46, otherwise so anomalous: "The foregoing Article shall not be construed so as in any way to encourage the overthrow of any State Government of the United States; and look to no dissolution of the Union, but simply to Amendment and Repeal. And our flag shall be the same that our Fathers fought under in the Revolution."

The rationale behind Brown's curious Constitution is obviously this: He badly needs the support of Canadian and other blacks, and this is the proof of his seriousness, the earnest of his plan. The soldiers of his Gideon's army will fight for clearly defined objectives. Like the patriots of '76 they will inaugurate a new order in the United States, restoring, as the Preamble puts it, "those eternal and self-evident truths set forth in our Declaration of Independence."

Hinton also supplies us with a good eyewitness report of Brown's remarkable incursion into Missouri, his capture of the eleven slaves, his hegira up the continent in the dead of winter, a step ahead of the law. The details:

December 19, 1858. Brown (or Shubel Morgan) is in southern Kansas, not far from where he once lived. He and his men have little to do, Kansas being quieter than ever, and he's preparing to leave. Then comes a "heaven-sent" chance to carry the war into "Africa"; also to engage in a dry run for the larger events of the future. A member of the Shubel Morgan company has run across a Missouri slave who's about to be sold with his wife and children. Brown decides quickly. One contingent is to go to the owner's place (the Lawrence estate) and free the family; a second contingent is to raid other estates and liberate all the slaves they can get. Late the next night they attack.

It goes off well. Brown and a party of twelve or so take Lawrence's slaves (the family of three plus two others) along with a considerable amount of property. Brown and his men free five more slaves from another farm. Two white men are brought along as hostages. The caravan moves back toward the Kansas Border. Encountering no trouble, Brown releases the hostages.

A few miles away the second party of six (headed by Brown's chief lieutenant, Aaron D. Stevens) breaks into a planter's house and takes a woman slave. In the course of the action Stevens kills the planter in a gun duel. Before leaving, Stevens and his men help themselves to mules, horses, oxen, and a wagonload of goods. They rejoin Brown in Kansas.

(On the matter of property: two opposing ethics at work. To the slaveholder, and under American law, forcible liberation of the slaves constituted theft, no different in kind from the looting of any other form of property. On this view Brown was a thief pure and simple. Most slaveholders, most whites in fact, even those opposed to slavery, must have found it inconceivable that some among them would gratuitously attempt to liberate blacks. What motives could they have had but plunder? Brown and radical abolitionists for their part assumed not only that it was right to free blacks without compensation—this went without saying—it was right to expropriate the owner's property in general which, after all, he owed to his bondsmen's toil. Further: There could be no guilt, no crime, in acts of violence against a slaveholder.)

The authorities know the man behind the disguise and put a price on Brown's head. Brown enjoys the notoriety: It helps his cause, brings him to the attention of a wider public, reminds his New England friends of his prowess. He's irrepressible.

The eleven-hundred-mile journey begins on January 20, 1859, from Osawatomie (where Brown et al. have had to hole up because one of the slave women has given birth to a boy; his name:

John Brown). Day after day they trudge along in their ox-drawn wagon, relying on the benefactions of abolitionist sympathizers along the way. There is no question in anyone's mind that they would fight to the death. This serves to inhibit his pursuers. The ordeal lasts two months. On March 12 the ex-slaves board a ferry in Detroit for Windsor, Ontario, where they will be forever beyond the reach of American law.

Hinton's book possesses one demonstrable virtue: its poignantly informative account of John Brown's men as they awaited the summons of their fate at Kennedy Farm and Charlestown jail. Hinton points out that his is the first biography to do them justice, give them their due. Their neglect he ascribes less to Brown's overwhelming presence in history, less to the length of the shadow he casts, than "to the strange fact that their lives were given for the negro; that they fought for those who were then the poorest and most wretched of all Americans." They had offended "the canons of good taste," "a spirit which worships success." A plausible reason I thought.

Of the twenty-two revolutionists, only three (Brown, his son Owen, and Dangerfield Newby) were over thirty; three weren't yet twenty-one (Barclay Coppoc, Oliver Brown, and William H. Leeman). Five belonged to Brown's own household (his sons Owen, Watson, and Oliver and Henry Thompson's brothers William and Dauphin). One was foreign-born (Stewart Taylor of Uxbridge, Canada). And there were five black volunteers (Osborn P. Anderson, a printer who left safe and secure Canada; Lewis S. Leary and his nephew John A. Copeland, Jr., both of Oberlin, Ohio, and active members of the Underground Railroad; Shields Green, the runaway ex-slave, Frederick Douglass's companion; and Newby, also a former slave who joined up in hopes of freeing his wife and seven children from a Virginia plantation). All in all they were men of parts, having experienced a good deal of life despite their youth, their characters already formed by the holocaust that was beginning to engulf America. Ten of them had fought in the Kansas wars (Aaron D. Stevens, Charles Plummer Tidd, Jeremiah G. Anderson, Edwin and Barclay Coppoc, Owen Brown, Albert Hazlett, John E. Cook, John Henry Kagi, and

Leeman). Some were well educated by the standards of the time
and their letters disclose a high degree of literacy and intelligence.
Here was no motley crew of irregulars and adventurers. Furthest
from it. Here was truly a Gideon's army, the cream of the American young.

What united them, fused them as a group, was of course their
aversion to slavery, an aversion too deep to be contained within
the vessel of formal and discreet abolitionism. Like Brown they
were the instruments of a higher law and owed no obedience to
statutes which bore the marks of Satan.

Samples from their letters speak eloquently for them. I excerpted a few.

Jeremiah Anderson to his brother: "At present I am bound by
all that is honorable to continue in the same cause for which I left
Kansas and all my relations. Millions of fellow beings require it of
us; their cries for help go out to the universe daily and hourly.
Whose duty is it to help them? Is it yours, is it mine? It is every
man's; but how few there are to help. But there are a few who
dare to answer their call, and dare to answer it in a manner that
will make this land of Liberty and Equality shake to the center."

William H. Leeman tells his mother why he's been away from
home so long: "I am warring with slavery, the greatest curse that
ever infected America. . . . I have been engaged in a recent association of as gallant fellow as pulled a trigger, with the sole purpose of the extermination of slavery. We are now all privately
gathered in a slave State [Kennedy Farm, Maryland], where we
are determined to strike for freedom, incite the slaves to rebellion,
and establish a free government. With the help of God we shall
carry it through. Now you will see, mother, the reason why I have
stayed away from you so long—why I have never helped you
when I knew you was [sic] in want, and why I have not explained
to you before. I dared not divulge it."

John E. Cook to a family of friends: "A light is breaking in the
Southern sky, and my glad eyes are gazing on its beams, for well I
know that they are heralds fair on the bright glories of the coming
day. My hours of watching and waiting now are over, and my glad
heart is thrilled with the joy which the morning light has brought.
My spirit seems to drink the inspiration of the scene, and I

scarcely feel the weakness of my body. I am ready, waiting for my task."

In a similar vein, John Henry Kagi, Brown's "Adjutant General," to his father and sister: "I believe there are better times dawning, to my sight at least. I am not now laboring and waiting without present reward for myself alone; it is for a future reward for mankind, and for you all. There can be no doubt of the reward in the end, or of the drawing very near of the success of the great cause which is to earn it."

Aaron D. Stevens, shortly before his execution, to a friend: "Without going into the mysteries of death, what a field of thought and action there is here to find out *how* to live and *how* to do our duty to our brothers and sisters, or to everything that lives. How little can we learn in the few years we spend here of the truth found in the infinite ocean of mind and matter."

And John A. Copeland to his family, a few days before his execution: "I am not terrified by the gallows, which I see staring me in the face, and upon which I am soon to stand and suffer death for doing what George Washington was made a hero for doing. . . . Washington entered the field to fight for the freedom of the American people—not for the white man alone, but for both black and white. Nor were they white men alone who fought for the freedom of this country. The blood of black men flowed as freely as that of white men. . . . And now, dear brother, could I die in a more noble cause? Could I die in a manner and for a cause which would induce true and honest men more to honor me, and the angels more ready to receive me to their home of everlasting joy above? I imagine that I hear you, and all of you, mother, father, sisters, and brother, say—'No, there is not a cause for which we, with less sorrow, could see you die.' "

One observation may be made from a reading of the letters Hinton has collected: the confidence they reveal. They convey no impression that the men were courting martyrdom, expecting to die.† Except in scale and importance, the attack on Virginia, they

---

† The one exception, it seems, is the Canadian, Stewart Taylor. He "somehow got the notion," writes Anne Brown (who kept house at the Kennedy Farm), "that he would be shot as soon as the party took possession of Harper's Ferry. We could not persuade him out of this. It did not seem to make him cowardly in the least, or act like flinching from what he consid-

believed, would be no different from the guerrilla campaigns they (or many of them) had fought in Kansas. It was to be the same war, greatly expanded, on another front.

I asked myself how John Brown's men could have been so insouciantly optimistic. Did they really think they could capture a federal arsenal, then take on the state of Virginia, the South, the country, and survive, much less succeed? Were they encapsulated in their own euphoria, psyched up by each other's professions of bravery and idealism and worthiness? But then again they were levelheaded men, neither stupid nor quixotic nor foolhardy. If they weren't embarking on a suicide mission and if they had a reasonably realistic understanding of their chances—what *was* their mission, their objective? What did they want with Harpers Ferry?

I was asking the same kinds of questions that I'd asked of the Secret Six, questions for which Sanborn too provides no satisfactory answers. Mystifying.

3

I looked forward to the next set of biographies—two of them, W. E. B. Du Bois's *John Brown* and Oswald Garrison Villard's *John Brown,* both published around the same time (1909 and 1910 respectively), by writers of some repute (and more or less well known to me), a refreshing change from the amateurishness and pietism of the hagiographical school, now safely left behind. Du Bois and Villard were born after 1859, and, deeply sympathetic though they were to John Brown, each openly affirming his solidarity with the abolitionist cause, each having taken a prominent part in the early days of the civil rights movement (when it all seemed so hopeless for black people), each bringing a measure of detachment to their studies (a result of their professional skill as well as their temporal and spatial distance from the 1850s and

---

ered his duty. He wrote farewell letters to his relatives and friends and sent them off. Then he seemed as calm and content as ever, even laughing when one of the men found him writing one day and called out: 'Boys, Stewart is writing his will.' "

1860s) which their predecessors were perforce incapable of achieving. They had no comparable need to justify themselves.

———◆———

I clearly remembered W. E. B. Du Bois. I remembered his troubles and persecutions in the 1950s when, an old man, his great career as a scholar behind him, he ended up in the orbit of the Communist party. He died in 1963 in Ghana where he'd settled down to spend his last days in self-imposed exile from the land of his birth. He died just as the civil rights movement was flowering in America, thanks in no small degree to his seminal labors. He died, mercifully, before Kwame Nkrumah, his host, was overthrown and became himself an exile, another sad terminus to one's hopes.

In my intellectual peregrinations I'd become vaguely familiar with the stages of Du Bois's career—his pioneer work in black history, folklore, and sociology (I'd read a couple of his earlier books, *The Negro Artisan* and *Souls of Black Folk,* the latter a beautiful evocation of the black past, etched on the tablet of *my* soul), his break with the accommodationist position of Booker T. Washington, his struggle to get a civil rights movement going within a liberal constitutional framework, his part in creating the NAACP, whose views he articulated for so many years as editor of *Crisis,* his growing disillusionment with liberals, his belief that class conflict was the answer to the race problem (reflected in his tremendous work of the thirties, *Black Reconstruction*), finally his drift toward communism and simultaneously his alienation from America. An extraordinary life, marked by accomplishments and failures, paralleled in some ways by that of another extraordinary black man of our time, much younger than he, Paul Robeson, who also grew more radical with age and who also recoiled against his hostile environment by going into exile. They make a sad diptych of our racism.

In his biography Du Bois is content to rely on and repeat pretty much what Redpath, Sanborn, and Hinton have written before him. It's *their* John Brown without, however, the romantic posturing and fulsome adulation. He's more careful, more guarded than they.

He's also a damned good writer, something of a novelist; he knows how to tell a story, and he sacrifices a lot to tell it well. John Brown flies through his pages like an eagle, pitilessly stalking the slavocrats, punishing them wherever he finds them, changing the course of history in the process. And so Du Bois depicts the Pottawatomie victims—the story ruthlessly demands it—as "the worst of the border ruffians who were harrying the free state settlers." He then takes off, his prose swelling to a crescendo:

"So Kansas was free. In vain did the sullen Senate in Washington fume and threaten and keep the young state knocking for admission; the game had been played and lost and Kansas was free. Free because the slave barons played for an imperial stake in defiance of modern humanity and economic development. Free because strong men had suffered and fought not against slavery but against slaves in Kansas. Above all, free because one man hated slavery and on a terrible night rode down with his sons among the shadows of the Swamp of the Swans—that long, low-winding and sombre stream 'fringed everywhere with woods' and dark with bloody memory. Forty-eight hours they lingered there, and then of a pale May morning rode up to the world again. Behind them lay five twisted, red and mangled corpses. Behind them rose the stifled wailing of widows and little children. Behind them the fearful driver gazed and shuddered. But before them rode a man, tall, dark, grim-faced and awful. His hands were red and his name was John Brown. Such was the cost of freedom."

But if we strip away the layers of rodomontade we discover an original interpretation, a unique angle of vision. Where other biographers see slavery and the black question through John Brown's eyes, Du Bois asks us to see John Brown as the blacks of his time might have seen him, he, Du Bois, being their spokesman, their chronicler. Brown, he writes, "worked not simply for Black Men—he worked with them; and he was a companion of their daily life, knew their faults and virtues and felt, as few white Americans have felt, the bitter tragedy of their lot." (Du Bois mentions the few "whom the sorrows of these children called to unselfish devotion and heroic self-realization: Benezet, Garrison and Harriet Stowe; Sumner, Douglass and Lincoln." Du Bois's point, inicidentally, is well taken: But for slavery they couldn't have appropriated from history their meed of immortality. Definitive proof of what "America owes to Africa.") For Du Bois, then, blacks are no invisible presence somewhere offstage; they're active participants, often the chorus, in the unfolding drama of John Brown's martyrdom.

It's his particular orientation that enables Du Bois to explain Brown's plan more clearly and coherently than anyone else has so far. He's established that Brown understood the black people, understood especially their deeper strivings, their potential (which accounts for the fact that he was also their stern critic, demanding [see "Sambo's Mistakes" and the statement of the League of Gileadites] that they strike off their thralldom to whites, adopt new habits of resistance and autonomy). Brown must therefore have known—so Du Bois assumes as a matter of course—just how vulnerable the South's "peculiar institution" was, how close it was to collapsing from within. Yes, he asserts, "the great black mass of Southern slaves were cowed, but they were not conquered. Stretched as they were over wide miles of land, and isolated: guarded in speech and religion; peaceful and lighthearted as was their nature, still the fire of liberty burned in them. In Louisiana and Tennessee and twice in Virginia they raised the night cry of revolt, and once they slew fifty Virginians, holding the state for weeks at bay there in those same Alleghenies which John Brown loved and listened to. On the ships of the sea they rebelled and murdered; to Florida they fled and turned like beasts on their pursuers till whole armies dislodged them and did them to death in the Everglades; and again and again over them and through them surged and quivered a vast current which only the eternal vigilance of the masters kept down. Yet the fear of that great bound beast was ever there—a nameless, haunting dread that never left the South and never ceased, but ever nerved the remorseless cruelty of the master's arm."

Brown's plan, according to Du Bois, was to unleash that beast. It's an ingenious explanation. Harpers Ferry, he informs us, "was the safest natural entrance" to what he calls "the Great Black Way." If we look at a population map of the 1850s (Du Bois our guide) we notice two paths leading southward to the heaviest concentrations of slaves in the country, more than three million of them by his reckoning. One, by way of Washington, was "physi-

cally broad and easy, but legally and socially barred to bondsmen." The other, off slightly to the west, ran down from Harpers
Ferry and was situated in a deep trough of the Alleghenies where
the Potomac and Shenandoah rivers converge. "One has but to
glance at the mountains and swamps of the South to see the Great
Black Way. Here, amid the mighty protection of overwhelming
numbers, lay a path from slavery to freedom, and along that path
were fastnesses and hiding-places easily capable of becoming
fortified refuges for organized bands of determined armed men."

In short, as Brown's guerrillas penetrated the heart of "the
Great Black Way," the slaves would be summoned to revolt, creating a civil war in the South with what consequences no one
could foresee. Du Bois refrains from speculating.

No doubt of it, Du Bois's explanation has the virtue of logical
coherence and intelligibility. But on reflection I thought it implau-
sible. In the first place he furnishes no evidence that Brown had
"the Great Black Way" in mind and even admits that the "exact
details of Brown's plan will never fully be known. As Realf said:
'John Brown was a man who would never state more than it was
absolutely necessary for him to do.'" Second, if Brown wanted to
set up a guerrilla unit deep in the southern Alleghenies, shouldn't
he have done so stealthily—familiarizing himself with the alien
surroundings, digging in, building well-protected enclaves before
launching an assault on the slavocracy? Wouldn't his men have
reconnoitered the area from Harpers Ferry on down? Third, a
closer look at the map, the very one Du Bois presents, reveals that
the truly great concentrations of slaves lay well below or beyond
the Alleghenies in the lowland arc that sweeps westward from
South Carolina through Georgia, Alabama, Louisiana, and Mississippi. The thickest segment of the black belt was nowhere near
any mountain range. Finally, Brown himself repeatedly, and with
some vehemence, denied that he went to "Africa" to incite slave
uprisings. Guerrilla warfare, yes—that he readily admitted. Insurrection, no. Was he lying? He had no reason to. When he said so,
he was about to die anyway.

I was disappointed that Du Bois had failed to clear up the mystery of John Brown's plan. It was as opaque as ever.

The last chapter of Du Bois's book ("The Legacy of John
Brown") is a summing-up and a prophecy, too. He's doing what

Brown did exactly fifty years before. Only Du Bois's vision is global, universal. The America he apostrophizes is imperial, the rising white star of the continents. He's speaking in 1909.

"Has John Brown no message—no legacy, then, to the twentieth century?" Du Bois asks. "He has and it is this great word: the cost of liberty is less than the price of repression. The price of repressing the world's darker races is shown in a moral retrogression and an economic waste unparalleled since the age of the African slave-trade. What would be the cost of liberty? What would be the cost of giving the great stocks of mankind every reasonable help and incentive to self-development—opening the avenues of opportunity freely, spreading knowledge, suppressing war and cheating, and treating men and women as equals the world over whenever and wherever they attain equality? It would cost something. It would cost something in pride and prejudice. . . ."

And the grand coda on which Du Bois concludes the book: "The building of barriers against the Negro-American hinders, but in the end cannot stop their progress. The excuse of benevolent tutelage cannot be urged, for that tutelage is not benevolent that does not prepare for free responsible manhood. Nor can the efficacy of greed as an economic developer be proven—it may hasten development but it does so at the expense of solidity of structure, smoothness of motion and real efficiency. Nor does selfish exploitation help the undeveloped; rather it hinders and weakens them.

"It is now full fifty years since this white-haired old man lay weltering in the blood which he spilled for broken and despised humanity. Let the nation which he loved and the South to which he spoke, reverently listen again today to those words, as prophetic now as then:

"You had better . . . prepare yourselves for a settlement of this question. It must come up for a settlement sooner than you are prepared for it, and the sooner you commence that preparation, the better for you. You may dispose of me very easily—I am nearly disposed of now; but this question is still to be settled—this Negro question, I mean. The end of that is not yet."

———◆———

Waiting for me patiently was Oswald Garrison Villard's forbidding tome, an epical piece of work, ponderous with weight (738 pages), accoutered in full scholarly battle dress (almost 90 pages of notes and bibliographical references), a definitive study in every respect. There's no faulting it as a compendium of facts, Villard having sedulously marshaled them all, sparing no expense, tracking down every conceivable lead (with the help of an assistant, Katherine Mayo, who evidently did most of the footwork and the other onerous labors). Here at last was an exhaustively thorough biography, "free from bias [to quote Villard] from the errors in taste and fact of the mere panegyrist, and from the blind prejudice of those who can see in John Brown nothing but criminal." Good! This was just what I wanted.

But before taking notes on it I did a few hours' research on Villard to supplement the little I already knew about him. I knew that he was once an editor of the *Nation,* a magazine I used to read regularly (less so now), that in the 1920s and earlier he was a reformer of the Mugwump stamp (naturally being both a Garrison and a Villard), and—small world—that a professor friend of mine, Mike Wreszin of Queens College, had published his doctoral dissertation on him.

I went at once to Mike's book (*Oswald Garrison Villard, Pacifist at War*), a good, well-researched exercise and nicely written to boot. While Mike honors Villard for his high-mindedness, his defense of unpopular causes and minorities, being in this a chip of the family block ("Villard's reputation was that of a maverick, a gadfly who subjected his society to continuous and uncompromising scrutiny. Like his grandfather, William Lloyd Garrison, whom he worshipped, he insisted on being heard and refused to equivocate"), Mike also brings into high relief Villard's weaknesses, mainly his obsession with himself, with his own moral rectitude, especially as a pacifist. Villard, it appears, would have preferred that fascism rule the world than see America arm itself (that being the choice in the late thirties), so enormously did he fear and hate the presence of a standing army and the creation of a war machine. Why then did he spend a part of his life writing a book on John Brown, a man of brutal deeds, "the meteor" of the bloodiest conflict in American history?

I hoped Villard's autobiography, *Fighting Years, Memoirs of a Liberal Editor* (published in 1939), might tell me why (Mike's book didn't). But Villard reveals very little about himself, about his real feelings, personal relations, the daily texture of his life. It's his career as an idealist he discusses (and not all that informatively either), a career, he would have us believe, that was ending in failure as the United States prepared for war again. He dwells on John Brown only long enough to say that the idea for a biography came to him while he was going to Harvard in the early 1890s and that, despite the many serious books he wrote in a long life, he regards *John Brown* as the only really good "job" he's ever done. Altogether an odd bird.

I wondered: What would crusty old Villard think of America if he were alive? The Pentagon, the Vietnam War, the limitless power of the President, the fact that liberal administrations, from FDR's to Johnson's (New Deal, Fair Deal, New Frontier, Great Society, etc.), turned out to be the most bellicose in foreign affairs, each of them having involved the country in war abroad, each having added significantly to the militarization of American life. Villard, had he been with us, would have said: "I told you so. I knew it would end up this way. I warned you against sowing the dragon's teeth of war and armaments. Now they've sprouted. You have only yourselves to blame."

Villard's book contributed vastly to my carefully nurtured portrait of John Brown. I was able to add new lines of definition, new details, new colors and shades. I perceived contrasts and ambiguities in his character that I hadn't perceived before. I made special note of the following:

A. It describes as no other work does the extent of Brown's humiliation and suffering after the 1837 crash demolished him and rendered him bankrupt. After the court was done with him, Villard tells us, he owned nothing more than eleven Bibles and Testaments, a book titled *The Beauties of the Bible, The Church Members' Guide,* and two mares, two cows, two hogs, three lambs, nineteen hens, seven sheep, and three pocket knives. Nothing more.

From Villard we also learn of one particularly unfortunate personal episode unreported elsewhere.

Just before the crash Brown borrowed six thousand dollars from a bank. Six men stood surety for him. He was unable to pay it of course, and the wealthiest of them, one Herman Oviatt, was held liable. Oviatt then sued Brown and the other five endorsees of the six-thousand-dollar note. Here the story gets complicated. Brown paid Oviatt not in cash but with a promissory bond for a piece of property called Wetland, which Brown hadn't yet bought. When he secured title to Wetland, he failed to tell Oviatt and instead took a mortgage on it. Meanwhile another one of Brown's creditors (there appear to be an army of them) got the court to sell Wetland. Brown then did the obvious: He asked a good friend of his, Amos P. Chamberlain, to buy Wetland from the sheriff. Oviatt, learning of the transaction behind his back, insisted that the promissory bond for Wetland be redeemed and that Chamberlain be removed from what he, Oviatt, rightly regarded as his property. Chamberlain naturally balked and the case eventually went to the Ohio Supreme Court, which ruled in Chamberlain's favor. Poor Oviatt was out six thousand dollars. Brown was legally safe; he couldn't be sued.

But this was only the prelude. Brown, believing that Chamberlain intended to give Wetland back to him, used the land for pasture. A conflict over ownership ensued. Brown and his sons, armed with muskets, occupied a cabin on the site and refused to leave. Chamberlain called in the sheriff, who arrested Brown, John, Jr., and Owen and threw them in jail, where they stayed briefly. Once he had his property Chamberlain let them go.

On the face of it Brown seems a scoundrel and a lunatic. But Villard prints in full a long letter from Brown to Chamberlain (written before he moved into the cabin) that illustrates the desperation of his plight, Wetland being the only bit of capital he had left, the only thing that stood between him and bankruptcy. It's full of pathos. "I have not forgotten the days of cheerful labor which we have performed together, nor the acts of mutual kindness and accommodation which have passed between us. I can assure you that I have ever been and still am your honest, hearty friend. I have ever looked with sincere gratification upon your steady growing prosperity and flattering prospects of your young family. I have made your happiness and prosperity my own instead of feeling envious at your success. When I anticipated a

return to Hudson with my family I expected great satisfaction
from again having you for a neighbor. This is true whatever you
may think of me, or whatever representation you make of me to
others. And now I ask you, why will you trample on the rights of
your friend and of his numerous family? Is it because he is
poor? . . ."

And yet, despite such episodes, despite his bankruptcy and failures and burgeoning debts—proof one would think of grossest ir-
responsibility and improvidence—his neighbors continued to
think well of him as a businessman, attributing his unhappy condition (so one would surmise) less to his personal faults than to the
ill-fated circumstances of his life.

B. The book helps clarify the complex Kansas events and the
part John Brown played in them.

If there were any doubts about why Brown joined his sons out
there and set aside his plan, Villard effectively resolves them. He
includes a letter (dated May 20 and 24, 1855) to Brown from
one of his sons at Osawatomie. After decrying the lawless power
of the slaveholders and the "cowardice" of the Free State settlers
the letter pleads for immediate military assitance so that opposition can be organized. "Now we want you to get for us these arms.
We need them more than we do bread. Would not Gerrit Smith or
someone furnish the money . . . ?" Brown's response was to take
the arms out there himself.

And, according to Villard, the situation in Kansas was quite as
bad as Brown's sons described it. By the spring of 1855 the fraud-
ulent practices of the proslave faction had swept everything before
it. "The violations of law and order, the stuffing of the ballot
boxes, the terrorizing of the Free Soilers, the expelling of Northern
election officials,—in brief, the subversion of our free institutions
was complete." Some months later the notorious Judge Lecompte
declared that anyone who resisted the laws of the proslave legislature, bogus to its core, would be "guilty of high treason" of the
United States and that anyone who even opposed them or sought
to change them would be guilty of "constructive treason," a term
never before or since used in American jurisprudence.

Now, Villard also points out that consideration of the rights of
blacks, free blacks, was no part of the Free State movement. He

makes it clear in fact that Free State whites loathed blacks at least as much as they did slavery. The first Free State platform, adopted at Big Springs on September 5, 1855, proved a "great disappointment to the radical Abolitionists of the John Brown type," Villard informs us, because it specified that Kansas must be a free white state and until then would support "stringent laws excluding all negroes, bound and free," from the Territory. And later in the year the Free State settlers by a margin of about three to one ratified a provision of their constitution that kept free black people out of Kansas. What was more, the heaviest vote for ratification came from Topeka and Lawrence, the two centers of the Free State movement.

This piece of information was new to me, and I wished Villard could have explored its significance more than he did. (He merely strings it on his bead of facts.) For I had a feeling—nothing more than that yet—that racism was central to the whole Kansas struggle, to Brown's strategy as well, even to his master plan for the liberation of the slaves. Just a hunch.

C. Villard's illuminating account of Pottawatomie. He refutes the myth propagated by the adulatory school that the five men Brown et al. murdered had been Border Ruffians or ruffians of any kind. "Excepting perhaps Wilkinson, the others were of the rough, brutal disorderly element to be found in every frontier outpost, whether it be mining camp or miners' settlement."

(Villard also prints an extraordinary document: a letter from Mahala Doyle to Brown, dated November 20, 1859, twelve days before his execution.‡

("Altho' vengeance is not mine I confess that I do feel gratified to hear that you were stopped in your fiendish career at Harper's Ferry, with the loss of your two sons, you can appreciate my distress in Kansas, when you then and there entered my house at midnight and arrested my Husband and two boys, and took them out of the yard and in cold blood shot them dead in my hearing, you can't say you done it to free slaves, we had none and never expected to own one, but has made me a poor disconsolate widow

‡ According to Villard, Mrs. Doyle, being illiterate, couldn't have written the letter. He assumes she dictated it because it betrays "her homely style of expression."

with helpless children, while I feel for your folly and I do hope and trust that you will meet your just reward. O how it pained my heart to hear the dying groans of my Husband and children, if this scrawl gives you any consolation you are welcome to it.

("N.B. My son John Doyle whose life I begged of you is now grown up and is very desirous to be at Charlestown on the day of your execution, would certainly be there if his means would permit it that he might adjust the rope around your neck if Gov. Wise would permit it.")

Villard agrees (with me) that the murders were ideological—more exactly, theological. Brown, he says, "pictured himself a modern crusader as much empowered to remove the unbeliever as any armored researcher after the Grail. It was to his mind a righteous and necessary act. . . . Naturally a tender-hearted man, he directed a particularly shocking crime without remorse, because the men killed typified to him the slave-drivers who counted their victims by the hundreds." The pregnant word is "typified." Wilkinson, the Doyles, Sherman, were for Brown only types; they were nothing in themselves.

Villard's verdict is judicious. But I felt that it omits a part of the equation—the political part. One comes away from Villard with the impression that Brown hardly calculated the larger consequences of Pottawatomie, that his motive was fundamentally moral, namely to settle accounts on his own for the wrongs done to the Free State people. Yet Villard himself tells us that the consequences of Pottawatomie were enormous: "as a war measure, John Brown's murders were beyond doubt successful; they were actually followed by more killings of Free State men than had taken place previously in the Territory; they led to the burnings of Osawatomie and other settlements, to attacks upon the Border Ruffian 'forts' and to the stand-up fighting at Black Jack and Osawatomie. If Brown intended to set men at each other's throats, to make every man take sides, to bring matters in Kansas to a head he was wholly successful when he lived up to the Biblical doctrine he often quoted, that 'without the shedding of blood there is no remission of sin.'"

Mark, then, what Villard has done here. Having described a widely ramifying political act (setting men at each other's threats, making them take sides, etc.), he turns right around and negates it

by attributing it all to Brown's Calvinism, the compulsion to extir-
pate sin by blood. This is consistent with Villard's view of Brown.
It's the easy and obvious explanation for Pottawatomie. And while
I was dissatisfied with it precisely because it neglects the political
dimension staring us in the face, I had no alternative explanation
(or intelligible hypothesis) to offer.

Another conundrum.

D. Villard spends considerable time on Brown's master plan for
"breaking the jaws of slavery." Patiently, systematically, Villard
goes through every trace of evidence, every piece of testimony,
however obscure or questionable, by Brown's children and friends
and acquaintances, demonstrating beyond a scintilla of doubt the
depth of Brown's passion, the seriousness of his commitment to
destroy slavery, singlehandedly if need be. His plan was the consummation of his whole being, all that he was.

Villard's portrait is persuasively drawn, no question of it. Something about it, however, bothered me, and it was a while (punctuated by walks through the porno zones of Forty-second Street)
before I could identify and articulate it to my satisfaction.

Villard convinces us that Brown was a man of ideals, differing
from other abolitionists in the means he chose, in the sacrifices he
was prepared to make; that is, in the plan he devised and sought
to execute. Now, as Villard analyzes it the plan had absolutely no
chance of succeeding, an adventure doomed from the start. Not
that Villard thinks the less of John Brown for it. He thinks the
more of him for it, Brown having selflessly offered himself up as a
martyr against the "sum of iniquities." And though his gesture of
resistance was futile, its effects certainly weren't. He triumphed
when the nation came to recognize the martyr for what he was.

What bothered me was having to take the plan seriously only in
the distorted image of Brown's extraordinary idealism. Villard
asks us to forgive Brown his plan, or rather to understand sympa-
thetically how an exalted soul, biblical in its innocence and devotion, would *necessarily* dream up something so hopelessly imprac-
tical, so completely foredoomed.

But I refused to believe that this was an accurate portrait, that
Brown was a naïf, an armed Prince Mishkin. Such a man could
never have led a large-scale conspiracy, could never have com-

manded and gone to battle with so much support. How does Villard explain the willingness of so many to follow Brown? Like him they all knew they would die, he says. They knew it in their bones. He writes: "only a few believed in the plan of campaign, or looked upon the arsenal adventure as anything but a death trap. Yet it was in an exalted frame of mind that they spent their last Sabbath and came together for their last meal. For them the hour had struck; their sacrifice was ready for the altar of liberty." But Hinton has told us at great length and with ample documentation that they looked forward to a drawn-out conflict, Harpers Ferry to be the first of many such engagements, a sort of Bleeding Kansas below the Mason-Dixon line.

(A parenthetical note. For Villard the Provisional Constitution provides a striking example of Brown's grotesque impracticality, the obverse side of his vaulting idealism. The "whole scheme," in Villard's words, "forbids discussion as a practical plan of government for such an uprising as was to be carried out by a handful of whites and droves of utterly illiterate and ignorant blacks. As has already been said, it is still a chief indictment of Brown's saneness of judgment and his reasoning powers." I'd concluded, however, that the Provisional Constitution was hardly as outrageous as Villard presents it. It was, after all, a constitution for a guerrilla army and an occupied territory and a population of blacks and whites, all treated as equals. The main part of it, it seemed to me, was that Brown wanted this liberated space to attract sympathizers and become the focus of national attention. Again, none of his accomplices—who cannot be accused of lacking intelligence—objected to the Provisional Constitution. None thought it an "indictment of Brown's saneness of judgment and his reasoning powers." And neither did Frederick Douglass or Martin Delany or his Brahmin partners think so.)

E. More and more the plan confronted me as an enigma, especially since I was tending more and more to take it seriously on its own terms. (So does W. E. B. Du Bois. But Du Bois's interpretation of it—that Brown sought to invade "the Great Black Way," the soft underbelly of the South—I'd rejected as inadequate.) And so, going back over Villard's text, I laboriously copied down those references to the plan which I thought worth recording, worth pondering in the future, references whose meaning Villard, I felt, fails to apprehend or explicate clearly enough.

1. One of Brown's "memorandum-books" contains an arresting note, entered probably in 1855. It's a cryptic statement about a recent biography of the Duke of Wellington, specifically about the Spanish guerrilla war against Napoleon during Wellington's Peninsular campaign. Brown is calling attention to "some valuable hints" and "imporant instructions to officers" which he found in its pages. And those pages, Villard says, describe Spain's mountainous landscape and the way the guerrillas conducted themselves. Then, opposite this note in the "memorandum-book" is a list of Southern towns and Pennsylvania cities. Villard say nothing further about these strange entries.

What struck me straightaway was the obvious difference between Brown's plan and the Spanish guerrilla movement before 1812. One was to consist of a group of outsiders going in to disrupt the established order of things, a legitimate order so far as the majority of native inhabitants were concerned. The other consisted of natives fighting against an alien army and government, Napoleonic despotism. Now, was Brown unaware of the difference? I couldn't imagine it. And why, I wondered, did he list the Pennsylvania towns along with the Southern ones? Did it have something to do with the presence of a more sympathetic population in Pennsylvania, fish swimming in their own waters, like the guerrillas of Spain? How else to explain the juxtaposition of the two items?

2. Villard briefly discusses "the purpose behind the plan and the object to be attained." That discussion for all its brevity (a page long) I considered the most illuminating in the whole book. It's a summary of a letter or statement written by Salmon Brown's daughter Agnes to a Mr. J. H. Holmes of Portland, Oregon, dated October 15, 1902, giving her father's views on the plan. Here, quoting Villard, is a précis of it:

"At one time, as his son Salmon points out, John Brown hoped to force a settlement of the slavery question by embroiling both sections. This was in line with his whole Kansas policy of inducing a settlement by bringing armed pro-slavery and Free State forces to close quarters, and letting them fight it out. After the Kansas episode, John Brown planned agitation for the purpose of setting the South afire. The Southern leaders in Congress having continually threatened secession, John Brown hoped to help them carry out their threat or force them into it, saying that the 'North would then whip the South back into the Union without slavery.' Salmon Brown declares that he heard his father and John Brown Jr. discuss this by the hour, and insists that 'the Harper's Ferry raid had that idea behind it far more than any other,' the biographers of his father having failed heretofore to bring out this central far-reaching idea to the extent it merits."

Yet, having said this (and implicitly subscribing to it), Villard himself repeats the failure. He refrains from exploring Brown's attempt to provoke sectional conflict, this being the "central far-reaching idea" behind his plan, if his son Salmon Brown is to be believed. Why the failure? I supposed it was because Brown left hardly any evidence on his real or concealed purpose, as distinguished from his manifest or apparent one. Villard is content to say merely that Brown sought "to come to close quarters with slavery, and to try force where argument and peaceful agitation had theretofore failed to break the slaves' chains." True to be sure. But it's like saying the purpose of Brown's violent response to slavery was to engage in a violent response to slavery.

Nonetheless I was immensely pleased. Thanks to Villard's (or Salmon Brown's) remarks I could now perceive a link—a possible link, a hypothetical link, maybe an imaginary link—between Brown's master plan and the politics of the time, between his vaunted idealism and the practical exigencies that engaged him and carried him into the stream of history.

I began to pay closer attention to those references in Villard bearing out the existence of that link (or my perception of it). For example:

a. A letter, September 11, 1857, from Sanborn to Higginson telling why Brown is momentarily lying low in Kansas (Higginson having complained about Brown's inaction): "You do not understand Brown's circumstances. . . . He is as ready for a revolution as any other man, and is now on the border of Kansas safe from arrest but prepared for action, but he needs money for his present expenses, and *active* support. I believe he is the best Disunion champion you can find, and with his hundred men, when he is put where he can raise them, and drill them (for he has an expert drill

officer with him) will do more to split the Union than a list of
50,000 names for your Convention, good as that is."

I wanted to know what "Disunion" meant to Brown and his
coconspirators. Was it secession, the breakup of the Union? Unlikely. Probably it meant a crisis that would precipitate a civil war.
For radical abolitionists a perfectly reasonable strategy.

b. The details of Hugh Forbes's celebrated letter of May 14,
1858, setting forth the reasons why he would have to blow the
whistle on the plan and the people backing it (causing a year and
a half delay in its execution). In the course of his long letter
Forbes explains his own role in helping develop and refine the
plan. In the early stages, he claims, Brown expected to make a
dash for Harpers Ferry, picking up a number of slaves, a hundred
or so, on the way. Then, as Brown fought off United States troops
in the mountains, a political movement in the North would quickly
rise to his support. "New England partisans would in the meantime call a Northern Convention, restore tranquility and overthrow the pro-slavery administration." In short, trigger a revolution.

Forbes says he disagreed with Brown, arguing that the slave insurrections would be "either a flash in the pan or would leap beyond his control or any control and would become a scene of
mere anarchy." And Forbes considers the "dream" of a Northern
convention to be "a settled fallacy." "Brown's New England
friends," he's certain, "would not have the courage to show themselves so long as the issue was doubtful."

Weeks of discussion followed Forbes's criticisms during which
time, Villard contends, a new plan emerged, one to which Brown
"acquiesced or feigned to acquiesce." At a minimum, Villard adds,
it had "its influence on Brown."

Forbes proposed that Brown's guerrillas organize "a series of
stampedes of slaves" over a period of months along the Virginia
and Maryland "slave frontier," "only resorting to force if attacked," and that the stampeded slaves be transported immediately to Canada so that "pursuit would be impossible." In this
fashion, Forbes reasoned, the guerrillas would wear down the
South in a war of attrition. "Slave property would then become
untenable near the frontier; that frontier would be pushed more
and more Southward." And finally the denouement, the ultimate

hope which Brown and his New England friends and Forbes all shared: "it might reasonably be expected that the excitement and irritation would impel the pro-slaveryites to commit some stupid blunders."

In other words, however much Forbes's modification of the master plan might have differed from Brown's original version, its purpose and object was the same: to bring on a condition that would convulse the nation, destroy slavery in a pillar of fire. Here was solid reinforcement of the link between the plan and the politics of the day.

F. Villard's description of the abortive raid on Harpers Ferry is a masterpiece of clear prose, the best account of it by far. A gruesome, heart-rending narrative, all gore and death. I struggled hard, largely for mnemonic reasons, to reduce it to a synopsis.

On Sunday night, October 16, 1859, John Brown and eighteen members of his Provisional Army leave Kennedy Farm and move by wagon and foot toward Harpers Ferry a few miles away. Two of the bravest men, John Henry Kagi and Aaron Stevens, form an advance party and capture the Maryland bridge and its watchman. Brown and the others go on to the armory, subdue the watchman there, and occupy the buildings. They also occupy the rifle works. Meanwhile more "prisoners"—people found on the street and on the second bridge—are brought to the armory and held. Brown then dispatches a raiding party, three blacks and three whites, to the home of Col. Lewis W. Washington, a descendant of George Washington, the owner of a substantial estate, slaves included of course. (Before they depart with Washington and his male slaves, they appropriate an ancient sword which, as legend had it, Frederick the Great gave to George Washington. Brown always put considerable stock in such symbols.) On the way back to the Ferry the raiders stop at another house, liberate six more slaves, and bring along the owner and his son. When the slaves arrive at the armory, Brown arms them with special pikes and orders them to guard the "prisoners."

By now things have begun to go awry. The relief night watchman on the Maryland bridge eludes capture and manages to inform the conductor of the train about to cross over from Harpers Ferry to Maryland. The train turns back. (Just then a gruesome ironic incident: The baggage master, a free black named Shephard Haywood, is shot by Brown's men after failing to halt on command; later he dies.) The next morning Brown allows the train to continue on its way. This evidently proves to be a blunder, for naturally as soon as the conductor reaches the other side of the bridge he telegraphs the astonishing news of a white-led slave rebellion to Baltimore. The Baltimore and Ohio Railroad president gets wind of it and transmits it directly to President Buchanan, Governor Wise of Virginia, and the commander of the First Light Division, Maryland Volunteers. The federal troops are alerted.

Meanwhile a doctor, John D. Starry, has been drawn to the scene of action by Shephard Haywood's cries and witnesses everything. Inexplicably Brown's men don't take him prisoner; they let him go on treating the dying man. At daybreak he rides off and arouses the local citizenry. Then he informs the inhabitants of Charlestown eight miles away that an insurrection is going on at Harpers Ferry. The white people's deepest fears come to the surface. Few need be reminded of the Nat Turner horror twenty-eight years earlier. An unspeakable image is evoked: The slaves are wielding pikes again. Would the heads of whites be impaled on them again? A Charlestown militia (the Jefferson Guards) is formed on the spot and proceeds to the Ferry by boat.

It's the early morning of October 17. Brown and his men have no idea the world is closing in. He has some thirty or forty prisoners; more keep coming in as they arrive for work. Brown and the others have a leisurely breakfast, ordered from a captured rooming house. Kagi, guarding the rifle works, pleads with Brown to evacuate Harpers Ferry while there's still time. But Brown dawdles and the precious hours drain away.

At around noon the Charlestown militia, a ragtag outfit, storms across the Maryland bridge, closing off one avenue of escape. Another is closed off by a contingent of Harpers Ferry townsmen who occupy the Shenandoah Bridge. In an exchange of fire with the townsmen Dangerfield Newby, father of seven slave children, is killed, his body mutilated by the mob.

Brown now realizes that all's lost. He sends William Thompson out with a flag of truce; Thompson's taken prisoner. Another flag goes out with Stevens and Watson Brown. Stevens is shot and captured; Watson Brown is hit too, but musters the strength to drag himself back to the armory where he will endure in quiet agony for another day.

Brown takes up a well-protected position in the fire-engine-house adjoining the armory. With him are eleven prisoners, the armed slaves, and several of his men. One of them, William Leeman, tries to escape. He's discovered and surrenders to a citizen who shoots him point-blank in the head; his body is torn to pieces by bullets.

The shooting intensifies. Two of the townsmen are killed, including the well-liked mayor of Harpers Ferry. Oliver Brown is struck down at the door of the enginehouse—a "mortal wound that gave horrible pain." In retaliation for the mayor's death the citizens shoot their prisoner William Thompson dozens of times and throw his body into the water. (His last words: "Though you may take my life eighty million [or thousand] will arise up to avenge me. . . .") The citizens want to similarly dispose of Aaron Stevens; they decide against it thinking he'll soon die of his wounds anyway.

Along with the Charlestown militia and the local volunteers, groups of irregulars, mainly Baltimore and Ohio railroad workers, are pouring into Harpers Ferry. It's crowded and confused, at once a celebration and a shoot-out. Nothing like this has ever happened to tranquil old Harpers Ferry and vicinity. John Brown has brought the people a holiday.

Three of his men—Kagi, Leary, and Copeland—are cut off at the rifle works. They try to break out of their encirclement. Kagi is slain at once; Leary is wounded and dies a few hours later; Copeland is taken and lives because his captor's gun fails to go off. Another miracle: The mob is about to lynch and dismember him when Dr. Starry—the "Paul Revere" of Harpers Ferry—intervenes to save him for the gallows.

An eerie scene that night, Walpurgisnacht. The festivities are in full swing. The drinking has been going on through the day and evening. The swelling crowd is working itself up for the final paroxysm of release.

Meanwhile, in the cold, heavily barricaded enginehouse are Brown, strong and alert and imperious as ever, and the hostages, the slaves, and the pathetic remains of his Provisional Army—Edwin Coppoc, Dauphin Thompson, Shields Green, Jeremiah Anderson, his two badly wounded sons, and the body of Stewart Taylor, the Canadian. (During the night Oliver Brown dies. "He had begged again and again to be shot," one of the hostages later recalled, "but his father had replied to him, 'Oh you will get over it,' and 'if you must die, die like a man.' ")

A detail of Marines makes its way through the roistering crowd and takes responsibility for the battle of the enginehouse. In charge of the Marines are Lt. Col. Robert E. Lee of the 2nd U. S. Cavalry and Lt. Jeb Stuart of the 1st U. S. Cavalry. Both men have conferred with President Buchanan and the Secretary of War. The importance of their mission has been brought home to them: The nation and the world are watching Harpers Ferry.

In the early morning of October 18 Stuart, bearing a truce flag, asks to speak to Brown. When Brown opens the door, Stuart recognizes him at once as "old Osawatomie Brown"; the two men crossed swords out in Kansas years before. ("No one present but myself," Stuart later said, "could have given us so much trouble in Kansas"—flattering testimony to Brown's skill as a guerrilla fighter from an expert.) Brown promises to stop fighting if he and his men can go free. Stuart demands unconditional surrender. The parley breaks off.

At the stroke of dawn the Marines batter down the door and with drawn bayonets storm the firehouse "like tigers." One Marine is killed, another wounded in the onslaught. Jeremiah Anderson and Dauphin Thompson are bayoneted through and die instantly. The officer who leads the assault, Lt. Israel Green, leaps at Brown in a fury, raining sword blows down on Brown's head until Brown lies prostrate and still. But fortune decrees that Brown should live: He suffers only minor wounds. Lieutenant Green, it turns out, failed to wear the regulation army sword, and that's what has made the difference. Prompting Villard to observe: "Men have carved their way to kingdoms by the stoutness of their swords, but here was one who by the flimsiness of his blade permitted his enemy to live to thrill half a nation by his spoken and written word."

G. And so a day and a half after Brown moved out of Kennedy Farm the battle of Harpers Ferry was over. His master plan, so long in the making, had proved a complete and catastrophic failure.

Was it a failure of design or execution? Villard argues it was both. No surprise, given his assumption that martyrdom was Brown's real motive. Brown, he claims, laid down no "clear and definite plan of campaign," "appointed no definite place for the men to return to, and fixed no hour from the withdrawal from the town." Also, by dispersing the men too widely he made "his defeat as easy as possible." "So far as he thought anything out," Villard concludes, "he expected to alarm the town and then, with the slaves that had rallied to him, to march back to the school house near the Kennedy Farm, arm his recruits and take to the hills. Another general, with the same purpose in view, would have established his mountain camp first, swooped down upon the town in order to spread terror throughout the State, and in an hour or two, at most, have started back to hill-top fastnesses."

These defects in the planning, according to Villard, come down to two fundamental errors of execution: Brown's procrastinating on the morning of October 17 (when he and his men ate a leisurely breakfast), giving the townsfolk and the Charlestown militia time to block his best escape routes; and his permitting the train to return to Maryland and spread the tidings of rebellion.

On the whole I thought Villard's criticisms reasonable and fair. I had one major objection, though. I wondered if he wasn't too harsh with Brown, too demanding. Why was it imperative for Brown to map out his plan of attack as thoroughly as Villard proposes? Obviously Brown and his men believed that they would assemble with their liberated slaves and hostages and arms, leave Harpers Ferry, and set up their defense perimeter in the Alleghenies rising above the town off to the west. But Brown's purpose —as Villard acknowledges—was to "spread terror through the State," alert the country, provoke a crisis, and to accomplish this he couldn't simply launch a swift foray and then retreat (as Villard suggests). I could understand why Brown *wanted* the train to return. He of course knew that it would report the frightful news to Washington and the nation. And by the time the government could do anything about it he'd be gone. And the Marines in fact did not arrive until late evening, long after his men had been trapped and decimated, just in time to perform the *coup de grâce*.

Brown's main miscalculation as I saw it was in not realizing that the civilians would be on the scene so quickly. And their presence, after all, was adventitious—because Dr. Starry was able to flee and sound the alarm. Had the Harpers Ferryites and Charlestowners shown up a few hours later than they did, Brown and his men would have been in good shape, maybe home free. No plan, not even the most brilliantly wrought, the most fastidiously laid, can account for contingencies, unforeseen circumstances. Brown's plan, for all its crudity, served his object adequately, sufficiently. So it seemed to me as I surveyed the battlefield situation in those critical early morning hours of October 17 from my eagle's perch on the third floor of the New York Public Library.

H. Finally, from Villard a fascinating little vignette: the gallows scene, an encounter full of ironies, portents, and anticipations. On that "warm and beautiful" December day thousands of troops and militiamen surround the gibbet. Some will soon make their mark in the pages of history. Robert E. Lee and Jeb Stuart; Stonewall Jackson, heading a group of Virginia Military Institute cadets; Captain Turner Ashby (commander-to-be of the Confederate cavalry), "of knightly bearing and superb horsemanship," riding back and forth on his "snow-white horse"; and, standing with a rifle on his shoulder, a private in the Richmond Company, John Wilkes Booth. Together they witness the hanging of John Brown and hear the presiding officer declare: "So perish all such enemies of Virginia! All such enemies of the Union! All such foes of the human race!"

Villard ends his book on an elegiac note, at once sad and upbeat. He has John Brown transcending the violence and misdeeds of his life, so vast and inclusive in his spirit, coming to rest at last in the sublime company of the other abolitionists, the preachers of righteousness whom he'd once held in contempt but who in fact "had prepared and watered the soil so that his own seed now fell upon fertile fields, took root, and sprouted like the magic plants of children's fables."

Nicely said. But why does Villard feel compelled to cover over with eloquent balm of conciliation the differences between Brown and the other abolitionists? This is what Ruchames and the hagiographers do, too: He was only an abolitionist of another sort, using other means. Yes, but I wished more could be made of their *differences*. I wished to compare their conflicting positions, doctrines, principles, keeping an open mind about all of them and presuming nothing.

4

Oswald Garrison Villard is one of the last of John Brown's friends. The remaining books bristle with animosity, or lower with contempt, an astonishing turnabout of sentiment. Suddenly the hero and saint and archangel of redemption disappears, replaced by a villain, a thief, a mountebank, an insensate fanatic, the harbinger and symbol, moreover, of much vaster evils: the Civil War, the conquest and rape of the South, the horrors of Reconstruction, the tyranny of industrial capitalism—the undoing of a whole generation. And all, all traceable to the cause that John Brown epitomized.

Now as a sometime student of American history I could understand how such a metamorphosis came about. It seemed to me to correspond rather closely to a change of attitude that had been taking place in the country at large. The critical works on John Brown were published between 1912 and 1942, a period marked by the resurgence of racism and nativism, by the imposition of wide-ranging Jim Crow laws at every level of government, by the exclusion and persecution of Orientals, by the passage of legislation designed to keep out undesirable immigrants (those from southern and eastern Europe) and bring in desirable ones (those from northern and western Europe). From the turn of the century on, the doctrine of white Anglo-Saxon supremacy advanced by leaps, rising by the 1920s to the status of an official national credo. Looking back on their past, Americans naturally tended to blame the Republican-abolitionist North for the troubles they were experiencing and to see the South, even the Confederacy, in the reflected afterglow of innocence. In this climate of opinion who would dare come to John Brown's defense except a brazen radical or nay-sayer? Who but the enemies of everything he represented would find him a fit subject for a biography?

———◆———

I immensely enjoyed reading the first book on the list, *John Brown, Soldier of Fortune,* by Hill Peebles Wilson. It's a 450-page screed, a rant. It never lets up, not for a single sentence. Hill Peebles Wilson (who published the book himself in Lawrence, Kansas, in 1913) goes after Brown as though Brown were the scurviest horse thief and scapegrace on earth. He's no "soldier of fortune," only a low, contemptible, petty larsonist and brigand.

Wilson's intention, he tells us, is to set the record straight, to rescue the truth from the "eulogists," chief among them Oswald Garrison Villard, next to Brown the worst culprit in the piece. "As a study of John Brown, Mr. Villard's book is misleading, and, in places, worthless. It is a jargon of facts and fancies; a juggling with the truth of history; a recital of the long list of Brown's minor peculations, and the bloody deeds which accent his career, interlarded with half-hearted denunciations of his moral obliquity and conspicuously fulsome panegyrics upon his character, and extravagantly illogical attributes concerning the nobility of his aims. The book seems to have been put forth not with reference to the truth, but to enable an ignoble character . . ." Et cetera, et cetera.

Even more than the old-fashioned hyperbolic prose, what endeared Wilson to me was the maniacal simplicity of his thesis. He permits absolutely nothing to divert our attention from it, to diminish our abhorrence of John Brown. He gives us a children's morality play on the power of evil: on how a man is seduced by greed and avarice (why this happened we aren't told; presumably he had an inborn proclivity for it) and loses the little humanity he might once have had. "The years of Brown's life were a constant, persistent, strenuous struggle to get money. As to the means which should be employed in the getting of it, he was indifferent. In his philosophy, results were paramount; the means to the end were of no consequence. A stranger to honor, he violated every confidence that should be held sacred among men; and in his avarice he trampled upon every law, moral and natural, human and Divine."

Everything follows from this definition of character. Brown's professions of Christianity? A fraud. His abolitionism and concern for the welfare of blacks? A pose, the better to win the confidence of fools and fleece them. Why did he settle in Kansas? To succeed in his vocation as a speculator and con man. Why did he organize a guerrilla force? That was no guerrilla force but a gang of thieves and cutthroats. ("Free booty, and not Free Kansas, was the slogan in the Brown camp.") Why Pottawatomie? Same reason: to steal the property of the five murdered men. Why the foray into Missouri, the running off of the slaves? Same reason. Why Harpers Ferry? To trigger a slave rebellion which would prepare the way for Brown, commander in chief of the Provisional Army, to take over the South and really get rich. At least he had large ambitions.

Wilson's biography appealed to me as a species of fiction, a farce, an extravaganza, too ludicrous or absurd (or downright stupid*) to take seriously except as a period piece, except as it betrayed an approach to John Brown and the antislavery movement and the black question that had come to prevail at the time it was written.

After this bit of entertainment I was eager to read the next book on the agenda, Robert Penn Warren's *John Brown, the Making of a Martyr,* pleased that a famous writer had also tried his hand at doing a biography of Brown.

Consulting some easily available references (i.e., *Twentieth Century Authors,* edited by Stanley Kunitz and Howard Haycroft; *Literary History of the United States,* edited by Robert E. Spiller

---

* An instance of Wilson's plain stupidity. He perceives great significance in one of Brown's letters to his wife. She'd written him saying that the children wouldn't join him in any future adventure. Brown's reply was that "while I may perhaps feel no more love of the business than they do, still I think there may be in their day what is more to be dreaded if such things do not now exist." These words, as Peebles Wilson interprets them, are "fatal to any theory that he was instigated by other than sordid motives when he engaged in his course of crime." For Brown was acknowledging "that what he and his sons had been engaged in, in Kansas, was *'Business,'* simply business." That, Wilson would have us believe, was what Brown really meant in his letter!

and others, etc.), I learned that Warren wrote *John Brown* (it came out in 1929) shortly after he graduated from Vanderbilt College, where he was part of a remarkable little coterie of Southern poets and critics, chief among them John Crowe Ransom and Allen Tate, "Agrarians" as they styled themselves (their famous manifesto, *I'll Take My Stand,* I'd studied in graduate school). They believed that the South carried a redemptive message for America—the South with its wholesome, authentic, deep-rooted values, nurtured by the soil and by a reverence for tradition, the unbroken continuities of history—in contrast to the urban, industrial, deracinated, competitive, meretricious, anomic North. Exactly the contrast the slaveholders once drew. The myth of old Dixie, tenanted by untroubled, carefree, contented people trying to live their lives in peace. The Agrarian coterie dissolved in the 1930s, most of them finding their audience and gaining their considerable reputations in the North. Warren himself ended up at Yale.

I'd read a few of his novels, none of his volumes of poems, and had liked *All the King's Men* (the movie too), a brutally realistic slice of Southern life, bearing scant resemblance to the romantic one of his Agrarian youth. The year before (1966) I'd read several of Warren's sympathetic sketches of young Southern black civil rights workers in *Who Speaks for the Negro?* Here was a different Dixie from the one he'd once celebrated. Here were rebellious *blacks* declaring en masse, in their own voices, "I'll take my stand."

This item, coincidentally, in the August 18 New York Times. *Stokely Carmichael, apostle of black power, speaking in Havana the other day, called on black Americans to arm themselves, revolt, overthrow the "imperialist, capitalist and racialist structures of the United States." Some leader, urging* others *on a suicide mission! I could see Carmichael in Havana or Africa or Jamaica carried away by the resonance of his own words, addressing imaginary crowds thrown up by the rage of his inflamed psyche.*

I noticed the Times *squib because Warren wrote an encomiastic essay on Carmichael in* Who Speaks for the Negro? *Should Warren have seen these demons stirring in Carmichael's depths three or four years ago during the sit-in and voting rights campaigns and warned us of what to expect? To ask this is to neglect the meaning of a revolution. The demons of Carmichael's character might not have been present then. He must have been a different person, the transformation of his consciousness telescoping whole epochs of black history in a few brief seasons.*

I was disappointed in Robert Penn Warren's biography of Brown. It's hardly more than a colorful, fast-paced synthesis of Villard and Hill Peebles Wilson: Villard has given him the raw material, the factual data, Wilson the interpretive frame. Not that Warren could ever be accused of Wilson's gaucheries, simple-mindedness, or unintended humor. He develops the same thesis much more politely, decorously, reasonably. Unlike Wilson he's willing to grant Brown a certain complexity of motive and temper. But it's the complexity of a hypocrite—of a man who had to hide his personal will *zur Macht* behind the veil of equal rights for blacks and liberty for slaves, being in this respect the embodiment of New England abolitionism in general. Warren finds "one of the most significant keys to John Brown's character and career" to have been "his elaborate psychological mechanism for justification." Which explains, to Warren's satisfaction, how Brown was able to write those extraordinary letters and statements from the jailhouse, a feat that cannot be passed off as deceit and posturing and mendacity (the Wilson thesis). Brown now "wielded 'the sword of the Spirit,' " but he was "still the same man who . . . embezzled the money of the Woolen Mills, slaughtered and stole in Kansas, organized the Provisional Government, and said to Colonel Washington, 'your life is worth as much as mine.' But that last month can only be understood in terms of the many earlier years of struggle, brooding, vicissitude, and prayer." And to reach that understanding, Warren concludes, "is the final aim of this book."

John Brown, the Making of a Martyr, then, is a case study of a character type, a specific kind of personality. Do we find it disagreeable, do we recoil with antipathy? We should, because John Brown is our own reflected image, we of New England and the North who shaped the land to our liking after the Civil War. *We* are his progeny. And if it's change for the better we seek, we must look to the South, the uncontaminated South, rooted in pristine virtues, where a different character type has been bred. There's where we will find the substance of our redemption.

(Was I being unfair to Robert Penn Warren? Interpreting more than I had a right to? Yes, insofar as I went beyond the strict ordering of the text itself. But then why did he write it? Warren's answer might be that the question is illegitimate, why he wrote the book being none of my business, that it should stand on its own feet. My rejoinder: I wasn't composing a book review; I was attempting to make sense of the John Brown literature in my own way, without yielding to constraints and formal encumbrances.)

———◆———

I was happily drawing to the end of my task. Only one more book to go: James C. Malin's *John Brown and the Legend of Fifty-six* (published in 1942 under the regal auspices of the American Philosophical Society of Philadelphia). And what a book! Enough to intimidate the most worm-eaten scholar. A behemoth of a book, nearly 800 pages, densely packed, all concentrating on John Brown's Kansas experience; 1856 at that. What would possess anyone to build such a mountain to bring forth such a mouse? That was what I asked myself after hastily perusing its contents.

James C. Malin was a name that had somehow clung to the filaments of my memory, one of my teachers at Columbia long ago having praised him as a historian whose faint reputation belied his large talents. Ruchames mentions him in a footnote as one of Brown's most acidulous critics. And Allan Nevins admits that he depended heavily on Malin for his Kansas chapters. Malin (as I discovered after making the rounds of the standard references) was a long-time professor at the University of Kansas who wrote a goodly number of books (the New York Public Library's catalog omits nothing), most of them on the politics and culture and geography of the Midwest, Kansas in particular. Despite the perfunctory reading I gave them—a skimming really—I came away impressed by his scholarship, his ability to weave together large themes and minute facts, and his brisk, muscular, combative style

—one worthy, it seemed to me, of a subject more ambitious than the grasslands of Kansas.

My survey of the Malin *oeuvre* convinced me that his elephantine book on John Brown, esoteric and narrowly specialized as it was, deserved the intensive study I gave it, and I sweated my Malin to completion through some of the worst dog days of August 1967.

Notable are his faults. *John Brown and the Legend of Fifty-six* allows Malin the scope and freedom to display them *in extremis*. He dismisses all biographies of Brown as amateurish or irredeemably partisan, claiming that he alone is objective because he alone could say (quoting Emily Dickinson), " 'I had no time for hate. . . .' " Being a "professional historian" he's the first to conduct a "strictly scientific study."

(He's wrong. W. E. B. Du Bois was a professional historian. Is that why Du Bois gets such short shrift: barely a footnote in 800 pages? "Only one biography of John Brown has been written by a Negro, Du Bois, and it is too badly done and relatively of too little importance to merit more than mention." And that takes care of that!)

Two things about Malin's formulation bothered me: first, that someone has to be a professional historian to do justice to past events, which effectively eliminates the likes of Thucydides, Macaulay, Parkman, Prescott, Rhodes, Bancroft, Beveridge, Lea, and a few others of their breed—amateurs all—who wrote for the public in general rather than for each other and who never wrote a scholarly monograph in their lives; and second, that objectivity is assured and science vindicated because the (professional) historian has no ax to grind, no personal interest in the outcome of the events he describes. I wondered why a historian ceases to be objective or scientific if he *does* have an ideological commitment to one side or the other in a past conflict that still engages him. How, for example, can one be objective or scientific (in Malin's meaning of the terms) about John Brown? Malin's error is to create a false opposition between values and facts. The historian makes a value judgment in the very subject he chooses to study, in the very facts he marshals and draws on. Whether he's aware of choosing, judging, selecting, appraising, organizing, etc., is beside the point.

That's what he does, apart from which there are no "facts" as such.

The very title of Malin's opus betrays his animus toward John Brown and Brown's apologists. He asks: "What is the meaning of the Legend about John Brown? Is it an endorsement of the application of direct action to social change, an approval of the overthrow of institutions by violence?" Note the assumptions implicit in these questions. Brown is presented as an apostle of "direct action" and "violence" who rose up against institutions and the ordinary processes of social change. We're not told that *slavery* is the institution in question. Malin tacitly accepts it as normal and legitimate (though Southerners admitted it was "peculiar") and so throws the entire burden of wrongdoing on John Brown. Malin is clearly operating in the realm of ideology and value.

He goes on to attack the people he thinks responsible for promulgating the John Brown legend. "A review of three-quarters of a century of the growth of the Kansas phase of the Legend," he writes, "emphasizes the fact that John Brown has had his strongest hold among the conservative classes of society. It has never been conspicuous as an inspiration of industrial wage workers or even of Marxian revolutionaries. It has served rather, perhaps, as a sort of psychological compensation for people otherwise most respectable and conservative socially. . . . Is it merely a strange paradox, or is it a form of practical or even a necessary balancing of social forces, that such a national Legend, grounded in a doctrine of violence, should become to such a degree an escape mechanism for a class of society which would be most injured by its application?"

Now, consider the logic of this assertion. Without offering a single piece of evidence (odd for a scientific historian) Malin establishes the "fact" that the conservative classes have been Brown's staunchest supporters. The contrary seemed to me to be the case. The Brahmins and intellectuals who unreservedly sided with him—Higginson, Sanborn, Howe, Thoreau, Emerson, et al.— were reformers or radicals throughout their lives; so were his sympathetic biographers down through the years from Redpath to Villard; so were the authors—from Frederick Douglass to Clarence Darrow—whose essays and speeches Ruchames includes in his collection. Where, I wanted to know, were the conservatives?

Having produced no evidence or cited a single name, Malin then maunders all over the lot in his silly, opinionated fashion on the putative needs of conservative people for compensation and escape.

None of this I would have thought unforgivable if it had come from someone more humble about himself and his vocation, someone just a little less certain of his own disinterestedness and objectivity, someone less prone to condemn the failings of others.

But Malin's primary fault is what I liked to call his facticity— his invincible love of documented minutiae, his tendency to lose himself in the complexities of the most trivial event. To Malin of course no event, no document, is trivial; if it exists it must be examined critically and fitted into the factual scheme of things. Facticity gives him his freedom, his power. He comes alive, his energy leaps off the page, when he cites a settler's diary, a rural newspaper, a squatter's claim—the more citations, the better.

Facticity also enables Malin to discard or bracket out anything not fully documented, anything ambiguous or unclear or vaguely limned. Facticity as a mode of thinking lends itself to minutiae, the registry and emplacement of precise and indisputable "facts," and as such becomes a weapon of attack in the hands of a historian like Malin. If a statement or idea can't be proved beyond doubt and backed by an army of evidence, it can't be seriously entertained.

And so Malin can call into question John Brown's abolitionism because he finds only four "authenticated episodes in which he was connected with the negro question": his 1834 letter to his brother asking for help to set up a school for ex-slaves; his "Sambo's Mistakes" article of 1848–49; his organizing the League of Gileadites in 1851; and his moving to North Elba, New York, for the purpose of aiding black farmers. These being the only "authenticated episodes," Malin argues, we may not generalize about what drove Brown to a life of lawlessness.

But, violating his own injunction, Malin does presume to know what drove him, and it wasn't abolitionism; it was the main chance, the desire to get on, make it, succeed. We are, in short, back to the Hill Peebles Wilson thesis served up now by a professional historian engaged in scientific study. "There was nothing unusual in the migration of the Brown family to the frontier,"

Malin writes. "He [John Brown] was not accustomed to settle down to the routine and drudgery of farm life. He was almost continually on the move, on the lookout for a business deal, frequently something on a large scale. Wherever he went he inquired about prices of land, livestock, corn and other farm products. His letters illustrate this abundantly. Possibly every rural community had at least one such character, who lived by trading, by buying most anything he thought he could resell at a profit, moving restlessly from place to place engaging in petty business but always pursuing that illusive, spectacular big deal which would bring fame and fortune."

If Brown was such a "character" why did he suddenly emerge as an antislavery guerrilla leader in Kansas? Unlike Peebles Wilson Malin refrains from expressly stating that failure turned Brown into a desperado who used abolition as a cover for his exploits. Malin after all lacks the documentary proof. But at every juncture he raises a plethora of questions about Brown's real motives. He digs deep into the available minutiae and discovers tiny factlets of support. He dissects Brown's behavior with the care of a brain surgeon.

(An example: On his way to Kansas in 1855 Brown stopped off at various places to raise money for the purchase of arms. What, Malin wants to know, "had Brown done with the money he had raised at Syracuse and in Ohio, and in Massachusetts to expend for arms? Did he spend all of that money for arms and still have so large a balance to pay? What became of such a quantity of arms as could have been purchased by these sums plus the amount of aid collected in the form of arms and ammunition? Or had Brown diverted to his own use sums entrusted to him, as he had done in the case of the New England Woolen Company funds? Why did he write Day specifying particularly that it was the arms bought of Carter that had maybe saved them from 'awkward circumstances,' when he had collected other arms in Ohio in considerable quantities? There was never any accounting of the total collections either of cash, arms or ammunition, or of their disposition or use. Without more specific information, each reader of the record is left at liberty to draw his own conclusions." I saw what Malin, master of facticity, is driving at. He expects John Brown to have been as exact as Price, Waterhouse in his multitudinous accounts and dealings, yes down to the last penny. It was Brown's duty to the historians of the future. Having failed to perform that duty, he's suspect, each of his acts are open to question, and the "reader of the record" can "draw his own conclusions.")

Malin's John Brown is a rather small man. Not as small and mean and contemptible as Peeble Wilson's, but certainly much, much smaller than the "Legend of Fifty-six" made him out to be. Malin wants us to notice the tremendous distance between the real person and the popular myth. He devotes almost 800 pages to the task of demythologizing John Brown, showing how the legend arose and took hold and, alas, made such an impression on the national conscience.

Right here, it appeared to me, lay the central defect of the book. Malin cannot explain why so many people, beginning with the abolitionists and their epigone, seized on John Brown, specifically *him,* no one else, as the bearer of legend—even assuming (as I emphatically did not) that they all had a need for a hero. "A frustrated generation of youth found its opportunity in an outpouring of emotion upon a cause and a man. . . . The Civil War was the climax of the cycle [of social reform] in the United States and it was American youth which caught up the banner of nationalism and abolition. John Brown became its first Hero, and had no serious rival until the assassin's bullet added the martyred Lincoln.") Malin admits that many were around to choose from. "So far as precedents are concerned, the technique of guerrilla warfare became standardized so quickly among the free-state and pro-slavery partisans as to give Brown no distinction or originality in that dubious trade." True enough. Why then did *he* win the adulation of so many? Was there in fact something in him that accounted for it?

It seemed unquestionable to me that there was. He alone among guerrilla fighters acted according to an overall plan or strategy. More than that: according to a set of ideological principles. That's what singled him out from the rest. That's why he became a legend even in Kansas, where so many other Free State guerrillas operated. That's why he went on to infinitely greater notoriety at Harpers Ferry.

I could understand Malin's problem. For him to concede this

distinction and originality in Brown is to undermine—worse, ne-
gate—his enterprise. It is to uphold the legend, justify it. Adamant
as oak, Malin concedes nothing. Brown was a violent and desperate man who did such and such and caused such and such to happen, all quite reprehensible. Period.

I had to check myself. My notebook bent under the weight of
the argument I was carrying on with Malin's ghost. The sin of facticity, as I discovered, had its attractions.

But what I learned from Malin easily repaid the Sisyphusian labors I spent reading his compendium. He silhouettes John Brown
against his Kansas background—not the Kansas where guerrilla
armies fought pitched battles, where men slew each other in cold
blood, where legends were made, but a prosaic unsung Kansas
where political conflicts were fought and rules of governing
defined. Malin's lengthy technical discussion illuminated whole regions of my understanding.

Of course he sets up the parameters of the discussion in a way
most favorable to his own predilections, his own structure of
values. He favors the popular sovereignty formula under which
Kansas was to be settled and the slavery issue resolved, voted up
or down by majority rule—a formula which assumed the moral
equivalence of freedom and slavery, a local choice like any other.
Now for the advocates of popular sovereignty, chief among them
Senator Stephen A. Douglas of Illinois, who sponsored the
Kansas-Nebraska Act (his meal ticket to the presidency), this
moral neutrality was the price that had to be paid for union and
peace, the only alternatives being disunion and war. That's where
Malin stands, too. Like Stephen Douglas he declares a pox on
both Northern and Southern fire-eaters or "extremists," those who
placed their sections or interests or private moral principles above
the well-being of the whole country—more accurately, those not
in the Douglas camp.

That I rejected the terms of his discussion went without saying.
I thought Malin was taking extraordinary liberties with history.
He has no warrant to order the conflicts of the past to his ideological specifications, determining, for instance, who is or isn't an
"extremist," a word freighted with meaning. Conflicts are fought
out according to their own rules. A deeply serious conflict will

produce "extremes"—the deeper they are the more "extreme." To treat the "extremes" as though they're somehow external to the conflict—as Malin does—is to deny its seriousness and implicity to accuse the actors involved in it of error or self-delusion or wickedness. Ah, if only the generation of the 1850s could have solved their problems in a peaceable, rational way. If only the "extremists" could have been effectively dealt with, put in their places. If only the importance of slavery hadn't been so exaggerated. If only . . .

Nonetheless Malin serves as our indispensable guide—this is his great virtue, his métier—in exploring the complex relations between the groups contending for power in Kansas, in particular those that comprised the Free State party. Sanborn and Villard only touch upon these recondite matters. Malin made me realize how much they miss by their failure and how much their works suffer for it.

I knew from Villard that most Kansas Free Staters were racist, that their constitution excluded blacks as well as slaves. Why this strong animus against blacks? Primarily, Malin points out, it was because of the large number of settlers from Southern and Border States who were in search of a pure white man's country virgin free of both race and class. By 1860, Malin informs us, almost 60 per cent of the Kansas inhabitants had come from slaveholding Border States. Their attitude can be summed up in a letter (quoted by Malin) from a New England settler to his folks back home: "The community here are very nearly united on the free state question. But the majority would dislike and resent being called abolitionists. . . . There is a prevailing sentiment against admitting negroes into the Territory at all, slave or free. . . . The western people are far the most numerous in the Territory. The country is no different from our Eastern country and the character of Eastern immigration is such . . . that I think one-half at least of the Eastern people return. Those who stay love the country as they get used to it. The Western people find much such a country as they left behind them, and settle right down, build their cabins, fence and break up their fields and drop their corn, before you hardly know they are here. They have a strong instinct against slavery, do not want it about them, but lack the strong moral sense of its injustice which we feel."

Malin nicely presents the dynamic interplay between the various factions of the racist Free State movement: the more militant racists versus the less militant. The more militant posed a clear choice: "slavery before free negroes"; the proslavery party over the abolitionists. The difference between these Free State factions —so I inferred—rested on the difference in their spheres of loyalty. The militant racists inclined toward the South in the emergent sectional struggle. The less militant inclined toward the North. Both, however, agreed on a strict policy of keeping out all black people, a policy written into Free State laws and constitutions.

The significant variable was the strength or danger of the proslavery party. When it seemed that the proslavery party would win, when the bogus legislature and courts and the Border Ruffians were riding high, more and more Free Staters, including a good number of militantly racist ones, were willing to countenance—even participate in—some form of direct action. Enter John Brown. He represented the *ne plus ultra* of the Free State "left." And because such an "extreme" tendency found a place in the Free State ranks, so many of the militant racists defected to the other side, joining the proslavery party. The ideological spectrum was broad and there was a considerable crossing of the lines.

Thanks to Malin I acquired a clear conception of how the middle of the road or majority Free State faction viewed John Brown. During the period of intensest struggle against the Border Ruffians, when it appeared that Kansas would opt for slavery— and once done nothing could undo it—Brown was highly useful, whatever his ulterior purposes, however detestable his convictions. The job had to be done and he was the man to do it. But the moment the crisis passed, the moment order was established (by the late fall of 1856), and the Free State majority could assert itself, John Brown became an albatross and had no further reason to stay.

What Malin brings into focus, in other words, is the nature of the conflict between John Brown and the Free State forces in general. Regardless of their differences, *all* Free State people (to labor the point) wanted the blacks out. Once that was secured, the issue, the contest, was over. "We look on the great question as now settled," one of the most influential advocates of the Kansas

Free State cause wrote in 1857 (in a valuable letter that Malin excerpts), "and all political movements in Kansas as having chiefly a local interest. . . . Now we must be magnanimous to the South. Slavery cannot be extended. Whether it can ever be got rid of in this country is doubtful. It is a curse imposed by the sins of our ancestors, and we must bear it patiently." What is this but a faithful expression of the Republican party's position in the 1850s? Quarantine slavery; confine it to where it is; do not disturb it; it might just die of inanition. It was a position that sanctioned the status quo, therefore the perpetuation of slavery.

Then and there, as I followed the dialectics of Malin's discussion, I realized that *John Brown's main quarrel was not with the Border Ruffians and the slavocracy; it was with the Free State people, his sometime allies.* The freedom of Kansas was their sole concern; the destruction of slavery was his. So that *their triumph necessarily meant his defeat.*

And for our further edification Malin summarizes the Free Staters' version of their differences with Brown, as their leader, Governor Charles Robinson, recounted it at length. "Robinson declared that John Brown told him he did not come to settle or establish a free-state government but to create difficulties; that Brown expected the Kansas troubles to spread into a general abolition war; that Geary's peace prevented the consummation of such plans in 1856." And years later in the course of an extensive argument with John Brown, Jr., on the Pottawatomie affair Robinson elaborated on his differences with Brown. He "assured the son," Malin writes, "that he did not look upon his father as a murderer in any ordinary sense as some others did, he gave John Brown credit for sincerity in his convictions that his course was justified in view of his objectives, but the real issue on which he and Brown had disagreed was this matter of objective. John Brown was making war on slavery as an institution and hoped to inflame the opposing forces to a war, which would result in general emancipation, while Robinson and the free-state party in Kansas were interested only in making Kansas a free state by peaceful procedure."

Now I paused to reflect on what I'd discovered, on what Malin had forcibly brought home to me. Suddenly I saw the broader national implications of Brown's struggle with the Kansas Free

Staters. If their ideology was roughly the same as the Republican party's, Brown must have been as apprehensive about its eventual success as he was about theirs. For in the Republican view both sections, the slave South and the antislave North, could live in peaceful coexistence, the South being left alone to govern its own affairs without let or hindrance provided it sought no further expansion. This arrangement, had it prevailed (and Brown had no way of knowing for certain it wouldn't), would have doomed the abolitionist cause or set it back indefinitely. Brown's strategy was to do everything in his power to sabotage the kind of modus vivendi that the Republican party was attempting to bring about.

I was able to perceive a new dimension to his master plan. Instead of putting the plan in narrow tactical terms—how Brown expected to induce a slave insurrection, whether Harpers Ferry was the best place to start it, why it went wrong, etc., etc.—I thought it might be more profitable to examine it in its larger political setting, keeping in mind Brown's antipathy to the Republican party's or the Free Staters' objective. I reviewed the passages I'd copied out of Sanborn and Villard which emphasized Brown's desire to provoke a crisis between the North and the South, to disunite the sections and so bring on a war between them. It was a plan that struck me as highly intelligent and reasonable. Here I parted company with his apologists who regarded the plan simply as an expression of his dauntless heroism and invincible will to martyrdom, W. E. B. Du Bois having been the only one to take it seriously as a rational enterprise. Part of the mystery surrounding the plan began to dissolve. As an operation directed to the achievement of far-reaching *political* ends, it made perfectly good sense to me.

But only at the most abstract level of my understanding. What did I know of the political situation in America in the 1850s? What did I know of the conflicts and accommodations between the various antislavery factions of the North? Between these and the abolitionists on the "left?" For that matter between the abolitionists themselves? And where precisely did John Brown stand? What was on his mind? Were his moves timed to coincide with, and therefore effect, the outcome of particular events?

These questions reverberated through the pages of my notes as

8. *(Left)* The youngest of the raiders, William H. Leeman was barely twenty when he died at Harpers Ferry. At seventeen he went out to Kansas and there he joined John Brown's band of guerrillas. Leeman suffered a brutal death at Harpers Ferry. He was killed point-blank when he attempted to surrender; the militiamen used his corpse for target practice. *(Compliments of the Library of Congress)*

(Right) Lewis Sheridan Leary was a sad
-and-harness maker from Oberlin, Ohio,
lack man, who (like his nephew John A.
peland) decided to throw in his lot with
legendary John Brown. He was the son
an Irish radical who'd fought in the
volution before marrying a mulatto from
rth Carolina. At Harpers Ferry, Leary
struck down trying to escape and he lay
inded for eight hours before dying.
mpliments of the Library of Congress)

John Brown's genteel co-conspirators in revolution and treason. For a detailed account of their political careers see Chapter Four.

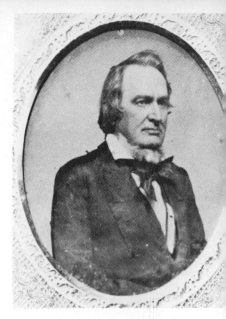

10. *(Right)* Gerrit Smith, immensely rich landowner and radical abolitionist of upstate New York, who supported John Brown after he was convinced that violent "revolution" was the only way to bring down the South. *(Compliments of the Boston Public Library)*

11. Dr. Samuel Gridley Howe, world-famous reformer, educator, and humanitarian, one of the more intrepid members of the Six. *(Compliments of the Library of Congress)*

12. George Luther Stearns, wealthy h[umani]manitarian businessman who surreptitiou[s] supplied Brown with money and weapo[ns] *(Compliments of the Library of Congre[ss])*

. Theodore Parker, the celebrated Trans-
ndentalist minister, apostle of violent re-
tance to slavery. *(Compliments of the
ston Public Library)*

14. Thomas Wentworth Higginson, Uni-
tarian minister, the most zealous of the Six,
who hoped that armed attacks on the South
would bring about "Disunion" and the civil
war. *(Compliments of the Boston Atheneum)*

15. Franklin B. Sanborn, a Concord schoolmaster who labored prodigiously in John
Brown's behalf—after Harpers Ferry as
well as before. *(Compliments of the Columbia University Library)*

16. *(Left)* John A. Copeland was hanged on December 16, 1859, at the age of twenty-five. He'd been a student at Oberlin College when his uncle persuaded him to join John Brown at Kennedy Farm. The Charlestown prosecutor called him "the cleverest of all the prisoners.... If I had the power and could have concluded to pardon any man among them, he was the man I would have picked out." *(Compliments of the Library of Congress)*

17. *(Right)* John E. Cook, born in 1830, came from a good Connecticut family and studied law. His specific task was to learn about Harpers Ferry from the inside, and in 1858 he settled in the area, marrying a local woman and doing odd jobs on the island. He was captured in Pennsylvania a week after the raid and executed in Charlestown on December 16, 1859. *(Compliments of the Library of Congress)*

I called a halt to my interrogation of James C. Malin. I thanked him for everything—for the documents and leads and insights, and for the querulousness and petulance and facticity, too.

5

August 1967 expired in a paroxysm of rain, a cleansing of the streets and air, New York's blessed rite of purification. The reservoirs, thank God, were in good shape (the new mayor taking credit). We had enough water now to see us through many a parched season. We had long since ceased to flush, bathe, and drink in direst guilt, measuring our quantities in drops. Yet, looking back, how quaint and innocent such municipal distempers seemed compared to what followed.

I returned to my work in progress and the welcome purlieus of the Columbia library and the Upper West Side. But I certainly wasn't shuffling off my silent companion of a month. John Brown was constantly at my side, a recurrent puzzle. My voluminous disordered notes told me what I well knew, that the original portrait of John Brown was giving way to a figure in a vast landscape. I had significantly enlarged the canvas and had reduced him in scale and proportion while filling in the details of the man's life and career. No longer did I see him simply as a violent abolitionist who did such and such to command history's attention. He was now bound up with issues of magnitude and complexity that far transcended his own role in them. He raised grave questions about the tactics and principles and politics of the whole antislavery movement—questions that hadn't occurred to me before, that might never have occurred to me but for this strange fortuitous excursion into his world.

Part Two
Figure in a Landscape

Chapter Four
The Secret Six

1

October marks the resumption of the busy season. The weather turns autumnally crisp and we settle into our fixed routines. We withdraw deeper indoors, awaiting the blasts of winter, the onset of early night. Not altogether a bleak prospect at that, for anticipated too are the cheery, rubescent cold-weather holidays, Thanksgiving to New Year, then, following a dark interregnum, another cycle in our lives.

My own fixed routine was well under way. The usual fare: dull evening courses given twice a week at Queens College, ill-paying and otherwise wretched (my chairmen were Neanderthals posing as historians), yet a source of bread hardly to be despised; and hack writing which ground on interminably, taxing every cell of my talents (being a wordsmith, standing as I did in special relation to my customers, I was privy to their anxieties, their caprices, their unsettled amour-propre). But I had only myself to blame. I chose the vagrant free-lance life. By rights I should have thanked my Queens College chairmen for those niggardly courses, thanked the people I hacked and ghosted for. So I swallowed my resentments and went on hoping for the day when I could strike off the gyves of those petty tyrannies.

The apocalypse, meanwhile, relaxed its hold on us. The autumnal equinox marked the end of this year's ghetto uprisings, enabling us to concentrate our energies again on the Vietnam War.

A march on Washington was scheduled for later in the month, the most ambitious so far. Antiwar marches had been swelling since that first one back in Eastertime 1965, a negligible affair, a misspent day in Washington (saved partially by a long visit to the National Gallery). Other marches and protests, conferences and meetings, followed, the most recent, the April Central Park rally, having also been the most impressive to date, attended as it was by multitudes, including Martin Luther King who (worth battalions himself) served notice of his full-throated commitment to the antiwar crusade. But the National Mobilization Committee always seemed two or three steps behind events, organizing strategies against yesterday's escalation of the war. Direct action, I'd come to feel, was the imperative course, physical resistance the only method that would bring home to Americans the enormity of the crime committed in their names, letting them understand the lengths we, its opponents, would go to stop it. I now supported the Vietcong and Ho Chi Minh, having abandoned the view that a third force in Saigon, neutral and non-Communist, might constitute a viable alternative (except of course tactically, as a short-run expedient)—a view still held by most anti-Stalinist enemies of the war, among them my fellow editors of *New Politics*. Would I myself take on the government? Go to jail? At a minimum, carry a Vietcong flag? I didn't dismiss any of these. Disobedience beckoned strongly.

An altogether different possibility was opening up. Democratic party insurgents were girding for the 1968 presidential election (the New Hampshire primary being only five months away). It was widely noised about that Allard Lowenstein, inveterate liberal gadfly, and several other like-minded reform Democrats were forming a stop LBJ coalition and were looking for an attractive candidate. According to the clotted New York grapevine (the least reliable on earth), Bobby Kennedy was to be that very candidate, was indeed masterminding the Lowenstein operation. Whoever the candidate might be, we prayed (for it would take a miracle) he'd do well enough to send LBJ packing, even if in the process the Democratic party disintegrated and passed into oblivion.

The antiwar movement, then, was beginning to march down several roads, from the radicals at one end who sided with the "enemy" and proposed (or practiced) civil disobedience, to the moderates at the other who sought to depose the President through the conventional machinery of electoral politics. And to reach our objectives we might without contradiction (except to invincible sectarians) find ourselves traveling at one time or another, or even simultaneously, on all of them.

I couldn't help reflecting on the similarities between the antiwar movement and the antislavery movement of the 1850s, on the complex of factions and tendencies separating Republicans from abolitionists at that time. For it must have been as true then as in the 1960s that someone who felt strongly hostile to the administration might essay a variety of tactics, changing as circumstances dictated, passing from moderation to radicalism (even of the extreme kind) and vice versa. I imagined the Vietnam crisis worsening, Lyndon Johnson sending more troops into the breach (and so calling up still more draftees), the dissidents growing more rebellious, more violent (there were signs of this already)—correspondingly, more and more respectable and distinguished people openly or clandestinely abetting the violence, encouraging it at every turn. It was John Brown's upper-class associates I had in mind, the Secret Six, returning (in appropriate dress, voice, manner) to haunt a nation that was again inflicting a savage, unspeakable wrong, this time on a land of peasants ten thousand miles away and with no end in sight.

Insensibly I picked up the thread of my distraction. It led straight to the Brahmin friends of John Brown. And during such time as I could wrest from my labors and family responsibilities I read what I could—what lay hidden in the stacks of the New York Public and Columbia University libraries—on the Six: Gerrit Smith, Samuel Gridley Howe, George Luther Stearns, Theodore Parker, Thomas Wentworth Higginson, and Franklin B. Sanborn. I was especially curious to know why they—they in particular—went over the edge and opted for violence, what they saw in John Brown and his plan, and what, incidentally, they might tell me about the other abolitionists and the antislavery movement in general.

That was how, in the high autumn months of 1967, I wandered back to the unfinished landscape of my canvas.

2

I gave the literature on the Six only a cursory reading, dashing through the repetitive and congratulatory parts, occasionally jotting down impressions of their personalities and accomplishments

—impressions that grew denser as I approached the abolitionist phase of their lives, especially their association with John Brown.

That reading, cursory as it was, made me realize first of all just how extraordinary they were, each standing out boldly in the pediment of his time. Gerrit Smith (1797–1874), the oldest and wealthiest (his father having left him at twenty-three with hundreds of thousands of acres of land in upstate New York), could easily rank as the leading humanitarian and reformer of the age. He seems to have helped every oppressed or dissentient group, every radical idea that sprang up in the rich soil of ante-bellum America; he sided with women, Indians, blacks (they above all), friends of the imprisoned and the "insane," apostles of international peace, food and health faddists, etc., etc.—the list was as inexhaustible as his pocketbook. Dr. Howe (1801–76) sowed his wild oats fighting with the Greeks in their war of independence, participating in the July 1830 Paris rising, and joining Polish nationalists in their struggles against the Czar (for which the Prussian government clapped him in solitary confinement). From the early 1830s on Howe presided over Boston's Perkins Institution, where he performed miracles in rehabilitating the blind, the deaf and dumb (Laura Bridgman was his pupil and source of greatest fame), and the feeble-minded, meanwhile providing tremendous assistance for such other crusaders of reform as Dorothea Dix and Horace Mann. It was standard procedure for distinguished foreign visitors to drop in on the famous Dr. Howe. (See, for example, Dickens's *American Notes*.) Intellectually, Theodore Parker (1810–60) towered over his contemporaries. Every biographer notes the incredible power of his mind, the number of languages and subjects he mastered, his ability to assimilate, effortlessly, the smallest details to the broadest range of ideas and historical currents. And though anathematized by the orthodox clergies for his radicalism, his subordination of Christianity to the laws of universal reason and the rights of man, he preached to multitudes in the Boston Music Hall and attracted his own enthusiastic following; Parker was *sui generis*. Thomas Wentworth Higginson and F. B. Sanborn were the youngest of the Six (thirty-four and twenty-six respectively when Harpers Ferry occurred) and lived the longest (eighty-eight and eighty-five), but each had already made his mark: Higginson as a radical minister and activist and lover of combat, physical and moral both (he'd amply demonstrate those virtues in the Civil War) and a first-rate essayist, a talent he would successfully pursue for the rest of his life*; Sanborn as a Concord schoolmaster, the friend among others of Emerson, Thoreau, Alcott, and assorted abolitionists of the direct action stamp, many of whom he'd later memorialize in his biographies (he wrote them by the shelf) and by his lifelong charity work in behalf of the poor, the disabled, the helpless, and the weak, continuing in this where Howe and Smith had left off. And even George Luther Stearns (1809–67), the least remarked of the Six, was a man of parts who made his fortune in business (manufacturing lead pipes), then threw in his lot with Boston's avant-garde writers and reformers and leaders of unpopular causes.

Such, very briefly, were the Six, as noble-minded, humane, and philanthropic a band of men as ever plotted to commit (or encourage) high crimes and misdemeanors against the government of the United States.

Now, the focus of my interest (I occasionally had to remind myself as I became lost in biographical miscellany) was their connection with John Brown. And here I encountered a problem, already familiar to me from my reading of the books on him, a problem of interpretation and perspective.

There's a celebratory literature of the Six sent out from a closed circle of their friends, relations, comrades-in-arms—for example: Sanborn, Higginson, Howe's wife and daughter (Julia Ward Howe and Laura E. Richards, both well-known writers in their times) on Howe; Sanborn and Octavius Frothingham (a member of the New York abolitionist movement and premier authority on the history of American transcendentalism) on Smith; Frank Preston Stearns on Stearns; a host of epigones, including Sanborn, on Parker; Higginson and his wife on Higginson; and Sanborn (lengthily) on Sanborn—which tend all in all to play down the John Brown conspiracy, explaining it away as one episode in a life of devotion to the oppressed, particularly blacks and slaves, dissolving it in the nimbus of their general humanitarianism. What's

---

* For most people Higginson is known today as the man who befriended Emily Dickinson and recognized her genius.

lacking in these family portraits is concretion, fact, detail, the precise accounting of their heroes' liaison with Brown, the objective or strategy that drove them ultimately to engage in "treason," the relation between their deed and their political milieu. To depict the Six as idealists pure and simple seemed ingenuous to me (amounting in some cases to a cover-up), especially since—as all their biographers tell, as they themselves clearly prove—they were such shrewd and levelheaded men of affairs, so attentive to the nuances of politics. What were those nuances? Their apologists neglect to say.

There's a critical literature of the Six, too. Critical in the sense of being dispassionate, distant, scholarly, a literature by academics for academics (hence its general flatness and torpidity, as though it were dissecting cadavers, the one exception being Henry Steele Commager's brisk, lively study of Theodore Parker). And as such it's unintimidated, unawed, holding nothing back, descending as far into the political fleshpots as the available data, the cold disembodied evidence (much of it destroyed, remember), will take it. I owed much to these unsentimental historians. Without them I couldn't have advanced beyond my all too general understanding of their abolitionism and their relation to John Brown.

But the historian-critics were also part of my problem. For they find that very relation between Brown and the Six puzzling, disturbing, inexplicable. They dismiss Brown as a fanatic or monomaniac or extremist. How could these men of such station and achievement have fallen for someone so palpably off base? Incomprehensible! Typical are the comments of one scholar, Dr. Howe's biographer, Harold Schwartz: "Howe, for over thirty years a respected and experienced man of affairs, ordinarily made clear judgments of men, but in Brown's case he lost all perspective." Schwartz proceeds to instruct Howe and the other five on what they should have done: "Instead of throwing their money down the drain, which is essentially what they were doing, The Six would have done well to have invested in projects designed to build up the country." And the height of audacity: "Unfortunately, they did not understand the actual conditions."

Gerrit Smith's chronicler, Ralph Volney Harlow, is amazed by the dual character of the Six (and abolitionists generally), the "contrast" between their "imagined" and their "real" selves. "For

after all these earnest advocates of freedom were Christian idealists who let their zeal and their words belie their true character,
and who, it must be admitted, resorted to words and to actions
which were bound to result in harm. Certainly Gerrit Smith was
no monster. . . . Possibly for every qualification revealing a display of violent zeal Smith's biographer should include one showing
his true kindliness." This particular biographer, then, is giving us a
psychological study, a study of excess "zeal" among otherwise
kindly and decent men. Omitted somehow from his calculations is
the specific object of their "zeal": slavery. And so we blame
them, not slavery, for the resulting "harm" to the nation. (It
should be noted that Ralph Volney Harlow not only despised abolitionism; he was an unabashed and rather crude racist.† Yet
he writes a 500-page biography of Gerrit Smith!)

Even Henry Steele Commager, usually so sympathetic to radical
dissent, chides Parker for his abolitionism: "Curious what came
over Parker when he dealt with slavery. He had balance enough in
most things, his feet were on the ground." But "on the subject of
slavery Garrison was not more uncompromising, Sumner not
more doctrinaire." Commager, it follows, doesn't take the conspiracy of the Secret Six very seriously; he sees it as a silly affair, full
of posturing and bravura and mock heroism: "So far it had all
been rather fun, and the Committee had enjoyed it—the hatchings
of plots, the secret meetings, the code ('How goes our little speculation in wool?' they would write slyly), the purchase of arms, the
tall talk and the rodomontade, matching the Southerners word for
word. It had all been a game."

† A few samples: "However if one wants to measure the intellectual ability
of the middle period of American history or to get a straightforward analysis of the problems of slavery one does not go to the abolitionists. Their
specialty was exaggeration and abuse, misrepresentation and invective,
qualities that call for a certain deftness in the choice of words, but certainly
not for brain power or penetrating wisdom. To qualify as a good abolitionist therefore one needed to be long on emotionalism and short, very
short, on honest analysis and readiness to deal with facts" (p. 134).

"Here in this letter" (by Smith to a slave whose freedom he'd bought)
"appears the abolitionist notion in its simplest form, that the Negro was a
black Anglo-Saxon, capable of being stirred as a white man would be by
this evidence of disinterested philanthropy. And at precisely this point appears the overwhelming weakness of every true abolitionist: an absolute inability to see the Negro as he was, and where the blacks were concerned, a
total lack of anything remotely resembling a sense of humor" (p. 273).

One recently published work on John Brown's friends and accomplices, *The Road to Harper's Ferry,* by J. C. Furnas, does
venture a hypothesis to explain their "treason," They succumbed,
it seems, to the same order of "romantic juvenilities," namely
those propounded by Sir Walter Scott, that their Southern counterparts did, identifying not with the Cavaliers and gentry but with
"the Scots Covenanters and English Roundheads of the 1600s—
God-minded, zeal-and-steel militants." And to appreciate "the actual importance of such identification between real persons and
literary figures" Furnas would have us "consider Wagnerian op-
eras of Nazi fantasies." But Furnas advances no proof that the Six
(a) were uniquely susceptible to Scott's influence and (b) assuming they were, ever acted on them. Besides, the question of *object*
remains. Why did they turn their "romantic juvenilities" (if they
had them) against *slavery?*

Dissatisfaction with both literatures, celebratory and critical,
compelled me to do what frankly I'd hoped to avoid. Retracing
my steps, I carefully, exegetically, reread the texts pertaining to
the abolitionist and conspiratorial periods in the lives of the Six. I
wanted to thoroughly comprehend the objective circumstances
that defined their position in the antislavery movement. I assumed
they were reasonable men who knew what they were about, who
chose their vocations as conspirators with the same sense of responsibility they exhibited throughout their lives, who weren't
"hypnotized" by John Brown or driven by some ludicrous myth or
swept up in the pervasive mood of violence and disrespect for institutions. I had to stake out my claims, reconstruct events from
my own standpoint, develop my own hermeneutic.

So it was borne in on me again: The painting I held before my
mind's eye demanded painstaking detail; it would be done brush
stroke by brush stroke or it wouldn't be done at all.

*The debate over the Vietnam War between President Johnson's
friends and enemies was heating up as demonstration day approached. On October 3 Senator Dirksen of Illinois said: "You
don't demean the ruler—the President is not our ruler—but you
don't demean him in the eyes of our people abroad. It don't sound
good and it don't look good. Have you heard the British demean
their king or queen?" Vintage Dirksen.*

(*Meanwhile the announcement in the October 11* Times *that Che Guevara was dead, the front-page story carrying a grisly picture of his corpse. It's what we'd long expected, since it was well known that his Bolivian campaign had petered out, that the peasants weren't supporting him, nor were the workers or radical intellectuals. His fate was sealed. The Bolivian government claimed its troops killed him last Sunday, the eighth, and Castro wasn't denying it.*)

Gerrit Smith was an abolitionist before any of his five compatriots were. By 1835 he was fully converted to William Lloyd Garrison's militant faith: He was advocating the immediate and unconditional emancipation of the slaves. Smith's abolitionism, I discovered, flowed directly from his sympathies for free blacks, his desire to see *them* completely emancipated, his fierce racial egalitarianism. Through Smith I realized for the first time that radical abolitionism required that society accept blacks as brethren and sisters, that unconditional integration must accompany unconditional emancipation. How, otherwise, could one be an abolitionist?

As the number of abolitionists grew, so more and more of them, those especially in the New York contingent, concluded that the struggle should go beyond the moral condemnation of slavery and look to the exercise—one day perhaps the conquest—of political power and with it the legal emancipation of the slaves, the legal equality of the blacks. Gerrit Smith was one of these political abolitionists. He came to believe that the Constitution and slavery were inherently at odds with each other and that, accordingly, abolitionists must learn to use the Constitution intelligently, as their instrument of deliverance. It "needs but to be administered in consistency with its principles," Smith wrote, "to effectuate the speedy overthrow of the whole system of American slavery. It is a power in the hands of the people which they cannot fling away without making themselves guilty of ingratitude to God and treason to the slave. . . . This shield which God has given us to put over the head of the slave we have traitorously made the protection of the slaveholder."

Hence the establishment of the Liberty party, of which Smith was the central figure, the chief hierophant, from its inception in

1840 to its extinction in 1854. He gave the Liberty party its name, supplied it with funds, chose its candidates. Its first candidate, ex-slaveholder James Birney, won a pitiful 7,000 votes in 1840. But four years later he won 62,000, enough to furnish the margin of Henry Clay's defeat in New York, therefore the nation. The Southern Democrat James Polk owed more to the abolitionist Liberty party than he might have ever cared to admit: his election as President.

The party was now a power to reckon with, the more so after Texas was annexed in 1845 and antislavery factions in both major parties, Democratic and Whig, began soliciting its support. The system was agitated by crisis; forces were realigning; new possibilities were emerging. But what should Libertymen do? They faced a dilemma common to ideological politics: How much of their doctrinal purity must they give up in the hope of growing more effective? What compromises should they agree to? Would they be co-opted?

Now, Smith was willing to compromise within limits. And those limits were fixed: no yielding on the principle of immediate and unconditional emancipation and civil rights for free blacks. Concern over black civil rights, for example, prompted him in 1846 to seek an alliance with the hated New York Whigs. That was because a new Democrat-sponsored state constitution was being offered to the voters which proposed (among other things) to disfranchise all but a few of the state's fifty thousand blacks by laying a $200 property qualification on them, no small sum in those days. Libertymen across the state adopted Smith's resolution, "that Libertymen should never cease, no not for a day, to strive for a new Constitution for the State of New York, so long as its existing constitution fails to recognize the right of a man to his vote, whatever may be the color of his skin, or the right of a man to his honestly obtained home, whatever debts he may owe." A vain effort. The 1846 constitution passed and blacks were duly stricken off the electoral rolls.

(The whole thing struck me as odd. If abolitionism was making its effects felt [as I'd been led to believe], why were free blacks losing their rights instead of gaining them? And why in a state like New York, bastion of democracy? And why at a time when Southern expansion was stirring such strong animosity? When I

asked these questions I remembered the Kansas Free State struggle, how fiercely antislave and antiblack it was, and how much this
bothered John Brown and the abolitionists. A pattern was emerging, dimly, confusedly.)

Now, if Gerrit Smith could set *his* limits on compromise, other
Libertymen could set theirs. Especially since the antislavery factions in the major parties were moving closer to them. In New
Hampshire Libertymen and others joined forces to win a stunning
victory: They elected their own United States senator, a staunch
antislavery ex-Democrat named John P. Hale. But Hale was
strictly a Wilmot Proviso man who didn't go beyond demanding
that all territory taken from Mexico in the war must exclude slavery; his opposition to the slavocracy didn't include emancipation,
not even as an ultimate goal. The New Hampshire or Hale formula, at any rate, became the model for other such mergers in
other communities. In 1848 the Free-Soil party (it could have
been called the Wilmot Proviso party) was born, and the Liberty
party's own candidate for President (the same John P. Hale)
withdrew in the interest of the new broad-based antislavery coalition.

That left Smith high and dry. He would have nothing to do with
the Free-Soil party, hardly an abolitionist organization. So he and
the Liberty militants regrouped as the National Liberty party and
nominated Smith himself its presidential candidate on the platform—abolition and civil rights—of the old Liberty party. Smith
ran a symbolic campaign; he expected no more than a token vote;
he in fact received fewer votes than Birney did back in 1840.

I thought this would be a good place to try for clarity's sake to
identify the various political tendencies thrown up by the deepening conflict over slavery. At the center were of course the two
major parties, Whig and Democratic, each with its antislavery or
anti-Southern components. Further "left" stood the Free-Soilers,
their platform resting on the circumscription of slavery along the
lines laid down in the Wilmot Proviso. On the "extreme" left
stood Gerrit Smith and the unreconstructed political abolitionists.
And furthest left, at the tip end of the scale, stood the Garrisonian
abolitionists who never strayed from their refusal to truck with
any institution tainted by slavery, least of all political ones. How
similar (I mused) in outline, morphologically, to the radical poli-

tics I'd experienced and seen, the sects multiplying as social conflict, the revulsion against felt wrongs, intensify—how in the nature of things such attempts to bring about drastic change serve at first to reinforce the status quo, the insurgent groups being mainly opposed to each other, until the center itself falls apart (usually for accidental reasons).

But as I made my way through these ideological thickets, trying to discern the difference between the contending abolitionist and antislavery factions, I had the sense that I was missing something important, and that it might bear on the race question which I'd encountered again in the matter of the 1846 New York State constitution. I resolved to keep my weather eye out for further leads, though I didn't know yet exactly what I was to look for.

Of the others who would later comprise the Six—Howe, Stearns, Parker, Higginson (Sanborn was too young)—we hear little in the 1840s; they attended to their private lives. When they did begin to speak out against the slavocracy, during the imbroglio over Texas annexation and the Mexican War, it was as Free-Soilers, not abolitionists. But the tide of their indignation soon carried them to the leftward-most point on the political compass.

(Reading through the biographies of Parker, I found a reference to his views on race which took me aback. "Parker's estimate of the negro, intellectually and morally, was low," writes John W. Chadwick [*Theodore Parker: Preacher and Reformer*]. "He exaggerated the sensuality of the negro, as he did that of the Jew, whom he placed only a little higher in this respect. Moreover the negro had for him a certain physical repulsion."‡ Now, whether any of the others shared this "estimate of the negro," and whether such an "estimate" explains why they were Free-Soilers rather than abolitionists, I had no way of knowing. I could only conclude that the moment Parker did become an abolitionist he suppressed his bigotries, or at least didn't allow them to affect his behavior toward blacks one whit. The same could be said of the others.)

The 1850 Fugitive Slave Act made Howe, Stearns, Parker, and Higginson bona fide abolitionists, erasing at a stroke the

‡ Chadwick also informs us that Parker "was no sentimentalist and had no illusions as to the negro character," which tells all we need to know about *his,* Chadwick's, views on "negroes."

differences that once separated them from Gerrit Smith and the tendency he represented. To put it more exactly, the Fugitive Slave Act transformed all of them, Smith included, into abolitionists of a particular sort: It united them in a common project of violence, a common commitment to resistance and direct action. And their enemy wasn't only the slave power; it was also—and more directly—the federal government, which was responsible for carrying out the slave power's wishes. In Parker's words (publicly addressed to President Millard Fillmore, who'd signed the Fugitive Slave Act into law): "I am not a man who loves violence; I respect the sacredness of human life, but this I will say solemnly, that I will do all in my power to rescue any fugitive slave from the hands of any federal officer who attempts to return him to bondage. I will resist him as gently as I know how, but with such strength as I can command; I will ring the bells and alarm the town; I will serve as head, as foot, or as hand to any body of serious and earnest men who will go with me, with no weapons but their hands, in this work. I would do it as readily as I would lift a man out of water, or pluck him from the teeth of a wolf, or snatch him from the hands of a murderer. What is a fine of a thousand dollars, and jailing for six months, to the liberty of a man? My money perish with me if it stand between me and the eternal law of God!" And further (spoken on another occasion): "The man who attacks me to reduce me to slavery, in that moment of attack alienates the right to life, and if I were the fugitive, and escape in no other way, I would kill him with as little compunction as I would drive a mosquito from my face." The very sentiments of Gerrit Smith: "if any class of criminals deserves to be struck down in instant death it is kidnappers."

Not accidentally Parker and Smith (and the others) were the leaders of the rescue or "vigilance" committees that sprang up in their cities (Boston and Syracuse). And as the Fugitive Slave Act was invoked, so the committees grew more pugnacious in their resistance to it. Smith, Howe, Stearns, and Parker, despite their fame, reputations, marmoreal aspect of dignity, embarked on a career of adventure, conspiring and plotting, directing masses of men to commit deeds (some bloody) which they would have once considered unthinkable. For them the Civil War had begun.

They plunged themselves into a series of fugitive slave rescues.

A few weeks after the act passed Howe spread the word that warrants were about to be issued for a black couple, William and Ellen Craft, parishioners (it turned out) in Theodore Parker's very church. The Vigilance Committee went into action, hiding the Crafts (and giving William a gun for good measure), laying plans for their escape. Just before they left (England being their destination) Parker married them. He later wrote: "I noticed a Bible lying on one table and a sword on the other; I saw them when I first came into the house and determined what use to make of them. I took the Bible, put it into William's right hand, and told him the use of it. . . . I then took the sword; I put that in his hand and told him if the worst came to the worst, to use that to save his wife's liberty or her life. . . . I put into his hands these two dissimilar instruments, one for the body, one for his soul at all events."

A young black man called "Shadrach" (Frederic Wilkins) was arrested in Boston on February 18, 1851. That afternoon, during lunch hour in the courtroom, a group of armed men, many of them blacks recruited from "Nigger Hill," created a disturbance. Shadrach was seized and hustled into a carriage bound for Canada. The Boston Vigilantes celebrated with a rally. Parker, the featured speaker, described the rescue as "the noblest deed done in Boston since the destruction of the tea."

Whatever Bostonians did at this time was well publicized, and the rescues of the Crafts and Shadrach had their effect elsewhere. For one thing, they nerved Gerrit Smith to pull off his own widely heralded rescue.

On October 1, 1851, a fugitive, William Henry, known as Jerry, was captured in Syracuse and brought before the local commissioner of the U. S. Circuit Court. As it happened Gerrit Smith was that day in the city presiding over a convention of Libertymen. When they learned that Jerry was being held for hearing and would shortly be transported back to Missouri, a number of them led by Smith mobilized for action. That evening they drove a battering ram through the jailhouse door, retrieved Jerry, and packed him off to Canada. Smith was exhilarated. Every year for the next decade he and his accomplices faithfully commemorated "Jerry Rescue Day."

The authorities naturally took care to prevent a recurrence of such rescues. They waited for the chance to demonstrate how well they'd prepared themselves. It came on April 13, 1852, when young Thomas Sims was picked up in Boston. This time a large force of guards kept him under impenetrable security. The Vigilantes were stymied. The Reverend Thomas Wentworth Higginson, who had by now risen to some prominence as the committee's zealot, proposed storming the courthouse. Parker concurred. The proposal was rejected. Parker then suggested an attack on the ship waiting to carry Sims to Georgia. This was also rejected. The verdict was that nothing could be done. The Vigilance Committee suffered a poignant defeat, especially after it heard that poor Sims received a public whipping on his arrival "home."

(Higginson discovered a lesson in that defeat. The ad hoc responses to specific wrongs he would replace with a well-planned general strategy of resistance leading to the overthrow of the government and the destruction of the slave power. The Sims case, he wrote in his journal, "left me with the strongest impressions of the great want of preparations on our part, for this revolutionary work. Brought up as we all have, it takes the whole experience of one such case to educate the mind to the attitude of revolution. It is so strange to find oneself outside of established institutions; to be obliged to lower one's voice and conceal one's purpose; to see law and order, police and military, on the wrong side, and find good citizenship a sin and bad citizenship a duty, that takes time to prepare one to act coolly and wisely, as well as courageously, in such an emergency. Especially this is true among reformers, who are not accustomed to act according to fixed rules and observances, but to strive to do what seems to themselves best without reference to others."

(Higginson was anticipating the John Brown conspiracy by five years.)

The most famous of the fugitive slave cases also brought them their crowning defeat. On May 26, 1854, Anthony Burns of Boston was jailed as a runaway. The Vigilance Committee promptly organized a rally, to be addressed by Parker, Wendell Phillips, and others, for that evening at Faneuil Hall. But committee militants led by Higginson had their own scheme. They would assault the courthouse just as the Faneuil Hall meeting was ending. The crowd, confronted by an accomplished fact—the clash of arms—

would join the attackers and overwhelm such opposition as the authorities (having been diverted by the meeting) could muster on short notice. At the appointed time Higginson and his men (whites and blacks together) smashed open the courthouse door and rushed up the stairs. A club-swinging band of policemen met them head on. Higginson was struck in the face. A shot was fired; a policeman fell dead. The attackers behind Higginson fled in panic. (He shouted after them: "You cowards, will you defeat us now?") Military reinforcements arrived. Only then, when it was too late, did the Faneuil Hall crowd arrive. Parker and Higginson hadn't gotten their signals straight.* The scheme was undone. Burns's fate was sealed.

The day Burns was taken to the pier for his return to bondage was Boston's day of angry mourning. Immense crowds lined the streets (prompting Burns to remark: "There was lots of folks to see a colored man walk down the street."). Stores and offices were draped in black. Flags flew at half-mast. Soldiers with drawn bayonets surrounded Burns and kept the crowd at bay. Despite the tension, the taunts, the imprecations, nothing untoward happened. The ship departed. Howe wasn't the only one to weep.

Nor was the drama over yet. The federal government indicted Parker, Higginson, Phillips, and others for conspiring to foment rebellion. According to the bill of particulars, Higginson, the number-one culprit, "did unlawfully and riotously attack the Court House . . . did throw stones, bricks . . . did break the glass in the windows and did force in and break open one of the doors . . . did fire and discharge sundry firearms . . . did utter loud cries and huzzahs . . . to the great terror and disturbance of diverse citizens." A perfect opportunity for a national cause célèbre. Each defendant would deliver his condemnation of the slavocracy

---

* Here's Commager's all too graphic description of what happened. "There was a shout from the door. 'To the Court House! To the Court House!' The signal had come at last. The Hall was in turmoil. Empty your seats now, Faneuil Hall, turn out your galleries, burst open your doors. There is Howe, he never was so fast before, and young Channing by his side. There is the faithful Bowditch, and tall Phillips, and Parker, his short legs chumping along the cobblestones. Faster, faster, you never did such work as this, farm boy from Lexington." (Commager often lapses into such apostrophes, especially when he's Parker's alter ego. An unusual intimacy between a biographer and his subject.)

and its partner in vice, the federal government, invoking as justification for his disobedience the higher law embodied in the Revolution and the Declaration of Independence. Parker, master polemicist, composed a whole tract, a book in itself, the courtroom to be his stage, forum, lectern, pulpit. But this grand opportunity went aglimmering, too. The judge dismissed the indictment on a technicality and closed the Burns case.

On October 18 the announcement we'd been expecting. Allard Lowenstein's outfit, calling itself the Conference of Concerned Democrats, was definitely going to challenge Johnson in the primaries on the war issue. The task now was to find a candidate. Or was the conference a subterfuge for Bobby Kennedy?

I made special note of the fact that the Six (or five) never ceased to be *political* during the fugitive slave period of their lives, when they flouted the law and committed dangerous acts of derring-do. It was if they were fighting a two-front war. Smith ran for and was elected to Congress (serving a brief undistinguished term) only months after he helped rescue Jerry, and even as he persistently recommended tactics of violent resistance. Howe and Stearns labored strenuously to elect the radical Charles Sumner senator from Massachusetts (a victory doubly sweet, Sumner replacing the great Daniel Webster, archadvocate of the Fugitive Slave Act). And they, with Higginson and Parker, never ceased to play an important role in the Free-Soil party, as witness their correspondence with such antislavery politicians as Sumner, Hale, Salmon Chase, and William Seward. The five were simultaneously moral outsiders and political insiders.

After some effort I worked out the logic of this two-front war they were conducting, one within, the other above (or below) the law. It was the logic of political abolitionism. They were exploiting for their own ends whatever public event happened to present itself to them, whether it was the rescue of a fugitive slave or an election to office. They were seeking to generate conflict, encourage opposition to the slave power, enlist more and more and more people in the antislavery movement—seeking, in a word, to bring on a crisis, a schism, a breakdown. *Politics for them meant not the resolution but the exacerbation of differences.* By resisting the Fugitive Slave Act, Smith, Howe, Stearns, Parker, and Higginson were looking beyond the runaways themselves: They were attempting to destroy the 1850 Compromise, indeed all the compromises that legitimated slavery in the United States.

(An analogy came to mind: the tendency of radical groups—Communists used to be notorious for this—to yoke humanitarian causes to their political purposes. Typical was the Communist defense of Southern blacks [e.g., the Scottsboro boys] who faced the death sentence for allegedly raping white women. The condemned would thus become symbols, perhaps martyrs, to a larger political cause, their fate being secondary to the fate of humanity as represented by that particular radical group.)

Passage of the Kansas-Nebraska Act in 1854 answered the prayers of the radical abolitionists, achieving by a single blow what they'd been trying in vain to achieve for years, with all their rescues and rhetoric and provocations. (Parker to Seward, May 19, 1854: "I have been waiting a long time for some event to occur which would blow so loud a horn that it should awaken the North, startling the farmer at his plough and the mechanic in his shop.") Kansas-Nebraska gave rise to the Republican party, natural heir of the Free-Soil movement, whose one dominant issue was the restriction of slavery within its present (pre-1854) boundaries. The party's fortunes, then, depended on sectional tensions, and to that extent it had the same vested interests as the radical abolitionists. But only to that extent. Republicans certainly had no interest in emancipating the slaves. Now whether in the course of advancing those limited interests Republicans would in fact heighten the tensions irreparably, bring them to a boil—this was problematic, conjectural. For the Six of course it was a probability devoutly to be wished—and sedulously encouraged.

When the Kansas struggle got under way, the Six joined one or another of the Kansas committees that burgeoned in the North, New England and New York especially. These committees were broad-based and ideologically diverse. Their sole and official purpose was to help the embattled Free State forces by whatever means necessary (sending emigrants, arms, supplies, etc.) to secure the Territory from the Border Ruffians (and for that matter the federal government). The Six, constituting the left wing of their respective Kansas committees, tended to carry weight in their counsels disproportionate to their numbers: Smith and Stearns (who was chairman of the Massachusetts Committee) because of their great wealth, Sanborn (who served as secretary of the Massachusetts Committee) because of his youthful assiduity, Howe because of the respect he commanded, the prestige he lent, Parker because of his appeal to the public at large as the voice of righteousness, Higginson because of his audacity as the most militant member of the left. For all of them Kansas was the continuation of the Fugitive Slave Act. So far as they could influence public events, their objective was to see to it that Kansas went on bleeding, its blood being the surest guarantee that the tensions wouldn't abate or be contained, no not even (or above all) by Republicans.

Such, I concluded, was the burden of their political strategy from 1854 on. Its terminus ad quem was Harpers Ferry.

Eighteen fifty-six seems to have been the critical year. The political temperature was rising as the presidential election drew closer and closer. The Republican party was fast becoming the first party of the North, posing a dreadful challenge to the South. All the more reason from the radical abolitionist standpoint why Kansas must bleed profusely, interminably, why the John Browns of Kansas must be strengthened. Gerrit Smith put it succinctly to a Buffalo audience on July 16, 1856 (while Kansas was bursting with violence): "You are looking to ballots when you should be looking to bayonets; counting up votes when you should be mustering armed, and none but armed, emigrants; electioneering for candidates for civil rulers when you should be enquiring for military rulers." Higginson was prepared to take up arms. In the summer of 1856 he attempted to organize a "free-soil army" which would attack federal troops and officials in Kansas, forcing the Northern states to come to his assistance and so precipitating a national "revolution" (i.e., civil war). Higginson went to Kansas as an observer and reporter (this being his cover) hoping to recruit soldiers for his free-soil army, and while doing so to seek out the fabled John Brown. ("I was tired of reading of Leonidas. I wanted to *see* him. I was tired of reading of Lafayette. I meant to *see* him. I saw in Kansas the history of the past, clothed in living flesh before me. And if I wanted a genuine warrior of the Revolution where could I better find him than in the old Vermonter [*sic*]

Captain John Brown, the defender of Osawatomie. . . . Old Captain Brown, the Ethan Allen, the Israel Putnam of today, who has prayers every morning, and then sallies forth, with seven stalwart sons wherever duty or danger calls, who swallows a Missourian whole and says grace after the meat.") Higginson's extravagant hope came to nothing, but it indicates what the Six had in mind as the 1856 presidential election approached.

They also traveled the road of conventional or "legitimate" party politics, for they—all but Smith at any rate—wanted the Republicans to win at any cost. They conceived of themselves as the standard-bearers of the party's highest principles, its "ethic of ultimate ends." These two roads—one subterranean and violent, the other open and political—weren't necessarily divergent provided one believed, as they obviously did, that the Republican party could be radicalized, could be made a vehicle of abolitionism. Now, Gerrit Smith kept his distance from Republicans precisely because (and for reasons his biographers fail to clarify) he didn't think they could be so radicalized; he "despaired" of them. But this difference between Smith and others was purely a tactical one, based largely on personal associations and friendships, the Boston Five having been close to men who had evolved in a little more than a decade from conservative Whiggery to "conscience" (antislave) Whiggery, to Free-Soilism, and now to Republicanism. The Five could properly assume that a Republican victory in 1856 might accelerate the train of evolution.

Parker (who kept up a running correspondence with leading Republicans, including Lincoln's partner William Henry Herndon) was undoubtedly thinking of such deep-dyed abolitionists as Smith when he delivered his famous speech about "The Present Crisis" before the American Anti-Slavery Society on May 7, 1856. It illustrates Parker's (the Six's) duplex political character.

"I am responsible to nobody, and nobody to me. But it is not easy for Mr. Sumner, Mr. Seward, and Mr. Chase to say all of their thoughts, because they have a position to maintain, and they must keep in that position. The political reformer is hired to manage a mill owned by the people, turned by the popular stream; to grind into anti-slavery meal such corn as the people bring him for that purpose, and other grain into different meal. . . . The nonpolitical reformer owns his own mill, which is turned by the stream drawn from his own private pond; he put up the dam, and may do what he will with his own; run it all night, on Sunday, and the Fourth of July; may grind just as he likes, for it is his own corn.

"The antislavery non-political reformer is to excite the sentiment and give the idea; he may tell his scheme all at once, if he will. But the political reformer, who, for immediate action, is to organize the sentiment and the idea he finds ready for him, cannot do or propose all things at once; he must do one thing at a time. He is to cleave slavery off from the Government, and so must put the thin part of the wedge in first, and that where it will go easiest."

But the Republicans lost the 1856 election, decisively if not ignominiously. The new President, James Buchanan, was an avowed "Doughface"; no one could have been friendlier to the slavocracy. The Six drew two melancholy conclusions from the results: that the Democrats would govern the country for years, perhaps indefinitely†; and that they would have to depend much more, if not exclusively, on tactics of violence and provocation. As Parker phrased it two weeks after the election: "I am more than ever of opinion that we must settle this question in the old Anglo-Saxon way—by the sword. There are two constitutions for America,—one written on parchment, and laid up at Washington; the other also on parchment, but on the *head of a drum*. It is to this we must appeal, and before long."

For the Six the situation was the more desperate because of the government's success in staunching the blood of Kansas. That success unquestionably contributed to Buchanan's victory and proved

† Typical was Higginson's prognosis early in 1857: "This very morning, I read in an able Republican journal, the statement that, after all, however it may have seemed in the past, the Slave Power is 'a weak thing,' when you come to look it in the face. 'A weak thing,' Mr. Chairman? If the power that has governed this nation since its formation, that has for half a century elected every President, dictated every Cabinet, controlled every Congress, the power that has demoralized the religion of the nation, and emasculated its literature, the power that outwitted Clay and stultifies Webster, the power that has ruled as easily its Northern creditors as its Northern debtors, the power that at this moment stands with all the patronage of the greatest nation of the world in its clutches, and with the firmest financial basis in the world . . . if this power be weak, where on wide earth will you look for anything strong? Weakness? Why slavery is King; King *de facto*."

(to the satisfaction of the Six) how fundamentally correct they were in affirming the political value of continued conflict and war.

I understood far better now why Higginson called his "Disunion" Convention of January 1857. And I better understood what he (and other like-minded militant abolitionists) meant by "disunion." It wasn't intended to establish the North's moral purity, to bring about a separation from the South, depraved beyond redemption, nor was it all a legal and constitutional matter; it was intended to incite disorder, treason, revolution—terms which Higginson freely and proudly asserted. Disunion was nothing more than "a practical problem which the times are pressing on us." The moment had come "for resisting the U.S. government in Kansas and sustaining such resistance everywhere else."‡ As it transpired, the plan for disunion, like the creation of the free-soil army, never got off the ground. The convention was sparsely attended. Radical abolitionists, while agreeing with its sentiments, were reluctant to act on them and follow Higginson's lead. Treason and revolution made a heady brew, especially if the effect was still to leave slavery untouched within an autonomous Southern nation. Even the other five, sympathetic as they were, maintained a wary distance. They might one day take the disunion road should it prove a viable alternative, but not yet.

What they did want was immediate action, the resumption of warfare. That desire, whetted by desperation and defeat (the aftermath of 1856), defined the context of John Brown's New England appearance early in 1857. The remarkable impact he made on the Six became fully intelligible to me—politically intelligible, that is. He was a miracle to them; they couldn't have invented his

‡ The venerable antislavery Jacksonian Democrat from Missouri, Thomas Hart Benton, appeared before the Disunion Convention to argue against it, representing as it did all he'd fought against in his sixty years in politics. Higginson described the scene some months after. "Said he (his eyes opening wide, and his face growing longer and longer), 'If you dissolve this Union, friends and fellow-citizens, twenty slaves will run away where one does now'; and a general chuckle of satisfaction ran through the audience. Thinking himself misunderstood, and wishing to deepen the impression, he said, 'If you dissolve the Union, you will bring Canada practically down to the lines of Maryland and Virginia'; and when he looked for sorrow and mourning the home shook with applause. . . .

"Everyone agreed that if we had driven the nail of Disunion, he had clinched it."

equal. (His age, religiosity, genealogy, helped too, qualities consistent with his reputation and demeanor.) It was clear to me now that John Brown and the Six found each other not so much because they shared the same moral ideals, the same aversion to slavery (this went without saying), *but because they believed in the same strategy.* Brown demonstrated to them that he and he alone would cause Kansas to bleed again. Which was why the Six, primarily Smith and Stearns, helped him as much as they did in 1857. He was their special agent provocateur in the Kansas Territory.*

(No wonder Dr. Howe's most recent biographer misses the point so egregiously. He writes: "They all felt so deeply about the cause of freedom that they were unwilling or unable to realize that Brown was an irresponsible guerrilla leader whose depradations had prevented peaceful settlement in Kansas without having aided the Free State side. Even if his tactics had once been desirable, there was no further need for them. Kansas was pacified, there was to be no further bloodshed." The pacification of Kansas was exactly what disturbed the Six so greatly and prompted them to support Brown. To them he embodied the quintessence of *responsibility.* If the author understood what the Six were about, he wouldn't gratuitously substitute his judgment for theirs, as though they were a bunch of naïfs.)

Oddly, Higginson at first regarded Brown as insufficiently radical—or rather revolutionary. He didn't think Brown's horizons extended beyond Kansas and so couldn't be trusted to partic-

---

* Stearns tried to swing the rather conservative National Kansas Committee behind Brown. He shrewdly made it seem that Brown was interested only in defensive operations to protect the Free State settlers. "I am personally acquainted with Captain Brown," Stearns assured the committee, "and have great confidence in his courage, prudence, and good judgment. He has control of the whole affair, including contributions of arms, clothing, etc. His presence in the territory will, we think, give the Free-state men confidence in their cause, and also check the disposition of the Border-ruffians to impose on them. This I believe to be the most important work to be done in Kansas at the present time. Many of the Free-state leaders, being engaged in speculations, are willing to accept peace on any terms. Brown and his friends will adhere to the original principle of making Kansas free, without regard to private interests. If you agree with me, I should like to have your money appropriated for the use of Captain Brown."

Of course Brown was too aggressively abolitionist to suit the National Committee's taste, and he received only a pittance from it.

ipate in the broader struggle to overthrow the federal government by force and violence. F. B. Sanborn, by now Brown's chief admirer, tried to change Higginson's mind. This was the occasion of his telling Higginson (in his letter of September 11, 1857) Brown "is as ready for revolution as any other man . . . the best Disunion champion you can find, and with his hundred men, when he is put where he can use them and drill them (he has an expert drill officer with him [the apostate-to-be Hugh Forbes]) will do more to split the Union than a list of 500 names for your convention—good as that is." And only when Brown disclosed his awesome plan to the Six several months later did Higginson give him his full unstinting support.

I was also able to make sense at last of Hugh Forbes's celebrated letter blowing the whistle on the plan and causing its postponement for a year and a half. What happened, evidently, was that Higginson and Brown in the course of their meetings pooled or combined their respective schemes; Higginson's pet idea, a disunion convention swelling to preponderance, was timed to coincide with Brown's attack on "Egypt" and the establishment of an abolitionist military base and government in the southern Appalachians.

The literature on the Six provides no detailed account of the plan as he originally proposed it to them and as they refined it in their lengthy discussions and correspondence. That they were actively and conscientiously engaged in the conspiracy was clear to me. Also that they thought well of the plan. Dr. Howe (to whom the others deferred on questions of guerrilla warfare) "insisted in after years," his wife Julia Ward Howe writes in her otherwise tight-lipped memoir, "that the plan had been a very able one, and its failure could not have been a foregone conclusion." Why did Howe think it was so able? We'd be vastly in his debt if he'd told us. The central difference between the Six appears to turn on whether or not Brown was supposed to provoke a slave insurrection. Some of them assumed he was supposed to. Only weeks before Harpers Ferry Gerrit Smith volunteered the following observations to his comrades of the Jerry Rescue Committee: "For many years I have feared, and published my fears, that slavery must go out in blood. . . . The feeling among the blacks that they must deliver themselves, gains strength with fearful rapidity. . . . No wonder then is it that in this state of facts which I have just sketched, intelligent black men in the States and Canada should see no hope in the practice and policy of white men. No wonder they are brought to the conclusion that no resource is left to them but in God and insurrections. For insurrections then we may look any year, any month, any day. A terrible wrong for a terrible wrong! But come it must unless anticipated by repentance and the putting away of the terrible wrong. It will be said that these insurrections will be a failure—that they will be put down. Yes, but will not slavery nevertheless be put down by them? For what portions are there of the South that will cling to slavery after two or three considerable insurrections shall have filled the whole South with horror? And is it entirely certain that these insurrections will be put down promptly, and before they can be spread far? Will telegraphs and railroads be too swift for even the swiftest insurrections? Remember that telegraphs and railroads can be rendered useless in an hour."

We also have evidence that Brown didn't look favorably on slave insurrections, that his plan didn't count on them, not immediately at any rate. In one of his autobiographical essays (from *Cheerful Yesterdays*) Higginson writes: "Brown's plan was simply to penetrate Virginia with a few comrades to keep utterly clear of all attempts to create slave insurrection, but to get together bands and families of fugitive slaves and then be guided by events. If he could establish them permanently in these fastnesses, like the Maroons of Jamaica and Surinam, so much the better; if not he would make a break from time to time, and take parties to Canada, by paths already familiar to him. All this he explained to me and others, plainly and calmly, and there was nothing in it that we considered either objectionable or impracticable. . . ."† And

---

† Elsewhere Higginson indicated that slave uprisings did figure in the plan. This is ominously brought out in a letter of November 1858 to Lysander Spooner, the abolitionist lawyer: "The increase of interest in the subject of Slave Insurrection is one of the most important signs of the times. It is my firm conviction that, within a few years, that phase of the subject will urge itself on general attention, and the root of the matter be thus reached. I think that will be done by the action of the slaves themselves, in certain localities, with the aid of secret cooperation from the whites.

"This is generally to be desired. The great obstacle to the anti-slave actions has always been the apparent feebleness and timidity of the slaves themselves. Had there been an insurrection every year since the American Revolution, I believe Slavery would have been abolished ere this. . . . The Northern people . . . would have been forced back on the fundamental

Brown himself always denied—even when he didn't have to—that
the slaves played more than an incidental role in his calculations.
They were (he insisted to his dying breath) the ultimate
beneficiaries of his plan, not the prime movers in its execution, the
spear (more accurately pike) carriers of his revolutionary brigade.

But it dawned on me that I might be wasting my time poring
over textual minutiae for clues, chance remarks, leads, anything
that would yield an insight into the precise nature of the plan—
that I was adding more layers of pigment to my John Brown portrait instead of integrating the plan (however imperfectly I understood it) with the landscape I'd been trying to work up. For the
Secret Six (we can call them that now) weren't so much concerned about the technicalities of the plan—exactly when and
where Brown would attack, how he'd dispose of his troops, deploy
the liberated slaves, take to the mountains and set up operations
there under his strange constitution, what the long-term logistical
problems might be (should he survive), etc., etc.—as making it
serve their over-all objective: to bring on a crisis, then a "revolution" (disunion or whatever), finally a war for the abolition of the
slaves. Brown had come along when they most needed him, holding out to them the promise, balm to their souls, of a greatly expanded Kansas, a fresh bloodletting of Northerners and Southerners. How else, to their way of thinking, could the Republican
party win the local elections of 1857, the state and congressional
elections of 1858, above all the presidential election of 1860?
How else could the Democratic party be driven from national
power for good? The North radicalized, public opinion pushed
leftward? This, it seemed to me, was the inescapable logic of their
political strategy; this was why they formed their conspiracy of
"treason" behind John Brown.

I was satisfied with the plausibility of my hypothesis. It enabled
me to explain why the Six acted as they did, in ways consistent
with their character, temperament, ideology. Yet when I drew
back from my reading of the literature on them during those

---

question of liberty, instead of the practical superficial aspects of the matter,
upon which the politicians have dwelt. A single insurrection, with decent
temporary success, will do more than anything else to explode our present
political platforms."

parlous weeks in October 1967 (and from the notes and conjectures I'd indicted), I found myself perplexed again, or rather anew. I wondered, as I had earlier, why they alone among all the abolitionists of the 1850s entered into such a conspiracy of death. What were the other abolitionists up to? I wondered why the Six thought the Republican party had to be prodded and provoked by incitations to general violence. Why couldn't the Six depend on the leadership even of the left Republicans, such as Sumner, Chase, Seward, et al., with whom they were otherwise so friendly to induce the desired crisis? What, I asked myself, was Republicanism really? For I doubted now that I understood it, especially in its relation to blacks, slave and free, and abolitionists. My study of the Six had made me aware of my ignorance of the whole antislavery movement.

And this much became obvious to me: If I was to do justice to John Brown and the Secret Six, if I was to deal with the questions that perplexed me (even as I answered others), I would have to further enlarge the landscape well beyond its present limits, the horizon having grown more elusive than ever. The prospect daunted me.

3

As the march on Washington approached, antiwar protests began mounting across the country, nowhere more violently than in California. The *Times* hesitantly reported them, wishing they'd go away, burying them in the back pages (with weather and shipping). But the protests were building up, surprising us by their size and vehemence. Everywhere, it seemed, students were burning draft cards, attempting to close down draft boards; the mood of rebellion was thickening palpably.

Meanwhile, Dave Dellinger, for the National Mobilization Committee (wasn't it the Spring Mobilization?), was meeting with people from the General Service Administration on working out the guidelines for the march. The agreement (according to the *Times*) specified that there'd be three demonstrations on Saturday the twenty-first: a morning rally at Lincoln Memorial, a march from there across the Potomac to the Pentagon (and if they fol-

lowed it far enough they would have gotten to Harpers Ferry),
finally a rally at the north parking lot (itself large as Manhattan).

I reflected on the astonishing freedom here in the midst of the
war. The opposition gathered, organized, moved about freely,
confidently. No crackdowns or massive repressions, though the
government no doubt had its agents—the FBI, the CIA, the military—everywhere, watching, taking notes, doing surreptitious mis-
chief. This was assumed by everyone in the movement and we
weren't offended, such spying being *de rigueur* even in the best of
times. But there was a world of difference between watching (for
future reference or troublemaking) and attempting to stop the action. The freedom and the violence coexisted, a uniquely American
phenomenon.

Preparations for the march went on apace—hectically. The
frenzied telephoning back and forth, the procuring of buses or
train tickets, the worrisome intractable details that had to be attended to, and the failures, all at the last moment, as though by
design, one bus operator after another reneging, deliberate sabotage (we took it for granted) on top of the normal disasters implicit in ad hoc planning.

And the decision at home that I'd stay to mind year-old Benjamin and that Edith, representing the rest of us, go to Washington and march to the Pentagon in a peaceful display of solidarity
with the movement. So it was arranged. And so she departed from
the Columbia University staging area in a quiet predawn hour of
October 21.

During that bright warm autumn day I tried to follow the
course of Washington events by listening to WBAI's amateurish
correspondent on the spot, but confess to spending the better part
of it in Riverside Park wheeling the stroller, reading desultorily,
occasionally picturing Edith and friends marching defiantly past
grim-faced troopers, observing certain realities of power, when the
sword of conflict is unsheathed and the civilities withdrawn. Anyway, it was my day off and I enjoyed it. I did manage to hear
Dellinger predict more active forms of resistance, the peace movement to become a kind of revolutionary or regenerating force in
America—an extravagant hope—and Dr. Spock lambaste Johnson as the man responsible for the murder of the innocents, Viet-

namese and Americans both. I'd learn more about the march from Edith and others.

Walter Cronkite that evening devoted some time to it (more than I'd expected), and what I saw hardly delighted me. Confrontation and panic scenes, protesters fleeing from the action, jailings as well, we were told (the number unremarked), protesters charging, and the government denying, that tear gas was used to effect the dispersion. Nothing wrong with such a clash (for I'd come to approve of direct action), except that Edith might have been swept up in the maelstrom of violence and pain. All I could do was wait, tempted by anxiety. As to the size of the crowd—an ideological, not a numerical equation—the estimates varied according to who gave it. Whoever did, it was vastly more than the government had prophesied and maybe even more than we'd realistically anticipated. Proof again that the movement was burgeoning on all fronts.

My anxiety dissolved into torpor, then by 3 A.M. (of what had turned into a cold Sunday) sleep. Distant reverberations of a door opening waked me, and a frozen apparition came in, undressed, and got into bed. Edith was solid ice. She'd shivered for nine hours in the rickety children's bus and now she lay there without thawing at all.

Through chattering teeth she managed to describe what happened in the brief time she marched (late morning to midafternoon). She did notice the trouble—the shouts, the melee, the running to and fro—but couldn't make much sense of it; she saw what we did on TV. But she and everyone there smelled the tear gas, smarted from it, a fact unmentioned by reporters.

In the months after, Edith paid penance enough for the President's crimes in Vietnam. The illness she came down with on the bus lasted well into other seasons, beyond even Johnson's term of office; an unfair *quid pro quo*.

Sunday morning the President went to the National City Christian Church and heard the minister, Dr. George L. Davis, sermonize on "the Spirit of Christian Reconciliation." "There are those in this nation who do not deserve to be free, but they have the right to be free and to play fast and loose with that freedom.

What do they know, these bearded oafs who listen to the strumming of lugubrious guitars? To be loved is not the end of greatness."

4

I should have laid my John Brown project—my unfinished canvas—quietly to rest (as I had so many other projects) and concentrated my attention on matters closer to home, to which I'd already committed myself and for which I could expect some immediate return, not to say remuneration. That's what I should have done. It's not what I did.

Doubleday accepted my book on American socialism (only partly done). But in lunchtime conversation with my editor I told of my interest in John Brown, what I'd so far learned, what tentative conclusions I'd so far reached, and in an unguarded moment, my tongue outpacing my thoughts (though perhaps in touch with the deeper layers of my psyche), said I might consider embarking on a study of my own of John Brown's life and times. She picked it up at once and asked that I submit an outline of such a study. I wrote it one evening off the top of my head, hoping (consciously) it wouldn't elicit a favorable response. The response in fact came quickly. The other editors had liked it, Doubleday offered me a contract on the spot. I remonstrated. Maybe I should have turned it down flatly, categorically. But I didn't; I supposed (I've since speculated often about my motives) that I really wanted to be persuaded, that I really believed a book of some interest and originality might emerge from the research I'd done and might in the future do, that my notes and conjectures, yards of them, might amount to something after all. And I was undoubtedly susceptible to persuasion because that year's end (when a multitude of debts fell due) found me strapped and reduced as never before. I succumbed. In January 1968 I signed my fateful contract, having decided provisionally on a title that excluded no possibility: "John Brown's America."

The existence of a contract didn't make the project any more palpable to me. I knew then, when I signed it, that I couldn't be compelled (or rather couldn't compel myself) to do the book, order it into existence, under the drumbeat of a deadline (although I was accustomed to working that way), that I'd need a Dionysian inspiration to complete it within or near the allotted time. In my heart of hearts I knew that my John Brown opus would take its own circuitous route and answer to its own chronologue, not mine.

Chapter Five
Black and White

1

In January 1968 I set up a new workshop (with the help of a student friend, Steve Buttner) in a modest-sized cubicle on the sparsely inhabited ninth floor of Columbia's library. The sense of heavy monasticism was relieved by the view: lower Manhattan on one side, the campus (the statue of Alma Mater and beautiful Low Library straight ahead) on the other. There I dutifully performed my chores, hacking for bread, preparing my two classes at Queens, researching my book on American socialism, editing and writing pieces for *New Politics*. John Brown was safely out of reach, the formidable body of notes (along with the contract, the lien on my future) consigned to a bedroom drawer. When I did occasionally think about him I didn't experience the tremors of anxious curiosity that had earlier driven me into his embrace.

The apocalyptic mood was closing in on us again, pursuing us wherever we went, even to the furthest sanctuaries on the topmost floors of libraries.

Events seemed to be heading madly, uncontrollably toward a climacteric. The new year began with President Johnson's familiar peace offer, the prelude invariably to another escalation of the war. And indeed the war did escalate, or rather take an unforeseen turn (unforeseen by the administration, not by us), with the awful Tet offensive launched by the Communists in early February. This trauma was enacted before us in full dress on television. (Who will ever forget the scene of the Saigon police chief— the cameras trained on him for our edification—blowing the head off that boyish-looking prisoner?) Here, clearly, was a Vietcong victory, even though Americans did recapture—at egregious cost—everything that had been taken. The enemy, after all, wasn't supposed to be capable of mounting such an assault, whatever the outcome.

But we drew back in terror. Second thoughts occurred to us. Wouldn't Johnson and his advisers (the brothers Rostow and Bundy, Secretary Rusk, General Taylor, et al.) interpret Tet as a fresh provocation requiring a response in kind? And in fact they did soon assert that the Communists had acted out of desperation and were wounded badly, that an infusion of more troops—as many as 200,000, the figure openly bruited about—would turn the trick once and for all.

And so we were mired in gloom during those supremely tense days of late February and early March. More and more of us entertained the possibility of trespassing the limits of direct action, going beyond nonresistance, beyond mild civic protests. What had been unthinkable from every point of view, tactically and morally both, we could now seriously contemplate.

(But I didn't think much of the Peace and Freedom party which a number of assorted radicals and antiwarriors tentatively inaugurated at a meeting in a Village apartment. I hoped opposition to the war would concentrate our energies, dissipate our sectarian differences. It didn't. The meeting provided another occasion to cast wide the net of reform, from marijuana to community schools, the war being one crime among many that had to be fought and overcome. I decided to maintain a healthy dissociation from the Peace and Freedomites, wishing them luck of course all the way. I remembered John Brown's abolitionist friends, the Secret Six, who did separate their passion for general reform from their abolitionist politics.)

The Tet offensive proved important beyond our reckoning. Senator Eugene McCarthy of Minnesota, who'd offered to lead the "dump Johnson" tendency in the Democratic party and whom very few (myself included) had refused to take seriously— McCarthy, thanks to Tet, won an astonishing 40 per cent of the New Hampshire primary vote; it was an unmistakable plebescite on the war. If he did so well there, in that conservative outpost, how would he do in such liberal centers as Massachusetts, Wisconsin, New York, California? The possibility of dumping Johnson began to tantalize us, the more so after Bobby Kennedy announced that he too would challenge LBJ, displacing McCarthy —so we assumed—as leader of Democratic insurgents. There was no containing the rebellion.

Especially tense were the weeks that followed. Everyone felt in his bones that enormous and fateful decisions were in the offing. The choices were clear enough. Would Johnson go all the way, stripping down the last vestments of his sanity? And would he thereupon go after dissenting Americans as well? For how could he allow his domestic enemies, their numbers proliferating and growing bolder by the day, aid and abet his foreign enemies? Repression would surely accompany escalation. Or would he draw back, offer some startling concession, steal his opponents' thunder? Few of us expected the latter from our Captain Ahab, our Davy Crockett. Some of us assumed the worst and pondered our own escalation, an ugly prospect. It was up to LBJ.

How his speech of March 31 stunned us! I was lying on the bed in front of the TV screen, tingling with dire anticipations (reminiscent of the Cuban Missile Crisis days), then hardly believing my ears as he droned on in familiar lubricious style. Was it conceivable? Ahab renouncing the whale? Crockett returning home to the plow? Yes, he'd stop bombing most of North Vietnam (Ho Chi Minh's condition for peace talks), send in no more troops, and— catching us completely off guard—*remove himself as a presidential candidate*. In a trice he'd converted from warrior to disinterested statesman. So it appeared. Was it in fact a conversion? And if it was, what did it mean? How did it happen? The media commentators and editorialists had a field day.

The conversion (it was obvious to me at any rate) was no epiphany but an accommodation to certain brute facts, namely that escalating the war to the extent thought imperative for victory might just bring about the disintegration of the country, not to say his party, assuredly his administration; it might compel him to use as many troops to keep order here at home as wage war in Vietnam (another summer of ghetto uprisings being only months away, the rhetoric of black violence already rising like a cloud on the horizon—this on top of the antiwar protests); and it might bury his name in infamy for all time to come. He was petitioning for clemency.

April 4, the day North Vietnam publicly affirmed its willingness to negotiate (the feeblest beginning of a beginning), was also the day of Martin Luther King's assassination, a blow which sent me reeling after I heard it on Walter Cronkite's seven o'clock news. I wept like a child. I couldn't imagine his absence, he who was our conscience and hope and moral teacher, who more than anyone else embodied the life of our times. We loved him and now he was gone, too, another victim of the bestial rage and violence of the day. (I concluded it was a conspiracy; we all did.)

If anyone was irreplaceable at that moment it was King, though he seemed to have been bypassed by black nationalists—the Rap Browns, Stokely Carmichaels, Eldridge Cleavers, et al., who were cutting a wide swath through the media—and by masses of people who'd reached the limits of their patience and self-discipline (the virtues King preached and sought to inculcate through Satyagraha) and were burning down the neighborhoods they themselves tenanted. For as a political strategist King represented a viable alternative to these, an alternative best suited to divide the white majority and build a left coalition which would establish those conditions of equality and dignity which the poor, white as well as black, desperately sought.

King's death was a political calamity, and it left us doubly bereft.

———◆———

It was shortly after King's unforgettable funeral (which cracked our hearts) that I returned to my John Brown canvas. The prompting was inexplicable. I simply began to think about the project, about the questions I'd put to myself months earlier when I was reading up on the Secret Six and trying to make sense of their lives as political abolitionists. I wondered again about their dual role (all but Smith) as both Republics and "revolutionaries," simultaneously open and clandestine. They were active Republicans

in good standing, yet the party, speaking for the antislavery movement, went to vast lengths to anathematize abolitionists of every
stripe, as though abolitionists were bearers of the most lethal
plague. And it occurred to me then (in mid-April 1968) as it
hadn't before that the Republican party wasn't soliciting *Southern*
votes; it was in fact anti-Southern, it was confined to the North.
Why were Republicans so hostile to abolitionists? How did abolitionists threaten Northerners? What difference did it make that
abolitionists favored the immediate rather than the ultimate extinction of slavery? In what sense, that is, did the antislavery North
regard abolitionists as "extremists"? What, I was asking, was so
objectionable about their "extremism"?

It was as though an old flame, reduced to imperceptibility, was
suddenly rekindled. No matter what I was working on, my mind
would turn back to the issues of John Brown's epoch and the
questions I'd raised about them.

I went to the bookshelves where the antislavery and abolitionist
literature lay and spent more and more time on it despite the
claims of my other obligations. Only now I made no effort to hold
back; I submitted to the demands of my obsession (no longer gra-
tuitous, no longer the urgings of idle curiosity) and gave myself as
wide a berth as I needed. Happily, I'd just finished a few assign-
ments and so had enough money to tide me over, for a few
months anyway.

———◆———

No sooner did I get started on my regimen—hunting down articles and books (they relentlessly multiplied behind my back) and
insatiably compiling notes, commentaries, exegeses—than the Columbia students conspired to distract me from it by rising in rebellion outside my window.

It caught me by surprise. I often observed SDS (Students for a
Democratic Society) at their rallies, held usually at the sundial in
mid-campus, and always had the impression they didn't take
themselves very seriously. They seemed too informal, too in-
souciant, too unorganized to do anything; it was as though they

were performing political theater (or charade). The new-style
radicalism of the youth culture was strange to me.

Now, like any proper-thinking citizen of New York's Upper
West Side–Morningside Heights community, I sympathized with
the cause SDS had taken up. Columbia's depredations of the
neighborhood were of long standing. Columbia was a mammoth
landlord, feared for its ruthless buying up of properties and dis-
possession of tenants, many of them old and otherwise defenseless. Most recently (adding Ossa to Pelion) Columbia had
begun constructing a new gym a few blocks below the college on a
piece of Morningside Park. Here was land owned by the city, i.e.,
the people, the community, being surrendered to Columbia in return for a promise that some residents would be permitted to use
the facility. The gym brought all the deep-smoldering resentments
to the surface. SDS seized on them. The point, according to SDS,
was that Columbia was more a money-making than an educational institution, that it was part of the corporate-military-bank-
ing establishment: hence its receipt of such egregious subsidies
(almost half its income) from the Defense Department and other
government agencies. The SDS was able to draw the connection
between the gym in the park and the war in Vietnam.

On the evening of April 22 I saw the SDSers from my ninth-
floor library window haphazardly, unseriously, march off from the
sundial to President Grayson Kirk's mansion overlooking Morningside Park (Harlem steaming in the valley below). I thought
nothing of it; more theater, another bit of rodomontade. Next
morning I learned that they'd seized the college dean's office
(having proceeded there from the mansion) and were holding the
poor dean captive. They were engaged in this "action," they
claimed, to protest the university's complicity in racism, imperi-
alism, war, etc. Protest it was. Within a few days they'd taken and
barricaded the entrances to several buildings; also, in a lightning
attack, the president's own office in Low Library.

Meanwhile black students and outsiders were capturing—
"liberating" was the ubiquitous term—old Hamilton Hall and
were holding it as their own separate and equal enclave.

SDS then had its crowning triumph, a gift bestowed by Kirk and
the trustees. I'd thought these worldly-wise, successful men of

affairs would patiently let the uprising run its course, exhaust itself as the school year petered out. Instead they panicked, lost their nerve. They committed the irrevocable act: They called in the police. (I witnessed the whole bloody campus-clearing operation early that morning of April 30). Overwhelmingly radicalized now, and firmly commanded by SDS cadres, the students shut down the university, thereby accomplishing what the police had been brought in to prevent. If there was a lesson to be drawn from the experience (repeated over and over in the weeks and months to come on campuses across America, Columbia having set off a great conflagration), it was this, that colleges, like governments, like most institutions, are legitimate offspring of the Bourbon monarchy: They forget nothing and they learn nothing.

The rest of that spring and summer was heavy with foreboding, failure, pathos. The stylistic and personal differences between Kennedy and McCarthy degenerated into deep enmity while Humphrey picked up the support, never tested in the primaries, that would have gone to LBJ. And just when it appeared that Kennedy, thanks to his exciting victory in the California primary, would prevail as leader of the insurgent Democrats (giving him a clear shot for the nomination), he too was struck down, obscenely, practically before the TV cameras, on the very night of that historic triumph. So the way was open for Humphrey, who repeatedly declared his enthusiasm for the policies of the President—his sponsor, his meal ticket. He rubbed salt in our wounds.

Nor was there a political alternative to which defeated opponents of the war could repair in dignity. The Peace and Freedom group (hardly a party), riven into racial and ideological factions (one of them calling itself Freedom and Peace and as such offering its own presidential candidate), was a jest, a parody, an expression of futility, a dead end.

I was tempted to travel to Chicago for the mid-August monster protest against Humphrey's nomination. I had no illusion that this extravaganza would accomplish anything beyond registering a personal statement, a thunderous disruptive show of negation. But I decided not to go because I didn't think the psychic gratification it might yield was worth the effort and the cost (and the prospect of a lonely trip).

I really didn't need to go. TV brought me (and the rest of America) into the thick of the carnage as it unfolded on Chicago's streets, presenting a view I couldn't have had as a participant, eliciting feelings of impotent rage I couldn't have experienced as a victim, at the same time as it was recording the serenity of Humphrey's nomination and the despair of the insurgents (a sizable minority) inside the besieged hall. The Democratic convention was the coping stone of our disappointments, forcing upon us once again the conviction that self-reliance through direct action was still our best recourse.

Yet throughout those tense melancholy months of 1968 (April through August) I pertinaciously managed to continue my study of the antislavery movement, my painting of the landscape of John Brown's America, keeping always in mind the parallels between that era and this; between two similarly tempestuous, crisistorn periods in our history, one which I was reading about, the other living through, when normal modes of political accommodation break down, when idealism (embodied usually in militant sectarian groups and extraordinary individuals) intrudes upon the settled habits of everyday life, when "moderates" and "extremists" commingle, interpenetrate, adopt each other's views, strategies, principles (sometimes to their own astonishment), when indeed the very terms of ethico-political discourse, such as "moderate," "extremist," "radical," "conservative," "idealist," "realist," etc., take on new meanings, new definitions, new consequences.

The raucous sound of discord outside my windows was the counterpoint of my solitary labors, my reflections and scribblings on events of a distant time.

2

The antislavery movement confronted me as a huge amorphous subject, a boundless literature. I lacked the easy guideposts—the biographies of John Brown and his six cohorts, the emphasis on *individual* action—that had lightened the task of my earlier explorations of the bookshelves. Now I was on my own. I had to create my own guideposts as I went along; I had to proceed on a course of my own mapping. But my discoveries were compensation enough for the strain of the effort, the drift and confusion, the waste.

I began by trying to clearly identify the assumptions I'd always taken for granted about the antislavery movement. This procedure —of isolating and critically appraising an idea—was the more imperative, I felt, because I held those assumptions so tenaciously, because they were fundamental to my understanding of that whole epoch.

I saw the history of ante-bellum America as a teleology: The end was implicit in the beginning. And that beginning was the abolitionist crusade launched by William Lloyd Garrison. Not that Garrison was the *first* of the abolitionists, a rich tradition having preceded him, one that included the Founding Fathers. It was that he was more vehement, more biting and uncompromising, more demanding than anyone else before him; also that he didn't seek to convert the slaveholder (besotted with sin) so much as his fellow Northerners. Garrison insisted that one had to place the evil of slavery first on one's moral agenda, that if one didn't act against it *hic et nunc* he was necessarily *for* it. And Garrison did place it on the agenda. He raised the issue, not least by his unpopularity, his ability to antagonize and disrupt, his polemical genius. Garrison attracted a following, first in New England, then elsewhere. Abolitionism, like early Christianity, spread in the teeth of tremendous public resistance, even mob violence, which took the life of one abolitionist and threatened many others, including Garrison himself. Abolitionism then split into factions. The New York State faction, led by the Tappan brothers, Gerrit Smith, et al., believed that immediate and unconditional emancipation could best be brought about by political means, and so in 1840 they established their own party and ran their own presidential candidate. Garrison had gotten off the locomotive of history. The rest of the teleology can be quickly summed up. The Liberty party conveyed the news of abolitionism to the people via the ballot box. The annexation of Texas alerted them to the danger of slavocrat expansion. Then came the Mexican War and the debate

over the Wilmot Proviso. The result, two years later, was the
Free-Soil party, successor of the Liberty party, which had accomplished its historical mission. The Compromise of 1850 temporarily stayed the sectional conflict, and the Free-Soil party floun-
dered. But of course the conflict was irreversible, entering its final
stage with the passage of the Kansas-Nebraska Act. The Republican party, Free-Soilism redivivus, sprang into being, grew mightily
as the crisis deepened, and in 1860 elected Lincoln President. The
South seceded. The Civil War was fought. Slavery was washed
away in a sea of blood.

When I held this teleological account up to critical scrutiny, I
found a flaw in it. The flaw had always been there of course; I just
hadn't noticed it (or if I had, made nothing of it). *The emancipation of slaves was an unintended, fortuitous consequence of the
antislavery movement; it was a movement that became the instrument of a purpose it hadn't wished to serve.* Had Free-Soilers and
Republicans favored emancipation, they would have been abolitionists. Nor were they simply *non*abolitionist; they were *an-
ti*abolitionist. And, as I now knew, a number of Libertymen—e.g.,
Gerrit Smith—opposed both the Free-Soil and the Republican
parties. The difference between abolitionism and antislavery—the
one advocating the extinction of slavery, the other its containment
—couldn't have been merely tactical, both having the same ultimate objective. What were these differences, these objectives?
That's what I sought to find out as I descended into the bowels of
the Columbia library.

The question facing me bore on the nature of the Free-Soil
party as it emerged (presumably) from the chrysalis of the Liberty party. And what I discovered (thanks to important work
recently published by scholars who were reconnoitering the same
terrain I was, pursuing the same hunches) fairly surprised me.

I soon realized that my initial assumption was itself faulty. The
Free-Soil party did not in fact grow out of the Liberty party. The
Liberty party platform concentrated on one issue: immediate and
unconditional abolition. Libertymen condemned slavery as absolutely, immitigably wicked in itself; they didn't condemn it as
wicked because it might lead to other unpleasantries. The Free-
Soil party, on the contrary, arose for strictly pragmatic reasons,

the slavocrats having demonstrated to a significant body of Northerners by 1846 that they were bent on enlarging their empire West and South and maybe North, too. Free-Soilers did not say—and went out of their way to avoid saying—that they thought slavery wicked if it stayed put; it wasn't wicked enough, at any rate, to openly denounce. The Free-Soil position could be interpreted—on logical grounds alone—as an indirect *defense* of slavery considered in and of itself, apart from any expansionist tendencies it might (or mightn't) exhibit. What then did Free-Soilers find so abhorrent in slavery?

The answer to this question surprised me.

Very helpful was a 1967 monograph, *Democratic Politics and Sectionalism,* by Chaplain Morrison, which definitely establishes (the effect on me was considerable) the profoundly racist motives behind the Wilmot Proviso and with it the Free-Soil movement. For good reason was the proviso called the "White Man's Resolution." (The racism of David Wilmot, Democratic congressman from Pennsylvania, is limned by his biographer Charles Buxton Going [*David Wilmot, Free Soiler*]. The "feature" of slavery that most "outraged" Wilmot, Going writes, "was not chiefly the oppression of the black race, but the degradation of the white race which inevitably accompanied it." And Going cites Wilmot's caustic aside: " 'By God, sir, men born and nursed of white women are not going to be ruled by men who were brought up on the milk of some damn negro wench.' "

The remarks of New York Congressman John A. Dix in behalf of the proviso typifies for Morrison the Free-Soil argument as it unfolded in the 1848 campaign: " 'One of the most interesting and important problems, both for the American statesman and philosopher, is to determine of what race or races this vast population shall consist; for on the solution which future generations shall give to it will essentially depend the prosperity of the community or communities they will constitute, and their ability to maintain such a form of government as shall secure to them the blessings of political liberty and an advanced civilization.' " Dix went on to define such a civilization; it was based on the rejection of blacks as an "inferior caste"; " 'Public opinion at the North—call it prejudice if you will—presents an insuperable barrier against its elevation in the social scale . . . a class thus degraded will not multiply. . . . it will not be reproduced; and in a few generations the process of extinction is performed. Nor is it the work of inhumanity or wrong. It is the slow but certain process of nature, working out ends by laws so steady and silent, that operation is only seen in their results.' "

(Author Morrison also comes up with a statement from the great anthropologist Lewis Henry Morgan, whose pioneer work on the Iroquois, *Ancient Society,* I'd once read because it influenced the thinking of Marx and Engels and Veblen among other radical social critics of the time. Morgan was a Free-Soiler too and he wrote the following to John C. Calhoun in 1848: "We are afraid of the indefinite propagation of the colored race, upon which the South seems determined. The feeling toward that race in the North is decidedly that of hostility. There is no respect for them. No wish for their elevation; but on the contrary a strong wish to prevent the multiplication of the race so far as it is possible to do so by such legislation as shall be constitutional and just." [I noted the judiciousness and objectivity of the observation, worthy of a great social scientist.])

Some trenchant articles by historian Eric Foner threw more light on Free-Soil racism.* I thought especially illuminating the fact that the most radical Democrats—the New York "Barnburners" —who represented workingmen if anyone did, who certainly spoke in the name of workingmen, were often the most extreme racists in the Free-Soil camp. These radical Jacksonians, says Foner, "emphasized that their opposition to the extension of slavery was motivated solely by concern for the interests of free white labor, who would be 'degraded' by association with 'the labor of the black race.' " Which was why the Free-Soil party—unlike the Liberty party—conspicuously omitted mention of the condition of free blacks. How could it?

(Quite by accident—while browsing in Columbia's darkened stacks—I came across an article in the *Chicago Jewish Forum* on "Whitman and the Negro." Now, Walt Whitman was a Free-Soiler through and through, a Jacksonian Democrat to his fingertips, the poet of the American workingman. Here's what he wrote in the

---

* Two in particular: "Radical Attitudes of the New York Free Soilers," *New York History,* Vol. 46; and "Politics and Prejudice: The Free Soil Party and the Negro, 1849–1852," *Journal of Negro History,* Vol. 50.

Brooklyn *Eagle* soon after the Oregon settlers, by a vote of eight to one, adopted a constitution barring blacks from the state and disfranchising the few who were there: "We shouldn't wonder if this sort of total prohibition of colored persons became quite a common thing in New Western, Northwestern, and even Southwestern states. If so, the whole matter of slavery agitation will assume another phase, different from any phase yet. It will be a conflict between the totality of White Labor, on the one side, and on the other, the interference and competition of Black Labor, or of bringing in colored persons on any terms.

("Who believes that Whites and Blacks can amalgamate in America? Or who wishes it to happen? Nature has set an impassable seal against it. Besides, is not America for the Whites? And is it not better so? As long as the Blacks remain here how can they become anything like an independent and heroic race? There is no chance for it.")

Foner informs us that some Free-Soilers—those who'd once been closely connected with the Liberty party—did display some concern for free blacks, but only in the abstract and *sotto voce* as it were, asserting that it should be "a local issue, irrelevant to the central problem of the extension of slavery." Which is to say a de facto abandonment of these blacks to their miserable fate (comparable to someone today professing concern for blacks but saying they could be best left to the mercies of local communities). And so in boarding the Free-Soil band wagon western abolitionists such as Salmon Chase and Josh Giddings had to adjust their convictions on the race issue. Both men, for example, publicly acquiesced in the resolution passed by the Ohio Free-Soil convention that "Ohio desires a homogeneous population, and does not desire a population of varied character."

Free-Soil racism explained to me once and for all, definitively, why Gerrit Smith and the other giants of political abolitionism—Birney, Weld, the Tappans, Frederick Douglass—refused to have anything to do with the party, why Smith kept the hopelessly minuscule Liberty organization alive, why he and Douglass in 1852 held their own little convention in which they bravely resolved that "the Liberty Party cannot consent to fall below, nor in any degree to qualify, its great central principle, that all persons— black and white, male and female—have equal rights, and are equally entitled to the protection and the advantages of the civil Government."

And I understood now why so much hung on the difference between the nonextension of slavery and abolition, why, in short, the difference between these antislavery groups was more than tactical. It was because the Free-Soil party was so blatantly antiblack; because it made racism the necessary condition of its resistance to the South; because it forged a fatal link (fatal to abolitionism) between opposition to slavery and white supremacism.

I was reluctant to draw the conclusion I did. I came to perceive Free-Soilism as a negative approval of slavery. The South had brought the curse on itself: It mustn't be allowed to spread it, to infect others with it. And what was that curse, that peculiarly Southern wickedness? It was to have been responsible for "the propagation of the colored race." *Free-Soilers thought slavery abhorrent*—to answer my question—*because they thought blacks abhorrent.* (Douglass in 1849 put it somewhat differently: "The cry of Free Men was raised, not for the extension of liberty to the black man, but for the protection of the liberty of the white.") So, under the circumstances, given the fact that three million or so slaves were concentrated in the South, didn't Free-Soilers have to *approve* of slavery, provided again it stayed put, at least until such time in the indeterminate future as the blacks could be transported en masse out of the country? And I could see, pursuing this line of reasoning, why Free-Soilers would detest the abolitionist formula. To immediately and unconditionally redeem blacks from bondage and let them migrate North and mingle with whites, as abolitionists appeared to advocate, must have struck antislave whites as the most grotesque unthinkable possibility of all. Hence the Free-Soil formula: "Keep upon the shoulders of the South the burden of the curse."

My insight into the Free-Soil movement gave me pause. I was aware of its distance from my previously held views. Its implications were unsettling. Was racism the mainspring of the antislavery crusade? What did abolitionism have to do with the explosive race issue? And what about the Republican party—to what extent did it owe its great triumph to the same racist ideology that animated Free-Soilism? I turned next to these questions, taking up leads I'd previously overlooked, rereading books I hadn't (as I now saw) properly grasped or construed or incorporated into my schema.

————◆————

First abolitionism. I could perceive more clearly now why the abolitionist position on *free* blacks couldn't be separated from its position on enslaved ones. *Immediate and unconditional emancipation implied as its logical corollary the immediate and unconditional acceptance of blacks as equals, as brethren, into white society.* One couldn't otherwise be an abolitionist, whatever else one was, whatever one's attitude toward blacks and slavery might be. Garrison beautifully summed up the credo of the whole movement: "O, if those whose prejudices against color are deeply rooted—if the assertion of the natural inferiority of the people of color, would but even casually associate with the victims of their injustice, and be candid to give merit its due, they could not long feel and act as they now do. Their prejudice would melt like frostwork before the blazing sun; their unbelief would vanish away, their contempt be turned into admiration, their indifference be aroused to benevolent activity, and their dislike give place to friendship." Abolitionism, then, was not only, or not even primarily, directed against slaveholders; it was a self-injunction. Abolitionists were expected to act as they preached, to assume all of the consequences of their beliefs. If manumission should lead to the appearance of countless blacks in their midst, and if this be the abiding white fear, so be it. That fear must be confronted head on. And to prepare for that miraculous day when the blacks do appear one must begin now, by demonstrating how they can be treated, how they can be taken in as equals, lifted up, humanized.† And so whenever abolitionists found little groups or cells

† Aileen Kraditor, in her fine study of the Garrisonians, *Means and Ends in American Abolitionism* (to which I owed a great deal [it came out just when I was working on this section]), puts it very well: "To have dropped the demand for *immediate* emancipation because it was unrealizable at the time would have been to alter the nature of the change for which the abolitionists were agitating. Even those who would have gladly accepted gradual and conditional emancipation had to agitate for immediate and unconditional abolition of slavery because that demand was required by their goal of demonstrating to white Americans that Negroes were their brothers.

("societies"), they conspicuously went among the despised black people and tried to educate them (e.g., the Prudence Crandall School in Connecticut, the Lane Seminarians led by Weld in Cincinnati, etc.), teach them industrial skills, give them land (as Gerrit Smith did), defend their elemental rights to vote, sit on juries, travel on public conveyance, and be left alone.

(Which isn't to say that abolitionists were free of racism themselves. There's plenty of evidence to the contrary, and even Garrison could be intolerably condescending to blacks he befriended—and insulting to those, chief among them Frederick Douglass, who crossed him. But what's important is the distinction between abolitionist and nonabolitionist racism. Abolitionists regarded white supremacism as an evil second only to slavery itself, an evil they perhaps had to struggle most against in themselves. Other whites struggled against nothing of the sort, for they affirmed black inferiority, took it entirely for granted. You needn't romanticize the abolitionists to acknowledge their courage.‡)

Once the nation had been converted on that point, other conditions and plans might have been made. Many documents indicate that most abolitionists would have accepted such conditions; most of them did in fact accept a moderate policy after the Civil War. Before the war, they refused to be drawn into the discussions on the problems that sudden emancipation might create or on 'plans' for easing the transition to freedom, for implicit in such discussions, they felt, was an assumption that Negro inferiority rather than white racism would produce the problems. This would not be so if the discussions were carried on by a society free of racism but merely anxious that the change in the Negro's status be as smooth as possible. But among whites unready to accept the Negro as inherently their equal, any such debate would feed the prevalent prejudice and provide an anaesthetic for consciences that were beginning to hurt. This was why Garrison's first great campaign was to discredit colonizationism. . . . That is why some abolitionists later could not accept free soilism as a tactic to strangle slavery to death in the Southwest; while they might recognize the practical utility of the tactic, they could not admit the legitimacy of slavery in any part of the country without denying their movement's fundamental principle."

‡ I agree completely with James M. McPherson ("A Brief for Equality: The Abolitionist Reply to the Racist Myth," *The Antislavery Vanguard*, edited by Martin F. Duberman) who observes: "Abolitionists insisted that the Negro was a human being, and that he was entitled to all the rights enjoyed by other men in America. Slavery and inequality could be justified only by denying the equal manhood of the Negro, and the supporters of slavery were finally forced to take this position. . . . Although slavery was finally abolished, the abolitionists' racial equalitarianism was ahead of its time. Not until the twentieth century was the validity of the abolitionist ar-

And I could now understand why abolitionists were so cruelly persecuted in the North. I'd believed they were persecuted because they were so "extremist" in their antislavery views, so far in advance of public opinion (such as, say, socialists have been in modern times). It was of course an unexamined belief, a cliché. It should have been obvious to me, had I bothered to excogitate the matter through, that Northern whites couldn't have cared less what these "fanatics" were saying against slavery, just as they didn't deeply care what the fanatical utopian socialists or fanatical millenarians or the countless other fanatical reformers were proposing in the 1830s and 1840s (and in any case abolitionist talk didn't free a single slave; no threat from that quarter). What irked Northerners, what lashed them to a fury, was *abolitionist behavior toward free blacks*. Here lay the cause of their persecutions of the 1830s. They were "nigger-lovers." Race, not slavery, was their undoing.

A subject opened up before me of which I'd been only dimly conscious until then—the subject of mob violence. I simply hadn't been aware of its dimensions. I certainly had no idea of the connection between race riots and abolitionism. A book just published, *Powder Keg* by Lorman Ratner, establishes that connection convincingly, pointing out how respectable, educated whites would accuse abolitionists of seeking the "amalgamation" of the races, with all that that suggested, sexually, aesthetically, intellectually, morally. Typical was the Massachusetts attorney general's comment in 1835 (antiabolitionist mobs having just roamed the streets of Boston): "Is it supposed they [blacks] could amalgamate? God forbid. . . . But I fearlessly aver that if this be the tendency and the result of our moral reformation, rather than our white race should degenerate into a tribe of tawny-colored quadroons, rather than our fair and beauteous females should give birth to the thick-lipped, woolly-headed children of African fathers, rather than the Negro should be seated in the Hall of Congress and his sooty complexion glare upon us from the bench of justice, rather than he should mingle with us in the familiar intercourse of democratic life and taint the atmosphere of our

gument confirmed. The history of our time has demonstrated that the abolitionists had perhaps a deeper understanding of the racial problem than any other men of their time—and many of ours."

homes and firesides—I WILL BRAVE MY SHARE OF ALL RESPONSIBILITY OF KEEPING THEM IN SLAVERY."

Nor did it take much in that age of free-wheeling democracy to translate the fear of "amalgamation" into direct action. This fact is brought out in frightening detail by James Bach McMaster, whose eight volumes on pre-Civil War America, *A History of the People of the United States,* I found an invaluable mine of information, a chronicle of popular events culled with old-fashioned assiduity (they were published before 1910), mainly from newspapers* By the mid-1830s, McMaster writes, "mobbing" of abolitionists and blacks "swept the country. Nothing like it had ever been experienced." I copied his description of two of these "mobbings." At Utica, New York, in 1835:

"While one mob was chasing Garrison through the streets of Boston, another was breaking up the Anti-Slavery Convention at Utica. The purpose of the meeting was to form a State anti-slavery society and Utica had been selected as a place geographically central. The people of the town, however, in mass meeting had denounced the abolitionists and their ways, had been urged by a political convention of Oneida County to close their churches, school-rooms, court-house and academy to the 'deluded men who were kindling the flame of civil strife,' and now heard with indignation that the Common Council had granted to the abolitionists the use of the court-room. Another meeting was thereupon called, and resolutions adopted setting forth that the people would not submit to such an indignity, that the building had been erected by the contributions of citizens for public purposes, not as a receptacle for reckless incendiaries, and that it was the duty of every citizen to prevent the meeting of the Convention. When the appointed day came people took possession of the court-room and bade a committee make known their will to the fanatics.

"Shut out of the court-room the delegates assembled in the Presbyterian Church, and had just finished the organization of their society when the committee, headed by the Judge, the county clerk and postmaster, and followed by a shouting mob rushed down the aisle and stopped all further proceedings. A demand was made that the Convention adjourn, and when this was complied

---

* I also consulted J. T. Headley's classic accounts of mob violence—*The Great Riots of New York* and *Pen and Pencil Sketches of the Great Riots* —but thought McMaster's much superior to them.

with, that the members leave the church. The minutes of the meeting were next taken by force from the Secretary, the delegates expelled, and later ejected from their boarding places. When night came the office of the Oneida Standard and Democrat was entered and types and cases thrown into the street. On the following day the abolitionists finished their business at Peterboro, a town some five and twenty miles from Utica."

(This riot, it might be noted, marked Gerrit Smith's conversion to abolitionism; it was Smith who invited the dispossessed members of the Utica Convention to come to Peterboro where he lived.)

And at Philadelphia in 1838:

". . . Driven from the churches, halls, and public buildings of that city, the abolitionists, anti-slavery people, and friends of free discussion had put up a building, named it Pennsylvania Hall, because the motto of the State was Virtue, Liberty, and Independence, and had dedicated it to Liberty and the Rights of Man. The ceremony of dedication took place in May, occupied several days, and afforded an occasion for addresses on Temperance, on the Right of Free Discussion, on the Right of Petition, on Indian Wrongs, on the Abolitionists, on Slavery and Its Remedy, and on Requited Labor. No trouble occurred on the first day; but on the morning of the second, manuscript placards were seen posted in several parts of the city. 'Whereas,' they read, 'a convention to effect the immediate abolition of slavery is in session, it behooves all citizens who respect the rights of property to interfere, forcibly if they must, to prevent the violation of pledges.' All so disposed were then called on to meet in front of the hall the next morning and demand the adjournment of the convention. Few came during that day; but the evening meeting was disturbed by stamping, yelling, and the throwing of bricks. The following day, the fourth day of the meeting, the mob gathered early. The managers in alarm applied, first to the mayor and then to the sheriff, for protection. Neither would do anything. About sunset the mayor announced that, if given possession of the building, he would disperse the mob. The keys were thereupon delivered; the mayor made a speech to the mob, and, when he had finished, the attack began. The door was beaten in, window blinds and books from the anti-slavery bookshop on the first floor were heaped on the speaker's platform, the gas pipes, pulled from the ceilings and walls, were bent toward the pile of books, a match was applied, and in a few hours the building was in ruins.

"All the next day the mob ruled the city and when night came attacked and set fire to the Shelter for Colored Orphans, stoned a negro church, and howled around the houses of several anti-slavery men. . . .

"When the excitement had gone down the mayor published a defense of his inability to scatter the mob, the Governor offered a reward of five hundred dollars for the arrest and conviction of each and every person engaged in the destruction of the hall or the asylum; the mayor offered two thousand dollars, and the Committee on Police made a report to Councils. The cause of the destruction of the hall was, the committee said, the determination of the owners to 'persevere in openly promulgating and advocating in it doctrines repulsive to the moral sense of a large majority of our community. Of their legal and constitutional right to do so there can be question.' But that they had a moral right the report attempted to disprove. The willingness of the citizens to countenance the mob, and the refusal of the onlookers to respond to the cry, 'Support the mayor,' were the causes of the inability of the mayor to save the hall.

"The press, the country over, united in lamenting or condemning the violence of the mob; but in the free States it was divided on the question where to put the blame. The *New York Gazette* laid it on 'the white-skinned damsels who promenaded the streets of Philadelphia arm and arm with their lamp-black paramours.' The Philadelphia journals denied that such a sight had ever been seen in their city. The *Baltimore Patriot* declared that 'this nation is the only one which presents the disgraceful spectacle of a set of women leaving the sphere of domestic duty to which they belong and voluntarily agitating which have rarely yet been touched upon without rousing the worst passions of the community.' The *Lynn Record* bemoaned the debased tone of the city journals that extolled women 'for dancing, singing, speaking, and acting publicly in a manner which decency would blush to witness, but express great horror when a sensible and benevolent female, personally acquainted with, and deeply feeling for, the injuries and outrages done her sex,' comes forward to plead for their removal. 'Who are the rioters?' said the *Philadelphia Spirit of the Times*. 'As a solemn truth we answer—the abolitionists. The liberty of speech and the freedom of the press are two of the strong pillars of the Republic, and we would be the last to abridge or destroy the one or the other. But what is a rioter? Now we contend that the abolitionists are the rioters, wanton, licentiously festive, seditious, turbulent, and that they knew the building of the Pennsylvania Hall would cause a riot in Philadelphia some day.'

" 'The destruction of this Temple of Amalgamation in the City of Brotherly Love should not be regretted by any American citizen who entertains just pretensions to patriotism,' said the *St. Louis Saturday News*. " 'We would as soon denounce the sages of our revolution as rebels as cast a shade of censure on the actors of the late Philadelphia affair. The abolition lecturers and the proprietors of this unholy temple may think themselves fortunate that their ashes have not been mingled with the rubbish of their edifice.'

"The example thus set in Philadelphia was quickly followed elsewhere. . . ."

Inexplicably, antiabolitionist mob violence fell off sharply in the late 1830s. And even antiblack violence abated by the time the Free-Soil movement got under way. Rioting as such, though (it might be mentioned parenthetically), kept growing in pervasiveness and ferocity. Only it was directed increasingly against Catholics, becoming a facet of the infamous Know-Nothing crusade. So again a familiar piece of irony: The Irish poor, so many of whom had been implicated in the terror against abolitionists and blacks, became themselves the victims of a worse terror.

(Riots against blacks flared up again in the early years of the Civil War. The bloodiest of these pogroms was of course the New York City draft riot of 1863 which claimed the lives of hundreds, possibly thousands, of blacks. The literature on that orgy of death makes one wince with pain.)

(With considerable interest I read the highly publicized report just issued—the summer of 1968—by President Johnson's high-level Advisory Commission on Violence, created in response to last year's ghetto uprisings. The report, generous and liberal-minded in approach [reflecting the views of the commission's leaders, Illinois Governor Otto Kerner and Mayor Lindsay], tends to reduce the subject to a criticism of national character, Americans having always been a violent people, having always resorted to mob violence, etc. True enough. The fallacy of the report is to place all forms of mass protest once they get out of hand under the same rubric, the same characterological defect. What counts, it seemed to me, is the *difference* between the mobs and riots and mass disorders that have punctuated American history, the difference, that is, in their tactics and ends, the composition and leadership of the participants, the social context in which they took place, and so on. If it weren't for mobs, would there have been an American Revolution? Any revolution?)

———◆———

I was satisfied now that I could explain why Northern whites felt as they did toward abolitionists; and why, for that matter, there were so few abolitionists. And this explanation led to another question which didn't bear directly on the issue at hand—the antislavery issue—but did excite my curiosity. I couldn't let it pass in the expectation that I might pick it up when I had the time (which might be never; I had to go after it then, while the anvil was still hot). And that question dealt with the condition of free blacks in the North. I wanted to know what forms racism took, why whites regarded blacks as pariahs. And I wanted to get an idea of the *dynamics* of this racism—whether it was growing or diminishing and to what degree antislavery politics reflected (or helped shape) it. I wasn't sure if the information I found would be useful for my project, if it would figure somehow in the background of my John Brown portrait. Nor did it matter. I'd discovered a lacuna in my education and filling it needed no justification.

The seminal work is unquestionably Leon Litwack's *North of Slavery*. I'd read it after a fashion years before (it appeared in 1961), and remembered being impressed by the data it bodied forth, the evidence it piled high of Northern racism, but saw no broader significance in it, the fact of racism coming as no surprise.

Now I was in a position to see its significance. In a sense I was reading the book for the first time.

Litwack is quietly objective, restrained, hardly voicing an explicit reproach as he catalogues one horror after another, as he shows how blacks were systematically reduced to the lowliest status possible within a putatively free society, a proud democracy. The crucial term for me was *reduced*. Litwack conveys a powerful insight (of which he himself isn't as aware as he should be), namely that there existed in Northern United States between 1800 and 1860 a cruel ratio between democracy and the condition of blacks, the first rising in proportion as the second fell. Every chapter in *North of Slavery*—on politics, education, economics, etc.—forces us to conclude that the triumph of the (white male) common man in the age of Jackson brought disaster to free blacks. And the disaster didn't consist simply in outbursts of violence (Litwack's illuminating on that, too). The disaster was *institutional*. In fact the institutionalization of racism appeared to obviate the need for random violence (explaining perhaps why mobs didn't bother so much with blacks from the mid-1840s on). As whites gained the vote in a succession of struggles against ancient oligarchies and assorted monopolies, so blacks lost it; they were steadily *disfranchised* in one state after another. It was the democratic political machines (e.g., Van Buren's Albany Regency, the model of them all)—celebrated in the encomiastic literature on Jacksonian democracy—that were mainly responsible for striking blacks off the electoral rolls even as they were putting unpropertied white males on them. (I was astonished to learn that the 1841 Dorr Rebellion of Rhode Island—Jacksonian democracy in extremis, the violent attempt of the masses of that state to secure the vote—would have disfranchised the blacks had it succeeded, the failure of democracy [and that proved only temporary] serving therefore to protect such political rights as they'd enjoyed.) And the most racist and exclusionary communities of all, it turned out, were those that best exemplified the ideals of yeoman democracy: the western states. The pattern began with those carved out of the Northwest Territory (Ohio, Indiana, Illinois) and was repeated—and surpassed—with each new settlement, with the admission of each new state into the Union. (What the Kansas Free Staters had done in 1855–56, what Brown and the other abolitionists had found so distressing, became more intelligible to me, consistent as it was with the pattern established everywhere else.) Litwack drove home the further point: The disfranchisement of blacks wasn't only superstructural—that is, political, legal, juridical—it permeated every aspect of their lives. He shows how blacks fell deeper and deeper into poverty, reinforcing the white aversion to them that had laid them low in the first place, accelerating the grim cycle; how white trade-unionists and workingmen were especially culpable, especially racist in deed if not in attitude; how the Irish immigrants, themselves reduced and persecuted, were thrown into competition with blacks, straitening their condition further; how blacks sought to resist their enforced suffering by holding their own conventions, creating their own abolitionist and self-help societies, calling forth their own remarkable group of leaders, among them Frederick Douglass (a giant of his times), Robert Purvis, Henry Highland Garnet, Martin R. Delany (one could go on)—their efforts in vain, however, before the remorseless engine of oppression; and how, accordingly, these leaders grew increasingly desperate, increasingly alienated from a society which, despite a few abolitionists, had become hopelessly racist, some openly advocating violent resistance by free as well as enslaved blacks, others the emigration of blacks to Latin America or Liberia,† a view to which even such long-time abolitionist friends

† Martin R. Delany wrote an interesting tract in 1852 (*The Condition, Elevation, Emigration, and Destiny of the Colored People*) which persuasively argues the colonization and black nationalist position. (He's a forerunner of such modern apostles of the idea as Stokely Carmichael and Rap Brown.) Delany summarized his reasons for espousing it in a letter to Garrison: "I am not in favor of caste, nor a separation of the brotherhood of mankind, and would as willingly live among white men as black, if I had an *equal possession and enjoyment* of privileges; but shall never be reconciled to live among them, subservient to their will—existing by mere *sufferance,* as we, the colored people, do, in this country. The majority of white men cannot see why colored men cannot be satisfied with their condition in Massachusetts—what they desire more than the *granted* right of citizenship. Blind selfishness on the one hand, and deep prejudice on the other, will not permit them to understand that we desire the *exercise* and *enjoyment* of these rights as well as the *name* of their possession. If there were any probability of this, I should be willing to remain in the country, fighting and struggling on, the good fight of faith. But I must admit, that I have no hopes in this country—no confidence in the American people—with a few exceptions—therefore, I have written as I have done. Heathenism and Liberty before Christianity and Slavery."

of black people as James Birney at last subscribed, so great was
his despair, his sense of futility and failure.

Litwack's book, in other words, argues the paradox that I was
wrestling with. While blacks were losing out in ways he describes,
the antislavery crusade was bounding ahead; the condition of
blacks was never worse than in the 1850s, when the Republican
party matured and laid the basis for its conquest of power. But it's
a paradox which Litwack himself doesn't draw.

If there's anything to criticize in Litwack's eye-opening study
it's his forbearance. He plays his theme close to the vest, avoiding
any statement beyond the evidence itself cautiously presented and
interpreted. I kept hoping he'd engage in some free-wheeling
(possibly errant) speculation on *why* Northerners were so racist,
particularly where blacks were fewest and couldn't conceivably
pose a threat to white workingmen. He doesn't try to relate trium-
phant democracy and black degradation, whites moving up, blacks
down. So we're left to assume that the relation was accidental or
due entirely to concomitant circumstances—for example, the arrival of hundreds of thousands of immigrants, the depression of
the 1840s, etc. Not that such circumstances, accidental or not,
were unimportant. Only they don't explain why blacks were
socially and politically disfranchised as democracy took root, why
the deterioration of their status was so general and categorical.

And beating against the enormous obstacle of his evidence is a
tiny angel of hope. Litwack's determined to retain his optimism,
despite the content of his book. "Although subjected to angry
white mobs, ridicule and censure," he writes in the preface, the
free Negro "made substantial progress in some sections of the
North and, at the very least, began to plague the Northern conscience with the inconsistency of its antislavery pronouncements
and prevailing racial practices. And although confined largely to
menial employments, some Negroes did manage to accumulate
property and establish thriving businesses; by 1860, northern
Negroes shared with white workers the vision of rising into the
middle class. Finally, on the eve of Civil War, an increasing number of Negroes were availing themselves of educational opportunities; either in the small number of integrated schools or in the
exclusive and usually inferior Negro schools." But in the concluding paragraph 280 pages later he writes: "In 1860 . . . despite
some notable advances, the northern Negro remained largely

disfranchised, segregated, and economically oppressed. Discrimination still barred him from most polls, juries, schools, and workshops, as well as from many libraries, theaters, lyceums, museums, public conveyances, and literary societies. Although he himself was responsible for this exclusion, the white man effectively turned it against the Negro. Having excluded the Negro from profitable employments, the whites scorned his idleness and poverty; having taxed him in some states for the support of public education, they excluded his children from the schools or placed them in separate and inferior institutions and then deplored the ignorance of his race; having excluded him from various lecture halls and libraries, they pointed to his lack of culture and refinement; and, finally, having stripped him of his claims to citizenship, and having deprived him of opportunities for political and economic advancement, the whites concluded that the Negro had demonstrated an incapacity for improvement in this country and should be colonized in Africa."

One question Litwack raises but doesn't explore in sufficient detail (understandably, given the scope of his inquiry) especially intrigued me: the part white workingmen played in the decline, the lumpenization as it were, of so many blacks—these white workingmen who epitomized the egalitarian ethic of Jacksonian democracy and the Free-Soil movement that arose from it. I wasn't looking for fresh insights and discoveries. I wanted to grasp more firmly the ones Litwack had suggested to me and refine them in the alembic of my imagination through my own reading of the documents and books (Litwack being priceless here too, his bibliographical essay a treasure in itself).

In this way I came to comprehend the *process* of black immiserization, their step-by-step *economic disfranchisement*. It was a process that obeyed its own implacable laws.

Now Northern slavery, as it petered out in the late eighteenth and early nineteenth centuries (varying in time and circumstance from state to state, community to community), left blacks with an important legacy: their skills. They were craftsmen or "mechanics" who possessed the same pride and integrity and stake in society that their white brethren possessed. And in large cities also, where thousands of them lived, they freely practiced their vocations. In New York City around 1800 some two thousand black men were engaged in a multitude of skilled occupations.‡ In Philadelphia, as late as 1820, blacks comprised a majority of the artisans.* Elsewhere it was pretty much the same. For free Northern blacks these were the halcyon days.

The beginning of their descent coincided with the organization of trade-unions in the 1830s. Such organizations (regarded as conspiracies by their enemies, sometimes by the law) were set up to protect their members, all skilled craftsmen, from the vicissitudes of an expanding market economy and the power of merchant capitalists. That protection meant, specifically, control of apprenticeship and employment—the labor market. But the protection wasn't extended to black workingmen. They were denied its benefits; to a measurable extent it was directed against them. As the unions got organized blacks lost the right to practice their trades, earn their livelihood. Frederick Douglass could thus lament to Harriet Beecher Stowe (years later, when the process was complete): "Prejudice against the free colored people of the United States has shown itself nowhere so invincible as among mechanics. The farmer and the professional men cherish no feeling so bitter as those cherished by these. At this moment I can more easily get my son into a lawyer's office to learn law than I can enter a blacksmith's shop to blow the billows and wield the sledge hammer."

Douglass's observation is borne out, for example, in a petition signed by a group of Connecticut workingmen in 1834 seeking remedial legislation against blacks coming into the state: Because of the presence of "black porters, black truckmen, black sawyers, black mechanics, and black laborers of every description," the white workingman "is deprived of employment or is forced to labor for less than he requires." (I found this item in Garrison's *Liberator* of February 1, 1834; the *Liberator* is a mine of such information.)

‡ Edgar J. McManus, in his solid study, *A History of Negro Slavery in New York,* informs us of this on the strength of a 1797 report by the New York Manumission Society.
* The estimate is by W. E. B. Du Bois (*The Philadelphia Negro*) and accepted by the most reputable authorities. (See, for example, Sterling B. Sporo and Abram L. Harris, *The Black Workers: The Negro and the Labor Movement;* also Charles H. Wesley, *Negro Labor in the United States, 1850–1925*).

There's also the testimony presented before the 1835 Ohio Anti-Slavery Convention. It's worth quoting from:

"A respectable master mechanic stated to us, a few days since, that in 1830 the President of the Mechanical Association was publically tried by the Society, for the crime of assisting a colored young man to learn a trade. Such was the feeling among the mechanics that no colored boy could learn a trade or colored journeyman find employment. A young man of our acquaintance, of unexceptionable character and an excellent workingman, purchased his freedom and learned the cabinet making business in Kentucky. On coming to this city [Cincinnati] he was refused work by every man to whom he applied. At last he found a shop, carried on by an Englishman, who agreed to employ him, but on entering the shop, the workmen threw down their tools and declared that he should leave or they would. 'They would never work with a nigger.' The unfortunate youth was accordingly dismissed. . . . This oppression of the mechanics still continues. One of the boys of our school last summer, sought in vain for a place in this city to learn a trade. . . . Multitudes of common laborers at the time alluded to above were immediately turned out of employment, and many have told us that they were compelled to resort to dishonorable occupations or starve. . . ."

Once launched, the logic of economic racism took on its own momentum. In excluding blacks from the skilled trades, white workingmen forced them to engage in open competition, *bringing about* exactly the situation the trade-unions were established to combat. Racism was bound to grow more virulent. Blacks were bound to become scapegoats whenever economic conditions worsened, whenever the threat of unemployment (hence competition) rose. So we find the *National Trades' Union,* journal of organized workingmen, repeatedly denouncing blacks as a race fit only for slavery or servitude. And we find the great leaders of the workingmen's parties, heroes of the Jacksonian left, men like Seth Luther and William Leggett, asserting that abolitionism was part and parcel of the aristocratic or Whig plot to strengthen privilege and monopoly. Emancipate blacks, give them the vote, bring them into competition with white workingmen, and the aristocracy of wealth would govern forever (which helps explain why in New York State Jacksonian Democrats of the Locofoco and Barnburner persuasion were so eager to disfranchise blacks).

The status of free Northern blacks seems to have collapsed quickly. New York and Philadelphia again provided striking indices of the change. According to the Colored National Convention of 1855, only 419 blacks were still working at their trades in New York, amounting to a few per cent of the black population there. In Philadelphia, out of a black population of above 10,000 Du Bois finds only 352 artisans were still plying their craft by 1840. The generalization needn't be qualified: Having been kept from their occupations, having in effect had their occupations taken away from them in an increasingly competitive market place, blacks were systematically *declassed,* victims of a campaign of economic terror.

With the condition of blacks deteriorating Northern workingmen became more and more fearful of what the South held in store for them. A double fear: of slavery expanding and slavery ending. It was in either case the fear of a black tide washing over the country, inundating its workers, reducing *them* to the status of blacks. We were back to Free-Soilism. So, according to the *Working Man's Advocate,* "It is not so difficult, therefore, to foresee in whose favor the competition between three millions of blacks and as yet greater number of whites would terminate; and who would first suffer from want of employment and the reduction of wages consequent on competition." Or as George Henry Evans, the radical worker-agrarian, father of the homestead idea ("Vote Yourself a Farm"), wrote in the same *Advocate:* Why "persuade the overworked *white* slaves (supposing they had the power) to vote the personal freedom only of the *blacks,* thereby enabling their former masters, by the lash of want, to get as much labor of two-thirds of them as they formerly got of the whole, throwing the labor of the other third on the already overstocked labor market?"

The inference couldn't be escaped. Workingmen believed they had nothing to gain, indeed everything to lose, by the emancipation of the slaves. Workingmen may even have had a vested interest in the maintenance of slavery (certainly not so bad an institution, many of their spokesmen said, as "wage slavery")†—

† According to just such a spokesman, New York labor leader and Congressman Mike Walsh: "The only difference between the negro slave of the South and the white wage slave of the North is that the one has a master without asking for him, and the other has to beg for the privilege of becoming one. . . . The one is the slave of an individual, the other is the slave of an inexorable class."

provided it was kept within the limits rigorously prescribed by the Missouri Compromise and, later, the Wilmot Proviso. The refusal of the slavocrats to oblige marked the genesis of the great crisis that followed. And we observe again how the race issue lay at the heart of the Free-Soil movement, how antislavery could also be seen (obversely) as *favoring* slavery—a slavery of the benign and quiescent sort to be sure, a slavery which knew its place and bore its "curse" alone.

(Too easily, it seemed to me, labor historians commit the same teleological error I did.‡ They assume that because antislavery led ultimately to abolition the two were really kindred movements, different tactics in behalf of the same objective. In other words, the racism of the white working class, the exclusion of blacks from the trades, etc. [which these historians—most of them—readily acknowledge], had nothing to do with their opposition to slavery, their joining the Free-Soil and Republican parties, their becoming de facto abolitionists. I'd concluded on the contrary [at the risk of repeating myself] that racism had *everything* to do with the workingmen's opposition to slavery and that if emancipation happened to be the end result of their opposition it was a wholly unintended one; it was precisely what they'd always sought to prevent.

(True enough, as many of these same historians point out, abolitionists tended to be indifferent, even calloused, to the affliction of the "wage slaves." Garrison for one was a downright apologist for the petty capitalist-cum-Protestant ethic and couldn't conceive why a freeman would complain about his lot in life. He and other abolitionists paid scant heed to the white workers' concern for the future—one which envisioned millions of ex-slaves entering the labor market. Being middle or upper class themselves, abolitionists never experienced that concern. No doubt of it, here was a blind spot in the moral retina of the abolitionists.

(But in the retina of *abolitionism?* That's an entirely different matter. Did workingmen reject abolitionism because of the people who espoused it? Or because its proponents stood aloof from them and took little interest in their struggles? Hardly. White

‡ I am referring especially to Bernard Bandel, *Labor: Free and Slave;* Herman Schlüter, *Lincoln, Labor and Slavery;* Joseph G. Rayback, *A History of American Labor;* and Williston H. Lofton, "Abolition and Labor," *The Journal of Negro History,* Vol. 33. The list can be vastly enlarged.

workingmen rejected abolitionism because they thought it wrong in itself, on *absolute* grounds, as something that should not come to pass, not in their lifetime anyway. The historic fact must be faced that on the question of abolitionism the white working class in general was retrograde and conservative.*

(And a considerable segment of it still is. In the late spring, early summer of 1968, while I was doing the research for this part of my project, black activists were picketing and closing down building sites because the construction unions involved—plumbers, electricians, ironworkers, etc.—had persistently kept blacks from practicing those trades, in direct contravention of the law, state and local as well as federal. But these unions were so strong, so well connected politically, they could contravene the law with impunity. Supporters of black workers [among them my friend Herbert Hill of the NAACP] had no choice but to resort to direct action. Interestingly, union spokesmen, mainly President George Meany of the AFL-CIO, would attack these activists much as white workingmen attacked abolitionists over a century earlier. Now such terms as "limousine liberal" and "radical chic" came into vogue to describe the middle- and upper-class intellectuals who stood in the forefront of one or another of the insurgent movements of the 1960s—movements from which the trade-union establishment was conspicuously absent, to which on occasion it was even more conspicuously opposed. The most disturbing question before us was how much of the working class would give its support to George Wallace and Richard Nixon, both appealing to the "law and order" vote, both dead set against any

---

* The single exception I came across (in an old book: George E. McNeil, ed., *The Labor Movement*) was a resolution passed by a convention of the New England Workingmen's Association held in 1846. It stated: "While we are willing to pledge ourselves to use all means in our power consistent with our principles to put down war, insurrection and mobs, and to protect all men from the evils of the same, we will not take up arms to sustain Southern slaveholders in robbing one fifth of our countrymen of their labor. . . . Let it no longer be said that Northern laborers, while they are endeavoring to gain their own rights, are nothing but a standing army that keeps three million of their brethren and sisters in bondage at the point of a bayonet."

A remarkable statement. One searches in vain for similar sentiments in the working-class press of the time.

of the insurgencies that had been moving and shaking the country since John Kennedy took office in 1961.)

A word about the Irish immigrants whose presence from the mid-1830s on contributed so enormously to the immiserization of the blacks. As Litwack and a whole literature on the subject attest, these two people fought it out among themselves for the few economic opportunities that were available. But the Irish, with all their handicaps, enjoyed incalculable advantages, one above all others: They were white. Once they were politically franchised they quickly obtained other kinds of power.† So that while the Irish were beginning their painful climb upward the blacks were descending more and more rapidly into the bottomless hold of pauperdom and anonymity.

This point, however, should be underlined: *The Irish may have completed the process of black immiserization; they didn't start it.* The system of white supremacy and exclusivity they found ready-to-hand for them when they arrived. Native Americans had prepared the way. It was only natural that the Irish would seize on any advantage in their own desperate daily struggle for survival. Frederick Douglass, clear-sighted as always, recognized the pathos of the Irish-black encounter (one which his people were destined to lose) and placed the blame where it belonged. "We see here the black man attacked in his vital interests," he asserted in May

† Some black citizens of New York City got together on February 28, 1838, to hold a protest meeting on this abominable state of affairs. One Peter Vogelsang (who'd emigrated to the United States thirty-five years earlier) spoke up: "Look at Europe disgorging her paupers from her alm-houses and work houses, by ship loads on your shores. London, Paris and other European cities eject from their jails and prisons their burglars and blacklegs on your shores. These men, after a temporary residence, before they can name the different states of the Union—the moment they register their intention to become citizens, are permitted to vote. Ignorant of the character of the candidates for whom they cast their ballots—ignorant of the common language of the land, they can approach the ballot-box—while YOU, natives of the soil, and I, a thirty-five year resident—acquainted with the public character of the prominent candidates for public stations, and (shall I say it?) well acquainted with the genius of the government as half the men that are elected to make the laws—are deprived of privileges granted to European paupers, blacklegs and burglars!!!" (Reported in *The Colored American* of June 24, 1838.)

1853, in a speech full of ironies. "Prejudice and hate are excited against him. Enmity is stirred up between him and other laborers. The Irish people, warmhearted, generous, and sympathizing with the oppressed everywhere when they stand on their own green island, are instantly taught on arriving in this Christian country to hate and despise the colored people. They are taught to believe that we eat the bread which of right belongs to them. The cruel lie is taught the Irish that our adversity is essential to their prosperity. The Irish-American will find out his mistake one day. He will find that in assuming our avocations he also has assumed our degradation. But for the present we are the sufferers. The old employments by which we have heretofore gained our livelihood are gradually, and it may be inevitably, passing into other hands. Every hour sees us elbowed out of some employment, to make room perhaps for some newly arrived immigrants, whose hunger and color are thought to give them title to special favor. White men are becoming house-servants, cooks, and stewards, coachmen, laborers, and floorkeeps to our gentry, and for ought that I see, they adjust to their stations with becoming obsequiousness."

One question remained to be settled before I could be done with my excursus into the antislavery movement—an excursus that had taken me to the outermost bounds, the barely discerned horizon, of the landscape I was adumbrating. Yes, I was willing to travel that far afield because I was surprised and intrigued by what I'd discovered, useful or not, and because I'd had no idea until then that racism counted for so much in the history of the North, particularly of the antislavery movement. My question was actually a hypothesis or inference: If Free-Soilers owed so much (perhaps its very existence) to white supremacy, didn't it stand to reason that Republicans owed at least as much to it? How much was what I wanted to know.

It was a question of moment to me. For as long as I could remember I'd had deep-set convictions about the Republican party of the ante-bellum, Civil War, and Reconstruction eras. It occupied a place of high honor in my pantheon of historical forces. It embodied for me the nobler values of the American experience. It affirmed its solidarity with the egalitarian ideals of the Declaration of Independence (to which it harked back over and over again in the 1850s and 1860s, as witness Lincoln's speeches, debates, letters, etc.). It mobilized workers and farmers and small entrepreneurs—those who lived by their own toil and according to a strict commitment to personal independence and self-reliance— to resist the slavocracy once and for all. So, under Lincoln it took on the South, refusing heroically to yield an inch in its resistance to the expansion of the slave empire. So, under its tutelage America underwent a traumatic rebirth: Equality became again the regulative ideal of the land, majority rule was vindicated, the integrity of the nation was upheld, slavery and the slavocracy were destroyed, the civil rights laws and the Fourteenth Amendment enacted. The Republican party had made a revolution.

(And like every revolution it also had its Thermidor, marked by the transformation of the party's character and aims, but that's another story.)

Now, I was familiar with Lincoln's racism and with the party's loudly proclaimed aversion to abolitionism. Having once helped edit and annotate a collection of Lincoln's writings, I'd had occasion to ponder his views on the subject, the distinction he customarily made between the *natural* equality of all men and the de facto *civic inequality* of blacks. He could say on the one hand, "All I ask for the negro is that if you do not like him, let him alone. If God gave him little, that little let him enjoy." And on the other, "I will say then that I am not, nor ever have been in favor of bringing about in any way the social and political equality of the white and black races—that I am not nor ever have been in favor of making voters or jurors of negroes, nor of qualifying them to hold office, nor to intermarry with white people." But I attributed Lincoln's racism to the fact that he sought office and therefore couldn't afford to alienate public opinion, that his humanity transcended his racism and waited only for the propitious event to demonstrate his true egalitarianism, that he did (despite all the reservations) emancipate the slaves and did convert the Civil War into a war of abolition, hence a war of penance and expiation. Lincoln's racism, in short, didn't perturb me that much, given his historic role, his genius as a leader, his capacity for growth. And the same could be said for the Republican party as well (until the 1870s).

As I was jotting down these thoughts I perceived how easily, insensibly, I fell into the teleological mode. I was explaining history retrospectively, in terms of its end results: antislavery in terms of abolition, as though the two were continuous, one the preparatory stage of the other. It was obvious to me that I was failing to do justice to Republicanism *as it was*—as a movement fearfully hostile to abolitionism. And to do justice to Republicanism as it was, before catastrophe overtook it and set another unforeseen train of occurrences in motion, I suspended (I could never erase) the teleos I'd assumed as a given. I tried to imagine the actors of the time (Brown and the Six among them) confronting a void, an uncertainty, an indeterminacy, not a future that we, their heirs, have imposed on them.

I was struck, often overwhelmed, by the depth and magnitude of Republican racism. Yes, *Republican* racism.‡ For wherever the Republican party gained ascendancy—that is, most Northern states by 1860, and nowhere more emphatically than in the newly settled western ones from the Great Plains to the Pacific Coast—there the policy of apartheid that had been gathering support for years was fully institutionalized and officially sanctioned. The Republican party, then, wasn't only the great antislavery party; it was also the apartheid party. I was astonished to learn this because I'd thought that while Republicans were racist, Democrats were more so (Lincoln after all wasn't nearly as bad as his archrival Stephen Douglas); Democrats weren't even averse to slavery, certainly not morally. But it hadn't occurred to me that the extraordinary rise of the Republican party could be largely accounted for by the presence of ex-Democrats in its ranks and that these ex-Democrats had to be cultivated, appealed to, propitiated. Republicans presented themselves as people who could be trusted to keep their communities blessedly white, "niggerless" as the saying went,

‡ Two 1967 monographs proved extremely helpful: Eugene H. Berwanger, *The Frontier Against Slavery,* and V. Jacques Voegeli, *Free But Not Equal.* They meticulously elaborate and detail points suggested by Litwack.

or failing that to keep the races entirely separate. Democrats of course couldn't be trusted to do either.

I was fascinated by how shrewdly Republicans played on the phobias of the masses. It's a study in the power of symbols. Republicans announced themselves as the party of uncompromising limits and negations, the party that marked out lines, borders, enclosures, unalterably confining slavery to its place and free blacks to theirs. They characterized Democrats as the party of promiscuity, the party that would bring about the "amalgamation" of the races, in the field, the kitchen, the nursery, the bedroom, everywhere. Democrats were held congenitally incapable of carrying out the program of apartheid.

The enormity of these fears enables us to understand the North's fierce reponse to the slavocracy from 1854 on. The slavocracy was guilty of lèse-majesté; it was attempting to foist negritude on the territories—the virgin territories bought a half century ago and held in trust (by God, Nature, Destiny) for the usufruct of white yeomen farmers and artisans and no one else. To open the land to blacks and slavocrats was an abomination, a stain on the nation's soul as ineradicable as the color of one's skin. By containing this negritude in hoops of iron, white America would through the ministry of the Republican party fulfill itself as a civilization unique on the face of the earth.

This Republican hope gave rise to certain problems (which I hadn't been aware of, whose implications I hadn't appreciated). Suppose the policy of containment didn't work out? Suppose somehow the slaves *were* or had to be emancipated? These questions bedeviled the party from the time of its victory in 1860 through the years of the Civil War.

Republicans came up with two answers. They trotted out the hoary doctrine of colonization; not apartheid but the removal of blacks from the country altogether. The Lincoln administration tried hard to get them out, as many as would go, because as Lincoln told a black delegation to the White House in August 1862, "You and we are different races. We have between us a broader difference than exists between any two races"; he thought it was "a great disadvantage to us both, as I think your race suffers very greatly, many of them by living among us, while we suffer from your presence" (the suffering therefore being equal, one canceling out the other!). Lincoln, good as his word, asked Congress to appropriate money for the transportation of blacks to Central America and the Caribbean, and he urged a constitutional amendment to authorize it. He even began negotiations with the Haitian government to permit the planting there of a black American colony, and he inquired into the possibility of buying land in Colombia (now Panama). Anything to get the blacks out.

But Lincoln wasn't a lunatic. How could he have envisioned the forced emigration of thousands, maybe millions, of Americans to the steaming jungles of Haiti, Panama, and like places? Because (as I also learned for the first time) he and white Americans generally took it for granted, as part of the prevailing racist mythos, that blacks would be happiest in such an environment, the most suitable to their "physical condition." Lincoln wanted to believe—and the mythos justified it—that he was also doing the blacks a humane service, putting at their disposal and for their well-being the facilities of the federal government. Further recompense for the sin of slavery.

(The political reasons for colonization were brought home to me; another illustration of the North's maniacal fear of the blacks. Lincoln advanced his colonization scheme in order to allay that fear because he was about to announce his plan of emancipation. Now, many whites, maybe a majority, regarded emancipation as rank betrayal, and antiblack uprisings broke out everywhere in the North during the hot summer of 1862. And the congressional elections that fall, in which Democrats critical of the war scored heavily, gave unmistakable proof of hostility to emancipation. It was then, in December 1862, that Lincoln pleaded for the adoption of a constitutional amendment providing for both the compensation of the slaves and their "voluntary" emigration.

(But here, incidentally, was another demonstration of Lincoln's greatness. He was willing to throw a sop to public opinion, but he wouldn't be deterred from his course: Come what may, he'd free the slaves. The North wasn't the only public he had to consider. There were the publics of Great Britain and France, both antislave. By making emancipation a war aim, Lincoln by so much diminished the chance that the governments of Britain and

18.   Osborn P. Anderson was one of Brown's few accomplices who managed to escape. He had been a printer in Canada, the only expatriate black (he'd been born in Pennsylvania in 1830) Brown was able to recruit. Anderson returned to the United States in 1864 and enlisted in the Union Army. He died in 1872. *(Compliments of the Library of Congress)*

19. *(Left)* According to historian Villard, J. J. Hawes of Boston took this daguerreo-type of Brown in 1858. The occasion of Brown's visit to Boston was scarcely a happy one. He'd just learned that his attack on "Egypt" had to be postponed, maybe even aborted, thanks to Hugh Forbes's letters which had revealed everything. *(Compliments of the Library of Congress)*

20. *(Right)* Watson Brown was twenty-four when he left his wife and infant son in North Elba and joined his father's war. At Harpers Ferry, he was shot carrying a flag of truce and dragged himself back to the engine-house where he died an agonizing death. *(Compliments of the Library of Congress)*

21. Oliver Brown was the youngest of John Brown's sons to grow to manhood and the next youngest to die at Harpers Ferry. Like his brother Watson, he died of excruciating wounds in the enginehouse. Oliver's wife Martha didn't survive him very long, dying in childbirth early in 1860. *(Compliments of the Library of Congress)*

. John Brown's third son, Owen, was (at rty-five) one of the older men in the guer- a army. He served faithfully, valiantly, all his father's campaigns, from the ear- st Kansas days through Harpers Ferry. managed to escape, having remained be- d at Kennedy Farm while the assault was king place, and lived to old age. *(Compli- nts of the Library of Congress)*

23.   In early July 1859 Brown ("Isaac Smith"), posing as a New Yorker on cattle business, rented this Maryland farm from Dr. Booth Kennedy. Here, Brown and his men holed up preparatory to the attack, and here the weapons—rifles, pistols, spears—were stored until the men, fresh from the raid, could carry them into the mountains. *(Compliments of the Library of Congress)*

24.   Harpers Ferry seen years after the raid from Bolivar Heights. On the extreme left is the Potomac River and the Maryland hills where (beyond the picture) Kennedy Farm was situated. Brown and his men entered the Ferry on one of the bridges (hidden from view) across the Potomac. On the extreme right is the Shenandoah River and Loudon Heights, Virginia, where the insurgents, their hostages, and the liberated slaves were to repair after the raid. Charlestown is several miles to the southeast. The enginehouse is missing. It had been removed and displayed in various places around the country as "John Brown's Fort" before finally coming to rest on the Shenandoah side of the island. *(Compliments of the Library of Congress)*

France, fearful of their own masses [1848 was still fresh in their memories], would recognize the South. Lincoln saw what Americans who were consumed by racist antipathies didn't, or couldn't, namely that it was a war of such world-historical import as to render any other concern—race relations, for example—trivial by comparison.)

To Northern critics of emancipation Republicans offered a second answer, akin to the first, really a variation of it. It amounted to a program for the *interior* colonization of American blacks. Exporting them to Africa or Latin America or the Caribbean might be impracticable in the short run. Why, then, shouldn't they remain in a region of the United States almost as congenial to them because almost as hot and wet and somnolent: the Deep South, where they'd lived as slaves for generations. Republican spokesmen were able in this way to turn racist stereotypes to their advantage. Emancipation, they argued, would be a blessing to everyone, especially to the white North, since it would encourage free blacks among them to return to where they most wanted to be; the only reason blacks stayed in the North was to escape from slavery. End slavery and they would go home en masse. Salmon Chase's remarks (in a letter of July 31, 1862, to the Union commander of the Department of the Gulf) were typical: "Let, therefore, the South be opened to negro emigration by emancipation along the Gulf, and it is easy to see that the blacks of the North will slide southward, and leave no question to quarrel about as far as they are concerned." "Nothing," wrote Greeley's *Tribune* (a week later), "ever drove the negro away from his genial South but Slavery, and the overthrow of Slavery will fix his residence where his welfare and his tenacious local attachments prompt him to stay."

Here was a persuasive argument indeed for emancipation; emancipation would induce blacks to "slide southward," relieving the North incidentally of the problem of apartheid. Blacks would be the South's problem. And rightly so. The South deserved to be punished. Having refused to contain its four million black slaves, it should forever have to contain its four million black freedmen. And if Southern whites for their part wished to leave for the "temperate climes," so much the better. It would hasten the time when the South became a black land and the North a white land. A prospect (for many Republicans) devoutly to be welcomed.

A question came to me as I was compiling this melancholy history of Republican racism. Why didn't Republicans say to the secessionist South: "Go in peace, erring sisters, and have your own nation of slaves and masters and poor yeomen; what a policy of containment couldn't accomplish your own sovereignty will." In fact, as I discovered (another surprise), some Republicans said exactly that. The most vociferous representative of this Republican "disunion" school was James S. Pike, a well-known writer for the liberal/radical New York *Tribune* (and years later the author of a famous tract, *The Prostrate State: South Carolina Under Negro Government,* condemning Reconstruction from the Republican point of view), who loathed the slavocracy about as much as he loathed blacks, who probably loathed it *because* he loathed blacks.* Here, in 1860, was Pike's summary of what the Republican (i.e., "Free State") position should be: "The slaveholder is claiming to spread the Negro everywhere, and the Popular Sovereignty man stands coolly by and says 'Let him do it wherever he can.' We say the Free Staters should say, confine the negro to the smallest possible area. Hem him in. Coop him up. Slough him off. Preserve just as much of North America as is possible to the white man and to free institutions." Small wonder Pike (and others with him) favored disunion or secession. What better method of hemming in, cooping up, and sloughing off the black population for good? Pike's boss at the *Tribune,* Horace Greeley, admonished him to lower his voice—but only for tactical reasons. "I know its propositions from our side would injure the Republican cause," Greeley wrote him, "and drive back thousands to Union saving. . . . Now if you really want Disunion keep still and let events ripen." It was apparently a desire so strong it had to be publicly muted.

(Pike's biographer informs us that Thomas Wentworth Higginson took an interest in Pike, saw a common bond between them.

---

* I owe much on this whole matter of Republican disunionism to Robert F. Durden's biography, *James S. Pike: Republicanism and the American Negro,* and article, "Ambiguities in the Antislavery Crusade of the Republican Party," *The Antislavery Vanguard,* edited by Martin F. Duberman.

"All the laws of nature work for disunion," Higginson assured Pike. "There is a mine beneath us, and the South will crash in powder quite as fast as we can touch it off." Which leads Pike's biographer to mistakenly assume they were men of like purpose. The quote itself suggests how completely *unlike* they were. Higginson worked for disunion in hopes it would "touch . . . off" a conflagration that would free the slaves. Pike hoped disunion would detach them and their masters from the rest of the country and he couldn't care less whether Southern blacks were slaves or free so long as they were gone.)

The question again. Why didn't Pike and Greeley and their fellow Republican disunionists have their way? Why, given the fact of Northern racism, weren't the eleven Confederate states permitted, encouraged, to depart? The answer is that racism didn't rank first in the Northern hierarchy of evils. It took the Civil War crisis to make that clear. Most Northerners, including many old-line Democrats,† feared the immediate possibility of disintegration or anarchy more than they did the distant specter of negritude. If states could disregard majority vote and secede at will—it was the argument Lincoln hammered home so brilliantly over and over again in the early days of the war—American civil society would either break into pieces or succumb to despotism, the country proving to itself and the world that it couldn't be at once governable and free. So in the moment of supreme choice the mystique of nationalism triumphed over the mystique of white supremacy, and the slavocrat South alone bore the onus of disunion. And by the time emancipation—negritude—did become a commanding issue, the war had progressed too far; there was no turning back.

My inquiry into Republicanism had so far been of the muckraking sort. I'd learned a good deal about its sordid side, and that told me why it was so successful, why it was so adamant in its resistance to the South, picking up where Free-Soilism had left off. I realized that I might be riding a thesis too hard, conveying to myself an unfair impression. For I knew that there was more to the

† Stephen Douglas, leader of the Northern Democrats and extreme racist who'd never said an unkind word about slavery, supported Lincoln to the hilt when the conflict started.

great Republican party than white supremacism, that it was also
the party of Charles Sumner and Thaddeus Stevens and five of the
Secret Six. I was curious to find out what they saw in it beyond
what I already knew (especially from research on the Six)
and for that matter how other abolitionists, those outside or in opposition to the party, felt about it. Rather than embark on a general survey of the antislavery "left" in the late 1850s (a useful
enterprise to be sure) I thought I'd concentrate on the period just
before and after Lincoln's election, when the future of the country
hung in the balance, when the question on everyone's mind (none
being vouchsafed a glimpse of the future) was what Lincoln and
the party would do once in office, what policy they would articulate. The antislavery left had a special interest in the answer.‡

It goes without saying that abolitionists in general didn't trust
Republicans, whose leaders throughout 1860 (Lincoln and Seward chief among them) were going out of their way to assure the
South that she had nothing to fear from them, that they had no
designs on the integrity and durability of slavery (and indeed this
was spelled out in the party platform) and wouldn't permit any
ideological jihad against it. We can understand, then, why nonpolitical abolitionists of the Garrison stripe dreaded Republicanism
as the expiration of their hopes. To Parker Pillsbury (one of Garrison's more militant lieutenants) the party was "really more dangerous to the cause of liberty . . . than any other party ever
formed since the foundations of the government were laid." The
political abolitionists, though not so hyperbolic, agreed. Gerrit
Smith (who never let up in his debate with Liberty people who'd
become Free-Soilers and were now Republicans) warned again
that "the mass of those who were once intent on abolishing slavery everywhere, do not go now for its abolition anywhere. The
calculating policy of nonextension has now taken the place of the
uncompromising principle of abolition." Frederick Douglass went
into active opposition to Lincoln and the Republican party. He
trembled at the prospect of Republican victory. "It promises to be
about as good a Southern party," he wrote bitterly, "as either wing
of the old Democratic party." And Douglass and Smith and the

‡ James McPherson's *The Struggle for Equality* was exceptionally helpful to
me in this part of my research. His quotes (some of which I excerpted) are
masterfully chosen.

other political abolitionists—no more than a few thousand at most
—formed splinter parties of their own (e.g., the Radical Abolitionists, the Union Democrats, etc.) to keep the Liberty tradition
alive.

Underlying the abolitionists' indictment of the Republican party
was the conviction that once in power it would seek to bring about
an accommodation with the South, that after all the alarums and
excursions and election-year distempers had run their course a
deal would be offered and perhaps consummated, such deals having been made many times before under similar conditions of
stress. And there's no doubt that most Republicans favored such a
deal, sought such an accommodation. They wanted nothing more
than peace and quiet, a restoration of the status quo before the
infamous Kansas-Nebraska Act shattered it. If only responsible
Southerners could prevail and agree to the easy terms the party
was giving them. These were the Republicans who had only
recently been Democrats and Whigs and Know-Nothingites and
whose sole objection to slavery was that it was too greedy, too expansionist, who had no objection to slavery where presently
confined; furthest from it. (With sound reason the famous English
abolitionist George Thompson admonished his American friends
[a week before Lincoln's election]: "You have now to grapple
with the new doctrine of Republican *conservation*. You have now
to make genuine converts of those who have as yet only been bap-
tized into the faith of non-extension, and whose zeal in that direction is mere *white-man-ism*.")

Left Republicans inclined toward the abolitionist view. They
too favored emancipation and they too feared an arrangement
that would freeze the status quo, legitimating slavery for the
indefinite future. They differed from the abolitionists, though, in
assuming that moral-theological truths were insufficient in themselves, that a political (or revolutionary) course of action was
feasible, and that the Republican party, conservative as it was,
could become the instrument for carrying it out. Within these
left Republican ranks were ideological gradations of every kind,
ranging from liberal to radical, gradations which I reduced (at
the risk of injury to subtlety and nuance) to their "ideal types":
Liberal Republicans believing that if slavery could be stopped
dead in its tracks and the South persuaded to remain in the Union

(these being admittedly tough to reconcile), a process of manumission would inexpugnably get under way, peacefully, step by
step, accompanied perhaps by modest compensation to the slaveholders and the one historic wrong of American civilization righted
in a spirit of national reconciliation and good will; and radical or
extreme left Republicans—Howe, Stearns, Higginson, Sanborn,
among others (Parker having died early in 1860)—holding to the
apocalyptic vision (or prevision, since it was theirs that came to
pass) symbolized by the Harpers Ferry raid and the martyrdoms
at Charlestown, looking to the South for vindication, seeing in the
very existence of the Republican party, however weak and pusil-
lanimous, the irritant that could goad the slavocracy to commit
acts of wild provocation. (In Lydia Maria Child's words: "If all
this excitement doesn't settle down into a miserable mush of concession, leaving the country in a worse state than it found it, we
shall owe less to the steadfastness of Republican leaders, than to
the utter impossibility of satisfying the demands of the South,
however patiently we may crawl in the dust, or whatever quantity
of dirt we may consent to eat.")

The radicals proved correct. Within weeks of Lincoln's election
South Carolina, good as its word, exited from the Union. By February 1, 1861, the other states of the interior South (Mississippi,
Florida, Georgia, Alabama, North Carolina, Texas) had followed
suit. And the Buchanan administration had given them leave to do
so by confessing its impotence to resist them, the Union being in
its view (it was also the Confederacy's) only a compact of the
separate states. Conservative or "Doughfaced" Republicans wa-
vered. Would the South be content with one more concession?
Many were tempted by Senator John J. Crittenden's "peace resolution" (to extend to 36°30′ line of the Missouri Compromise
clear across to the Pacific) and other proposals of a similar kind.
But Lincoln held fast, succumbing to none of the proffered compromises, proof again of his courage and wisdom. When he refused to accept secession, the Civil War began. The South had
played beautifully into the hands of the radical Republicans. Their
moment in history had arrived.

(Wendell Phillips, greatest of the abolitionist tribunes, had for-
seen everything [though he couldn't have imagined events moving

so swiftly nor anticipated Lincoln's role in them; who could?]. "If the telegraph speaks the truth," he told a Boston rally a day after the election, "for the first time in our history the *slave* has chosen a president of the United States [Cheers.] We have passed the Rubicon. . . . Not an abolitionist, hardly an antislavery man, Mr. Lincoln consents to represent an antislavery idea. A pawn on the political chessboard, his value is in his position; with fair effort, we may soon change him for a knight, bishop for queen, and sweep the board [Applause.] . . . The Republican Party has undertaken a problem, the solution of which will force them to our position.")

The last week of August 1968 I emerged from the Columbia stacks (an inferno which would have given Dante pause) where I'd labored part of every day for five months, satisfied that my inquiry into the antislavery movement was over and done with. I didn't think I needed to continue it any longer, adding more details, finding more evidence, pursuing more leads in the endless labyrinth that had opened up before me. For I understood now (to answer my original set of questions) why abolitionists were so despised, above all by the opponents of slavery and almost in proportion as that opposition flourished, why so few Northerners were willing to take direct action against the acknowledged evil of slavery (except for purely defensive reasons)—John Brown and his troops having been the only ones to plan and attempt to carry out an armed assault on "Egypt" itself, and why, therefore, given the public's fear of emancipation it made such good sense for the Secret Six (five of them at any rate) to retain close ties with the leaders of the Free-Soil and Republican parties. I'd discovered the singular fact that white supremacism lay at or near the heart of the antislavery moment and, further, that the great historic contribution of that movement—the emancipation of the slaves in the Civil War—(seen retrospectively, teleologically) *was precisely what it sought to avoid and would have avoided but for the vast imperial rapacity of the slave power.*

So much in brief was the fruit of my research, and I was pleased

I'd done it even though I was unsure of how I could integrate it with the rest of my work, unsure of where it belonged in my picture.

3

That picture came together fortuitously one rainy September day during lunch at the West End (a notable bar on Broadway across from Columbia) with my friends Jack Widick and Steve Buttner. Our desultory talk had turned from Che Guevara's pathetic demise in the Bolivian mountains—his diary of the campaign had just come out—to guerrilla wars in general, the point at issue being Che's failure to observe his own tenet, namely that a guerrilla war is possible only when the populace is *actively* sympathetic to the insurgents, when that populace has been sufficiently radicalized. Widick (whose own commitment to radical causes dated back to the labor and political wars of the 1930s) discussed the staggering difficulty of winning over a disaffected populace, even one, such as Bolivia's campesinos, that groans under the most savage repression. (The repression after all could always be worse: People could always lose the little they have.) How can the insurgents bring the neutral or suspicious or vaguely hostile majority over to their side? How can they unite disparate factions and ideologies? The problem, in other words, isn't simply opposing a despotic regime. The problem is how to provoke that regime into behaving in a way best calculated to drive the hesitant masses to support, at least sympathize with, the insurgent's political objectives. Somewhere in the midst of our table talk my John Brown project flashed before me in an epiphany of coherence, resolution. It appeared before me as an integrated, concinnated whole, a totality. (I said nothing of this to my friends.)

It was in fact a flash of recognition: recognition of an insight I'd long possessed, had gropingly tried to express in my notes, but couldn't have seen so clearly, so explicitly as now, following my research on the anti-slavery movement.

My work on the Secret Six the year before had substantiated my earlier hypothesis that John Brown intended not so much to incite a slave revolt as generate a cycle of provocations and retaliations leading to sectional warfare and through sectional warfare, emancipation. Now I was able to fully appreciate the soundness of his approach to abolitionism. The more I thought about it the sounder it seemed to me. *For the virtue of his master plan was that it bypassed the fractious race issue.* Racism was the death of every direct approach to abolitionism. If Northerners couldn't abide blacks, neither could they abide a slavocracy that kept threatening to burst its confines and circumscriptions. And as they demonstrated again and again, in their reponses to the Fugitive Slave Act and Bleeding Kansas, Northerners when pushed enough would physically resist the slavocracy and the laws that protected it. Here, in this willingness to resist when pushed, was something on which abolitionists could build, something on which Northerners could unite, however bigoted they were, indeed because they were so bigoted. *I interpreted the plan as an effort to create an extreme situation—the more extreme the better—that would induce such armed resistance on an increasing scale, that would bring Northerners over to the insurgents' side.* No other formula held out the remotest possibility of securing the release of the slaves; every other formula lay beyond the frame of political possibility, demanding, at most, a *moral* commitment without *political* effect. In sum: *John Brown represented a strategy of action, a relation of means to ends, inseparable from the over-all conflict between slavery and democracy, a conflict of polarities, irreconcilable by definition, and necessarily extreme or violent in its outcome.*

(Which isn't to say that the conflict had to be decided the way it was, by Civil War, etc. It could have been decided differently. But any decision—the establishment, say, of two countries, two political systems, slave and free, and without the shedding of a drop of blood—would have been extreme and violent, too. The outcome of such irreconcilable conflicts appears predetermined to future generations of historians.)

I felt an onerous weight—the puzzles, mysteries, conundrums that had been gathering over the past year—lifting from my shoulders. John Brown's life and career, set against the landscape of his day (a landscape requiring no further enlargement), confronted me as an intelligible whole. And my next task occurred to me as clearly as that flash of recognition at the West End: I would redo the picture on a fresh canvas; I would compose a rough, loosely drawn outline, in its entirety, omitting nothing consequential, of the book I'd contracted to write; it would be a final act of self-clarification.

Part Three
Composing the Picture

Chapter Six
Reprise

1

Dominating the fall season of 1968 was of course the presidential campaign. Everything fell into abeyance until that campaign ran its course.

We felt—those of us with strong feelings about the war, civil rights, and other issues of slightly lesser import—that the election wasn't ours. The candidates we might have supported were no part of it. Bobby Kennedy was dead and Eugene McCarthy was refusing to commit himself. We sympathized with McCarthy, agreed with him, because we too burned with resentment and indignation; nor had we forgotten the hecatombs of Chicago and Hubert Humphrey's seeming indifference to what had transpired on the streets (below his hotel suite in fact) while the convention was nominating him. And Humphrey was as much Johnson's servitor as ever. Yet a commitment had to be made. The choice, some choice, existed as an objective fact, whether we liked it or not.

Nixon was playing his familiar themes in conspicuously low key. He was serving notice that as President he'd redress the balance in favor of the "peace forces" in society and no longer "coddle" the "lawless" elements—criminals, rebellious kids, black militants, radicals of every persuasion (and all lumped together under one rubric)—whom a "permissive" Supreme Court had encouraged by its decisions in the past decade and a half (the exact period of Chief Justice Earl Warren's tenure). Nixon quickly played the demogogue, holding discussions with concerned citizens on TV, giving position papers on the radio (we were witnessing the new new Nixon in action) because he was so far ahead in the polls and because he contrasted so well with George Wallace, candidate of the American Independence party, whose program and views Nixon shared, whose thunder he was discreetly stealing.

On domestic affairs Nixon was a known quantity. There was no doubt in our mind he'd institute a "law and order" regime, cut back on civil rights and Great Society projects, favor the military-industrial establishment with even greater largess than it was accustomed to receiving, etc. All this to be sure. But if he'd also terminate the Vietnam War by means acceptable to the "enemy" he'd have merited our support and gratitude. Everything paled before that desideratum. And here too Nixon was found wanting. For he hadn't yet given the merest hint of what his "plan" was to end the war. He couldn't divulge it, he claimed, for fear of upsetting the delicate talks between the United States and North Vietnam going on in Paris. (They were at a standstill.) The last thing he'd do was take advantage of the administration's (hence rival Humphrey's) catastrophic weakness. He was, you see, a statesman who put America's welfare before partisan gain. Which we interpreted to mean that he had no plan, that he'd likely continue the war, though in ways less unpalatable to the American people than at present, that he was, beneath his several personas, the same anti-Communist ideologue who, we hadn't forgotten, had urged our entry into Indochina on France's side—and with atomic weapons—back in 1954, and whose only criticism of the war now being fought was that the United States wasn't winning it.

And so as the campaign progressed I found myself inclining toward Humphrey. It was almost too much to expect that he'd suddenly emerge a dove or half-dove, though he might emerge as one after his election. But nothing could be expected from Nixon. So, contemplating the choices (and wishing there were others), I began by late September, sometimes despite myself, to pull for Humphrey.

Most of my friends couldn't bring themselves to support him, however deep their aversion for Nixon. It was too much for them. Principled but shortsighted, I thought. The question wasn't ideological or personal; it was pragmatic. Which man, Humphrey or Nixon, could be better depended on, sooner rather than later, to come to terms with the Communists? Nor did the answer to that question have much to do with the antiwar movement. The movement would proceed on its own until the United States was out of the war irrespective of who became President. My friends failed to see the possibility of advancing toward that objective on several fronts. To back Humphrey, they feared, was to morally betray the movement; perhaps, on the other hand, it was to save it. (They could have learned something from Parker, Higginson, Sanborn, Stearns, and Howe, who as Free-Soilers and then as Republicans didn't feel they were betraying the cause of radical abolitionism.)

———◆———

I returned to my John Brown opus sooner than I'd thought possible and gave myself until the end of the year, about three months, to work on this, the final preliminary stage of the John Brown book, outlining what I'd put in it, pulling together the strands of my research and my notes, weaving them into a logical, comprehensive whole, now that I understood the whole, now that I knew where I intended to go and what I intended to say, what points I intended to make, guiding myself through John Brown's America, the America he symbolized, embodied, summed up, in his own person and deeds and fate.

With this act of self-clarification out of the way I'd be free to examine the various manuscript collections scattered here and there from Kansas to Boston, a job of indeterminate duration and expense (and no small source of concern to me). Then the conclusion of my labors, the writing of the book itself. It would be (changing the figure) the last of my canvases, for which all the others were the mere preparations, at once enormous in size and exact in detail, a unity of background and portrait, context and figure.

I didn't dare think of when it might be ready.

2

1. OWEN BROWN AND OTHER ANCESTORS

Can anything be learned about any of Brown's forebears beyond the general fact that they were yeomen farmers and artisans and goodwives, Calvinist to their marrows? Certainly the matter of their Calvinism deserves further elaboration. In the seventeenth and eighteenth centuries these frontier Connecticutters seem to have been the purest of the Calvinists, rooted unalterably in the faith, not to be tempted by heathenish reason and skepticism, the affliction of the cities and the higher classes, nor by antinomianism, the wish to establish far-out Christian sects (Methodist, Baptist, etc.) based on *unreason,* emotionalism. No, the Browns, generation after generation, yielded nothing to the deliquescent forces of modernity and were fixed in the imperishable creed of the 1600s.

Was I exaggerating? Not at all to judge from Owen Brown, John's father (not to speak of John himself), about whom we know something. We have portions of Owen Brown's letters and reminiscenses (recorded in Sanborn and Villard), some of them delightful, reflecting as they do the assertive self-reliance and native intelligence of these New England yeomen, salt of our American earth.

A few samples from Owen Brown's writings (as refined by fastidious Sanborn) will suffice: "I was born at West Simsbury [now Canton], Connecticut, February 16, 1771. I have but little recollection of what took place until the years '75 and '76. I remember the beginning of the war, and something that took place in 1775; but only a little until '76, when my father went into the army. He was captain in the militia of Connecticut, and died in New York, with the dysentery, a few weeks after leaving home. My mother had ten children at the time of my father's death, and one born soon after, making eleven of us all. The first five were daughters, the oldest about eighteen; the next three were sons; then two daughters and the youngest a son. The care and support of this family fell mostly on my mother. The laboring men were mostly in the army. She was one of the best of mothers; active and sensible. She did all that could be expected of a mother; yet for want of help we lost our crops, then our cattle, and so became poor. I very well remember the dreadful hard winter of 1778–79. The snow began to fall in November, when the water was very low in the streams; and while the snow was very deep, one after another of our hogs and sheep would get buried up, and we had to dig them out. Wood could not be drawn with teams, and was brought on men's shoulders, they going on snow until paths were made hard

enough to draw on hand-sleds. The snow was said to be five feet
deep in the woods. Milling of grain could not be had, only by
going a great distance; and our family was driven to the necessity
of pounding corn for food. We lost that winter almost all of our
cattle, hogs, and sheep, and were reduced very low by the spring
of 1779. . . ."

(Then follows the chronicle of his pilgrimage through life: his
learning to be a shoemaker and tanner, his marriage to a minister's daughter, his children's births and deaths, his migration
from one western Connecticut town to another, his decision to go
out to Ohio, which was just opening up to settlement.)

"In 1804 I made my first journey to Ohio. I left home on the
8th of August, came through Pennsylvania and saw many new
things. Arrived in Hudson about the 1st of September; found the
people very harmonious and middling prosperous, and mostly
united in religious sentiments. I made a small purchase of land in
the center of Hudson, with the design of coming at a future day. I
went to Austinberg, and was there taken sick, which proved to be
the fever and ague; was there a month, very sick and homesick. I
started for home against counsel, and had a very hard journey—
ague almost every day and night—but arrived home on the 16th
of October. I had the ague from time to time over one year; yet
my determination to come to Ohio was so strong I started with my
family . . . on the 9th of June, 1805. . . .

"We arrived in Hudson on the 24th of July, and were received
with many tokens of kindness. We did not come to a land of idleness; neither did I expect it. Our ways were as prosperous as we
had reason to expect. I came with a determination to help build
up, and be a help in the support of religion and civil order. We
had some hardships to undergo, but they appear greater in history
than they were in reality. . . .

"When we came to Ohio the Indians were more numerous than
the white people, but were very friendly, and I believe were a
benefit rather than an injury. In those days there were some that
seemed disposed to quarrel with the Indians, but I had never had
those feelings. They brought us venison, turkeys, fish, and the like;
sometimes they wanted bread or meal more than they could pay
for at the time; but were always faithful to pay their debts. In September, 1806, there was a difficulty between two tribes; the tribe

on the Cuyahoga River came to Hudson, and asked for assistance to build them a log-house that would be a kind of fort to shelter their women and children from the firearms of their enemy. Most of our men went with teams, and chopped, drew, and carried logs, and put up a house in one day, for which they appeared very grateful. They were our neighbors until 1812, when the war commenced with the British, the Indians left these parts mostly, and rather against my wishes. . . ."

(And so the chronicle continues in quaint biblical fashion as Owen Brown prospered, begot children—sixteen in all—buried two wives, and through a long life remained a steadfast and troubled Christian, concluding: "I have great reason to mourn my unfaithfulness to my children.")

The interesting question of western settlements was suggested by the elder Brown's odyssey. The planting of little New Englands throughout the Great Lakes region and upper Ohio and Mississippi valleys—the establishment of New England style institutions, architecture, manners, appearances, the germination of a potent seed. Specifically, the Western Reserve district of Ohio, "Little Connecticut," more specifically Hudson and neighborhood. (State and county histories—a dreadfully trivialized literature—would be useful here.)

A hypothesis: How many of these settlements can be explained as an attempt to preserve intact the *original* New England communities? The movement out to the frontier may have been prompted by the desire to re-create a stable, virtuous, Christian home, the Calvinist utopia, the promise of America after all. A hypothesis worth pursuing, even in the context of a John Brown study, because if valid (even in part) it would substantially modify the various "frontier theses," beginning with Frederick Jackson Turner's, which assume that the frontier reflected a progressive, future-oriented ethos, the democratic, capitalist, individualist ("legal-rational," as Weber phrased it) outlook of a young, robust people, unencumbered by a feudal legacy. Perhaps the frontier started out as a movement that sought to re-enact the *past* and build yet again a New Zion in the wilderness. When did rampant capitalism and the new-style frontier take hold? A good question.

The answer, obviously, must be sought in the state of the American economy. When Brown went to Ohio, America was still a land of villages, hamlets, little townships (like Hudson or the ones he inhabited in Connecticut), poorly connected by roads—as poorly connected as it had been 150 years earlier—each family having been self-sufficient in most things. (Turnpikes were scarce; canals to the west were many years off [the Erie, model and envy of them all, wouldn't be launched until 1815 and done until 1825]; railroads were a distant dream.) The world that formed Owen Brown hardly differed from the world of his fathers, back to the first of the Connecticut Browns, the seminal Peter, who arrived in the mid-1660s.

Now, Owen Brown was a staunch abolitionist, too. He'd been one since he was a boy. "When a child of four or five years old, one of our neighbors had a slave that was brought from Guinea. In the year 1776 my father was called into the army at New York, and left his work undone. In August, our good neighbor Captain John Fast, of West Simsbury, let my mother have the labor of his slave to plough a few days. I used to go out in the field with this slave—called Sam—and he used to carry me on his back, and I fell in love with him. He worked but a few days, and went home sick with the pleurisy, and died very suddenly. When told that he would die, he said he should go to Guinea, and wanted victuals put up for the journey."

Then Owen Brown recounts an interesting incident. During the Revolution a preacher named Thomson brought some slaves to Connecticut from his native Virginia. He bought a farm and assigned a slave family to look after it. Many years later, in 1798, Thomson returned to sell his farm and take the slave family back to Virginia with him. (In the meantime, it should be noted, Connecticut had abolished slavery.) The slave father ran away and hid among the tiny community of local blacks. Now Thomson served as a sort of guest preacher in the church. "The last Sabbath it was expected he would preach in the afternoon; but there were a number of church members who were dissatisfied with his being asked to preach, and requested Deacon Samuels and Deacon Gaylord to go and ask Mr. Robbins not to have Mr. Thomson preach, as it was giving dissatisfaction. There was some excitement among the people, some in favor and some against Mr.

Thomson; there was quite a debate, and large numbers came to hear. Mr. Thomson said he should carry the woman and the children, whether he could get the man or not. An old man asked him if he would part man and wife, contrary to their minds. He said: 'married thems myself, and did not enjoin obedience on the woman.' He was asked if he did not consider marriage to be an institution of God; he said he did. He was again asked why he did not do it in conformity to God's word. He appeared checked, and only said it was the custom. He was told the blacks were free by the Legislature of Connecticut; he replied that he belonged to another State, and that Connecticut had no control over his property. I think he did not get away his 'property,' as he called it. Ever since, I have been an Abolitionist, and I am so near the end of life I think I shall die an Abolitionist."

But we should be clear on what it meant for Owen Brown to be an abolitionist at the turn of the eighteenth century. Actually it meant little beyond the acknowledgment of his own convictions, his personal hatred of slavery and wish to see it extinguished. Who wasn't an "abolitionist" at the time? It was universally assumed that slavery would die, the only question being how and when. It was dying throughout the North; it was forbidden in the Northwest Territory; it was defended in the South only as a temporary expedient inconsistent with the progress of man and the destiny of the nation. Americans considered slavery an objective or institutionalized evil, which, alas, couldn't be undone in a day without inflicting harm on blacks and whites both. That it would be undone couldn't be doubted.

Which is to say that abolitionists at the time (like Owen Brown) didn't have to side with blacks. They didn't have to demonstrate (as they did later, with Garrison) that they embraced the full consequences of immediate and unconditional emancipation by *treating* blacks as equals and brothers. America was racist at the turn of the century, but it was still a *republican* (emphasis on small "r") form of racism, not yet a democratic one. What was republican racism?

In his *Notes on Virginia* Jefferson doubted that blacks had the cognitive ability to assume the burdens of republican citizenship —the burden, that is, of imposing the rule of reason on their passions (his slaves loved to sing and dance and tell tales, etc.), the burden of self-government. But while Jefferson was racist in the American grain he didn't *single out* blacks. Whites too fell under his republican ban if their passions got the better of them, if they lacked the talent and virtue to rise to the level expected of citizens. In the abstract all men started out as equals; and for those who didn't measure up, who fell victim to their vices, weaknesses, well . . . Republican racism didn't reify its white supremacism. It placed blacks at a level where, in fact, most whites were thought to belong as well. Republicanism was based on the principle of distance between the passion-ridden majority whose concerns were private, familial, petty, and the reasonable minority whose concerns were the public good, the whole society.* Republican racism enabled free blacks (we already saw this) to enjoy such rights and privileges as the white majority enjoyed. It was a tolerable modus vivendi. And it was the racial modus vivendi the country looked forward to adopting once slavery disappeared. (Jefferson hoped the black population could be diffused as homesteaders, yeomen, over the gigantic continental landscape. Winthrop Jordon's *White over Black,* [1968] is quite marvelous in showing the tragic-pathetic dimensions of that hope, that vision of Thomas Jefferson's.)

Racism grew virulent with the rise of democracy (to us an old story by now), and everything else changed correspondingly: the public's attitude toward slavery; the abolitionist response to that attitude; the white counterresponse to abolitionism (all this to be gone into in its rightful place).

At any rate there was nothing spectacular in Owen Brown's having been an abolitionist in the 1790s and early 1800s, nothing at odds with the dominant national commitment. So that he wouldn't have said in his youth—there was no need to—what he said in his memoir a half century later: "I am an Abolitionist. I know we are not loved by many; I have no confession to make for being one. . . ."

Seething below the surface of public equanimity, however, was

* The difference between Jefferson's radical republicanism and John Adams's or Alexander Hamilton's—in general the Federalists'—conservative republicanism rested on property: Conservative republicans assumed that property alone made possible one's capacity for self-government and virtue.

a new fact, a revolutionary fact, one too early in its development to be perceived for what it was and would become, namely the viability of slavery in the cotton-growing South. By the early 1800s the decline of the slaveholding class had been reversed. Cotton-growing was becoming more and more profitable (a discussion here of technical advances—the cotton gin and other machines, the industrialization of Great Britain, stimulated largely by the war with France, the increasing volume of overseas trade and expansion of the world market, etc., etc.), hence the need for fresh slaves, land, capital, etc., etc.

The point to be stressed is that while this revolution was beginning to take hold (we're still with Owen Brown at the turn of the century) its implications for the future went unnoticed. In its infancy King Cotton didn't challenge the governing ethic, the prevailing assumption, that slavery would one day disappear. But the everyday transactions of the market place would soon tell and duly assert its own sovereign claims; by then a qualitative leap will have been made (consciousness catching up to fact, to everyday life), the old ethic molting like old skin.

On October 1, 1968, banner headlines proclaimed Vice-President Humphrey's Salt Lake City speech. There was less in what he said than implied. As President he'd halt the bombing of North Vietnam in return for something, some proof that the Communists wouldn't take advantage of his generosity (!) by sending troops and matériel south in even larger quantities than now. ("I would stop the bombing of the North as an acceptable risk for peace because I believe it would lead to success in the negotiations and thereby shorten the war. This would be the best protection for our troops.") He was really saying that he acquiesced to North Vietnam's condition for moving ahead with the negotiations. The next question was whether Humphrey would also as President acquiesce to the other conditions for achieving peace—the abandonment of the Thieu regime and the creation of a government with Communist representation.

The speech was a step forward. But was it too late to make a difference in the campaign? Was he trying to cut his leading string to LBJ? He gave some evidence in the speech that he might be, that he was drawing closer to the peace forces. But was it too late to make a difference?

2. JOHN BROWN: THE FIRST TWENTY YEARS (1800–20)

The theme is how much John Brown grew up as an exemplar of the Puritan virtues of his father (himself a model) and forebears, how deeply he internalized their values.

No doubt of it, he was poured into the Freudian mold, his character traits drawn from the textbook. He was anal-compulsive par excellence. His neatness and cleanliness, his abilities as housekeeper and cook, betray him. Even more so his distended superego (he memorized the Bible through and through because it was for him the chronicle of holy norms, such norms being no remote and abstract ideal but a matter of immediate daily application and care, even down to the smallest detail, as though he were personally responsible for their fulfillment, as though the Pentateuch were placed in his hands for safekeeping). No wonder he struggled so hard, so painfully, to suppress his instincts—the attraction he felt for objects and the freedom of the forests—to escape from childish ways and desires and enter manhood as soon as possible.

Now, the psychoanalytic approach is valuable—within its limits. Outside those limits it displays the faults of its virtues. The fault is psychologism, the reduction of all subjects and questions to certain categorical, universal principles or rules or laws. This could lead to obvious absurdities: the lumping together, for example, of Stalin and Gandhi (and John Brown too) as anal-compulsive. Also, the psychoanalytic approach, pressed too far, becomes ahistorical, transcending time and place and social context. So while it's illuminating to know that Brown conforms to a universal character type it doesn't tell us why he chose his *specific* life's vocation. The same type could have chosen the opposite kind of life, could have been, say, an archapologist for slavery. Characterologically, John C. Calhoun showed marked resemblances to John Brown.

(Some post-Freudians attempt to avoid the pitfalls of reductionism by giving psychoanalysis a historical and social dimension, and I intended to make generous use of their insights in my John Brown study. I refer mainly to Eric Fromm, whose early writings, especially *Escape from Freedom,* have lost none of their perspicuity, and Erik Erikson, whose work—for example, his biographies of Luther and Gandhi—on the individual's discovery of and submission to a moral vocation leave us all profoundly in his debt. But I had no intention of following any formula or school of thinking.)

At issue, then, is the unique life experience of young John Brown, in particular his first experience with slavery at the age of twelve, when he saw the little black boy who'd befriended him (after one of his long cattle-driving trips) cuffed and beaten without remorse or compunction, with routine indifference, by a master not otherwise cruel, causing young Brown to reflect on "the wretched, hopeless condition of fatherless and motherless slave children" and vow then and there "eternal war with slavery." This response seems perfectly consistent with the kind of person he was, with his standards of moral rectitude. The encounter, I assumed, was as traumatic as he described it.

What slavery meant to John Brown was a question I had to grapple with (he kept his own counsel), demanding many an inferential leap.

He was of course nurtured in the belief that slavery was the premier evil, the evil that sprang directly from Satan, evil pure and pristine. Helpful to me in perceiving this was Paul Ricoeur's profound book *The Symbolism of Evil* (which I came across quite by accident in the summer of 1968). Ricoeur gets to the root of the human need, buried deep in the psyche of the collective soul, to identify and isolate the objective fact of evil, the afflictive primal stain. He does so with the skill of a surgeon, cutting into the layered myths and symbols, the poems, dreams, pictures, etc., through which it reaches consciousness. Slavery for John Brown was exactly that primal stain, evil reduced to its quintessence. Because slavery enabled some men to make others into whatever image—hence perform whatever acts, submit to whatever caprices —they chose, it went even beyond the sin of *human* pride, disobedience of God; it was *Satanic* pride, the de facto repudiation of God Himself, God having explicitly declared all humans His children, having made all in *His* image. Slavery for Brown inverted the whole moral order of the universe, turning everything into their opposites. This was what Satan had been trying to do all along.

But it appeared during these early years of the nineteenth century that Satan was losing out, that God in His infinite wisdom was letting matters take their labored, serpentine course. In swearing "eternal war with slavery" Brown could have meant an interior war, a recognition of the evil in all its magnitude, a commitment akin to his vow of Christianity a few years later. There's no evidence he or anyone in his family or community, the militantly antislavery Western Reserve region of Ohio, felt the need to *do* anything. Why should they? Abolition would triumph in its own good time.

Tragedy underlay this vast optimism, this faith in the workings of a beneficent future. Americans believed that the great mystique of expansion and prosperity, proof of their special status, their chosenness, would settle everything in the long run. And so far they were right. They converted the most incarnadine struggles of the Old World—religious, political, national, ideological, etc.—to mere private preferences, tastes, quarrels. Everything was subordinate to the task of getting on, seizing the main chance, following one's bent unfettered to the edges of one's capacities. For good reason, then, Americans thought slavery would yield to that same happy mystique and lapse into oblivion. But slavery was proving resistant. It was clear by the 1820s (if not sooner) that as the economy in general expanded so did slavery in particular. No sector of the economy rose so rapidly as cotton production. The slave population more than kept pace with the country's. Nor was there the slightest prospect that the future would be different, that the demand for cotton would diminish, that the source of slave labor would dry up because the slave trade was now strictly forbidden (the fecundity of native-born slaves, it turned out, assuring an adequate supply). To be optimistic or hopeful was therefore only to postpone, hence exacerbate, the time of reckoning. America insisted on seeing slavery as a problem; they couldn't (yet) bring themselves to see it as a tragedy.

Such musings were remote indeed from the John Brown who was growing up in his frontier hamlet, dutifully learning his father's trade, attaining his manhood according to Calvinist rite, marrying plain, mild-tempered Dianthe Lusk, and striking out on his own as a craftsman-entrepreneur—repeating, in a word (or expecting to repeat), the history of his forebears, envisioning for himself a life defined by sacred tradition, the eternal past.

On October 3, 1968, the long-awaited news introducing a bit of dash in this listless campaign. George Wallace made General Curtis LeMay his vice-presidential mate. In his press conference (as reported in the Times) *General LeMay, his swagger unsubdued, didn't disappoint us. "We seem to have a phobia about nuclear weapons. I think to most military men that a nuclear weapon is just another weapon in our arsenal. And the smart thing to do is when you are in a war—hopefully you prevent it, stay out of it if you can—but you get in with both feet and get it over with as soon as you can. Use the force that's necessary. Maybe use a little bit more to make sure that it's enough to stop the fighting as soon as possible." So the general wasn't retreating from his famous proposal (part of the lexicon of contemporary inhumanity) that the United States bomb the Vietnamese back into the Stone Age.*

3. JOHN BROWN AND HIS AMERICA: FROM YEOMAN TO CAPITALIST

From a biographical standpoint nothing's extraordinary or distinctive in the life of John Brown as he went from tanner and currier in Hudson to real estate speculator on a rather impressive scale. The transition from artisan to capitalist was swift, taking place in 1834–35, the years he returned to Ohio from his ten-year stay in western Pennsylvania. The unprecedented boom was reaching its apogee. Money was to be made in areas soon to be connected by canal and road to the burgeoning trade routes that led to New York and the East Coast, thence to the international centers of commerce. Brown and his partners, like hundreds of thousands of Americans, were going to take advantage of ripening opportunity.

As well as anyone Brown typified the conflicting values of the age. There he was, a skilled worker who'd built up a certain competence and reputation. He was reasonably successful; he employed apprentices and assistants; he was a respectable member of the community, his superego standing him in good stead as a leader and standard-bearer. (He sometimes went to quixotic lengths to do the right thing.) But he was swept up in the fury of expansion; the market permeated everything; not even the remotest frontier settlement escaped it. Less and less did one produce for his neighbors. Less and less was the buying and selling of goods confined to the local community. The coming of a national-international market began to wipe out local handicraft industries. For the shrewd entrepreneur the rise of such an economy was a blessing; for the rest it was or could be a curse. It threatened to reduce skilled artisans to wage earners or hands, subject to the will of merchants and nascent manufacturers; or, worse, to render them obsolete altogether in the face of new technologies, new sources of competition. Reacting to the same changes, John Brown went off in the other direction, abandoning his trade to become a full-throated recruit of the moneyed class.

It would be well to pause around 1835–37, the years of maximum prosperity for the nation (the world) when John Brown was riding high as a wheeler-dealer, on the way to making his fortune, to inquire into what sort of society had come into being. For this America wasn't the one he'd been born into a short time before, the change wrought in that interval of thirty-five years being greater than in the two centuries preceding it, defining the terms of the conflict over slavery and race and therefore the course of his own life.

The emergence of a money or market or commodity economy, accompanied by "the transportation revolution," gave rise to interest group politics, democratic politics. The wheat farmer in western Ohio, say, discovered that his personal well-being, his existence as a farmer, depended on his uniting with other wheat farmers or farmers in general to (a) promote national policies that would benefit them (lower tariffs, better roads, easy credit, etc.) and (b) what amounted to the same thing, oppose policies favored by competing groups, the enactment of which would injure them. The effect of a money or market or commodity economy was to *nationalize* politics, make the federal government the focus of people's attention, the object of their political passions. At the same time and for the same reason it set in motion a countervailing tendency: sectionalism. For each section roughly corresponded (with allowances for complexity) to a dominant interest or set of commodities: New England, manufacturing; the Northwest, wheat; the South, cotton. Now, some historians, following the lead of the great Frederick Jackson Turner, are persuaded that sectionalism was the grand motif of the period, the driving force of the American experience, at least until the Civil War. The interpretation is one-dimensional. Logic itself dictates that sectionalism and nationalism were twin facets of the same experience, that to depend on the federal government necessarily required a sectional orientation (no cotton being grown in the North, no industry to speak of down South), and to advance sectional interests required the implementation of national policies. Washington, not the state capitals or regional associations, became the main political battleground between conflicting interest groups and the parties representing them, mediating between them.

The point here being that by 1835 slavery was indistinguishable from the South's sectional, hence national, interest. Southern spokesmen, above all John C. Calhoun, regarded any criticism of slavery as a criticism of the South, an attempt to deny its parity with other sections and reduce it to permanent inferior status. And no longer were Southerners willing to concede that slavery was evil or wrong and that it should one day be ended. The official line—so official no one who valued his life or continued presence in the South dared challenge it—was that slavery was a worthy and desirable institution (compared to other forms of free labor), certainly for blacks (perhaps for "mudsill" whites, too: an open question), a humane institution, a sanctified institution (approved by Scripture), a super-efficient institution, an indispensable institution—in short, an imperishable institution. To be a Southern sectionalist was necessarily to prize slavery as her peculiar and unique institution.

The rest of the country nicely accommodated itself to this defense of slavery, this tacit assumption of its perpetuity. Moral sentiments gave way (as they always do) to reality, the acceptance of the mighty fact that over two million slaves—*a seventh of the country's population*—resided in the South. So while Northerners didn't approve of slavery, indeed viscerally disapproved it, they weren't condemning a practice that kept the slaves safely cooped and penned in a region exclusively their own. The vision of an America which affirmed equality and liberty for *all* men was fast receding into the horizon.

A money economy brought intimations of that other form of servitude, the more insidious for concealing itself behind the cloak of liberty and equality, the rights of man, and the inviolability of contract. Northern workingmen conceived themselves (their arguments were familiar to me) as victims of cruel and predatory monopolists determined to make them "wage slaves." They certainly weren't receptive to the idea of millions of penurious blacks competing with them in the labor market. (And what these same white workingmen were doing to their black brethren, how they were driving them out of the trades, condemning them to pauperdom, lumpendom, was also well known to me by now.) The advent of a market economy created a strange fellowship between the slavocrats and the Northern workers who feared for their livelihood.

The upsurge of democracy from the 1820s on was itself a response to headlong expansion, the imperial growth of a money society. For as people's needs came to be served by and through the government, the government (at every level) came to be subject increasingly to popular or majority will. And as the people came to rule, so free blacks, who'd enjoyed a modicum of civil rights under the aristocratic republican order, were systematically disfranchised, placed beyond the pale of citizenship. Racism and democracy were united in wedlock. Where democracy most prevailed—out in the West and in the cities—racism went furthest and government policies were most exclusionary. The triumph of democracy was the undoing of free Northern blacks. A melancholy truth which I hadn't wanted to believe.

Was there something in American democracy—repeating my questions of several months back—that *predisposed* it to racism? Did the presence of blacks, a symbolic presence often enough, actually *facilitate* the establishment of democracy? I was inclined to say yes to both questions, though my answers were highly speculative and tenuous.

The democratic ideology—and this is borne out in the best literature on the subject†—assumed civic virtue as its necessary condition: the capacity of the people to rise above themselves, discipline their vices, overcome their weaknesses, transform themselves into new men. This was a struggle, unremitting, unceasing, between two selves, the higher and the lower: if you will, the white and the black. Blacks, like Gadarene swine, exteriorized and objectified those vices—fecklessness, debauchery, dissipation, intemperance, obsequiousness, etc.—from which whites fled, thereby easing the struggle for the practitioners of virtue. Morally speaking, it was useful to have blacks around as noncitizens, as an irreducible limit which every white, especially the most humble, had it within him to transcend. Blacks simply *were,* possessing no self to which they could rise, never becoming what they weren't. Nature made blacks; whites made themselves.

Yet nascent democracy also produced abolitionism. It was no accident that Garrison and his intrepid band of dissenters appeared on the scene (in the early 1830s) just when Jacksonian democracy was coming into its own. Abolition was democracy's self-reproach, carrying the democratic idea beyond the bounds American democracy traced for itself. American democracy asserted that equal rights belonged to all white males. Abolitionists asserted that equal rights belonged to all people. Nor was it their egalitarian preachings that made abolitionists so unpopular among their fellow democrats; it was their actions, their defense of free blacks, their resistance to apartheid and white supremacism. Abolitionists couldn't have caused the stir they did had they only denounced slavery as sinful, wicked, etc., and called for the immediate and unconditional release of the slaves in the abstract (a demand so preposterous it would have been laughed out of court). Here is how the abolitionists might have put their case before the court of Northern public opinion:

† Specifically, Alexis de Tocqueville, *Democracy in America;* Marvin Meyers, *The Jacksonian Persuasion;* Frederick Grimké, *The Nature and Tendency of Free Institutions;* Moisei I. Ostrogorski, *Democracy and the Party System in the United States;* John W. Ward, *Andrew Jackson, Symbol for an Age.*

"Fellow Americans: It's not enough to oppose slavery from our privileged standpoint as whites. No one is threatening *us* with slavery, nor is there the slightest chance it will ever be instituted anywhere in the North. We must oppose slavery from the standpoint of the slaves themselves. 'Remember them that are in bonds as bound with them,' and remember that our nation was founded on the absolute conviction that 'all men are created equal' and are 'endowed by their Creator with certain unalienable rights.' Are we afraid of what might happen should the two million slaves suddenly be unshackled and released among us? Let us accept the consequences of that miracle. Let us prepare for it by banishing our racist fears and welcoming the chance to embrace these suffering children of God as our brothers and sisters and fellow citizens. The test of immediate and unconditional emancipation of the slaves is the immediate and unconditional equality of the free blacks."

But the court of public opinion rendered its verdict (a far from judicious one) long before it heard the case. Nothing could deter the march of white supremacism, advancing arm in arm with democracy itself. One could argue (and maybe I should in the book) that the rioting against blacks and the outrageous persecution of the abolitionists sharply abated at the end of the 1830s because the disfranchisement and exclusion of blacks had by then become firmly set throughout the North, had evolved into a national policy. Abolitionism thereafter remained a tiny radical schism (or series of schisms) in the burgeoning racist democracy of the North.

John Brown's own abolitionism at this time is a touching illustration of the abolitionist approach generally. He wanted to do something, as he wrote his brother Frederick in 1834, "in a practical way for my poor fellow-men who are in bondage." Abolition for Brown meant helping blacks become truly free. That's why he proposed to "get at least one negro boy or youth" (if necessary by buying him) "and bring him up as we do our own,—viz, give him a good English education, learn him what we can about the history of the world, about business, about general subjects, and, above all, try to teach him the fear of God." He'd been thinking for years of "some way to get a school a-going here for blacks" because "such advantages ought to be afforded the young blacks, whether they are all to be immediately set free or not." He went on to say that if "Christians" in the Free States could similarly teach young blacks, "the people of the slaveholding states would find themselves constitutionally driven to set about the work of emancipation immediately." "If the young blacks of our country could once become enlightened, it would most assuredly operate on slavery like firing powder confined in rock, and all slaveholders know it well."

John Brown's commitment to abolitionism, then, could be measured by his commitment to the rights or possibilities of Northern blacks, and it was in working to emancipate the latter that he rested his hopes on the emancipation of the former. What makes his famous letter so touching is his innocence toward his fellow whites. Obviously he wasn't aware yet of the impracticability of his very modest scheme. Oswald Garrison Villard is right: "he shows no knowledge of the prejudice in the North against teaching blacks which had resulted in his native state, in the suppression of schools for them in New Haven in 1831, and in Canterbury in 1834. . . . there is little to indicate that Brown was in touch with much of what was going on in the nation."

4. THE TRIALS OF JOB, 1837–46

John Brown, J.B.-Job (reverberations of Archibald MacLeish's bad allegorical metaphysical play of that title years ago), reduced, laid low, bereft, as though Providence was singling him out for punishment, a view of course he accepted and relied on as his source of strength. For in John Brown's universe everything possessed a meaning; nothing was undetermined, accidental, least of all one's suffering. Not to be tested by suffering was not to exist.

The story must be told in full, with much more poignancy than his biographers do (they're anxious to get to the John Brown of history)—how he loses his properties, gets into trouble with the authorities (the innumerable lawsuits that plagued him to his dying day), commits breach of contract, runs afoul of partners and friends, goes bankrupt, and then has nothing, literally nothing —in short, is stripped bare in middle age, with a huge family to support. And on top of this the unspeakable pathos of death, culminating in his burial of four young children within a few weeks, three of them at the same time.

Yet in experiencing these monstrous calamities was Brown so different from his neighbors? Death in the rural America of the 1840s was every family's steadfast companion, the chance of surviving to adolescence being about fifty-fifty. (To be sure even the angel of death usually showed more consideration than he showed the Browns of Ohio.) As for his poverty and humiliation—why that was common enough, too. Bankruptcy by the 1840s was as American as the family farm and nowhere more prevalent than among newborn capitalists in that epoch of the free and open market. The 1837 panic and subsequent crash was the worst economic crisis to strike the country. No mystery there since breakdowns were built into the system, were inseparably bound up with its strengths. Brown, like most Americans who were wiped out by it, saw nothing but their own failures. They were bankrupt—so they were convinced—for the same reason that they were guilty of being sinners. The fault was theirs alone. (Brown blamed himself for depending on credit; though if he'd prospered it would have been primarily because of that dependence.) They believed that the laws of a market economy were, in the end, subject to moral and theological imperatives. The system had it both ways; it was invincible.

(It's the more reprehensible, therefore, that historians and biographers also blame Brown for his terrible fall, some [Nevins, et al.] interpreting it as evidence of his instability, fanaticism, monomania, etc. A view we can dismiss out of hand.)

An aperçu on how his misfortunes might have affected his thinking on the slavery issue. His years in the wilderness as a middle-aged bankrupt might have given him the distance he had to have from the world to see it clearly, in its entirety. It might have been *then* that he came to perceive the futility of the abolitionist crusade as then organized: on the one side the unreconstructed anti-political Garrisonians affirming a strictly moral position and having no truck with any institutions that bore the taint of compromise with slavery; on the other side, the votaries of Gerrit Smith, the Tappans, Weld, and Birney, advocating the use of politics to bring about immediate and unconditional emancipation and so establishing the Liberty party in 1840. To John Brown, brooding in the Ohio countryside, these intramural conflicts may have been quite beside the point. Could he have failed to notice the racism? The intractability of the whites to whom these rightminded abolitionists were appealing? The increasing boldness of the South, the increasingly aggressive justification of slavery? The inexorable growth of slavery, regardless of the slump elsewhere?

We can assume—it's as good an assumption as any—that the change in Brown's thinking occurred in these straitened years, when he subsisted on the margins of society and looked upon it from a perspective he wouldn't otherwise have had.

(Though the foregoing's conjectural, there's an indication—hardly indisputable proof—of its validity. It's John Brown, Jr.'s testimony of an event which, he says, took place in 1839, though it may have been a little earlier. "Father, mother, Jason, Owen and I were, late in the evening, seated around the fire in the open fire-place of the kitchen, in the old Haymarket house where we lived; and there he first informed us of his determination to make war on slavery—not such war as Mr. Garrison informs us 'was equally the purpose of the nonresistant abolitionists,'‡ but war by force of arms. He said he had long entertained such a purpose— that he believed it his duty to devote his life, if need be, to this object, which he made us fully understand. After spending considerable time in setting forth in most impressive language the hopeless condition of the slave, he asked who of us were willing to 'break the jaws of the wicked and pluck the spoil out of his teeth,' naming each of us in succession, Are you Mary, John, Jason, and Owen? Receiving an affirmative answer from each, he kneeled in prayer, and all did the same. This posture in prayer impressed me greatly as it was the first time I had ever known him to assume it. After prayer he asked us to raise our right hands, and he then administered to us an oath, the exact terms of which I cannot recall, but in substance it bound us to secrecy and devotion to the pur-

‡ John Brown, Jr., is referring to some articles written by Wendell Phillips Garrison in 1890–91 under the title *Preludes of Harper's Ferry*.

pose of fighting slavery by force and arms to the extent of our ability.")

5. RECUPERATION AND DISCOVERY, 1846–55

John Brown's situation changed markedly for the better soon after reaching its nadir. He went back to tanning, cared for sheep (his favorite pastime), farmed, managing always to keep his family and soul together.

By 1846 he was on his feet again, an entrepreneur, this time in the wool business, the partner of a worthy Akron gentleman, Simon Perkins. He opened an office in Springfield, Massachusetts, to be closer to the New England market; there he also sorted and graded wool (he was a master at that, too) in behalf of a consortium of growers who needed someone to represent their interests against the manufacturers. Poor luck, though, galled his kibes. Only months after he arrived in Springfield the wool market collapsed (thanks largely to the Walker Tariff, just passed), destroying the prospects of Perkins and Brown and entangling him in further lawsuits. His life, then, was as unsettled as ever—as though he were pursued by Furies determined (this being their specific mission) to prevent him from putting down roots anywhere for any length of time. Here's an abbreviated account of his peregrinations from 1849 on: He goes to North Elba, in the North Country of upper New York State, on Gerrit Smith's land, where he settles to help blacks become independent farmers (another vain effort); to Europe for a few months where he hopes to sell his firm's high-grade wool, bypassing the New England manufacturers (a failed mission, too); back to Springfield (or rather back and forth between North Elba and Springfield), where he still has business to transact, suits to settle; to Akron again where he must fulfill his obligations to Perkins following the collapse of their New England operation; to North Elba again where, free at last, he looks forward to providing a permanent home for his family and resting his weary bones while working out the details of the destiny which calls him.

But by then—June 1855—his destiny's patience had run out. There'd be no rest for John Brown.

I imagined John Brown as a witness to that unfolding destiny, God's unfathomable design. I viewed history from his perspective.

Beginning in 1845 a gigantic new reality faced the tiny abolitionist movement. More and more Northerners, incensed by Southern expansionism, were joining the antislavery crusade. It was becoming a mass movement. The annexation of Texas, followed by the seizure of new territories during the Mexican War, provided incontestable proof that the federal government was being run by and for the South, that its announced policy was to guarantee the expansion of the slave empire. Hence the rise of the Free-Soil party (its motto: "free soil, free speech, free labor, and free men") dedicated to stopping the imperial South dead in its tracks, that is, keeping the slavocracy from moving into any of the new territories. With ex-President Van Buren as its candidate in 1848 the party received nearly 300,000 votes, outpolling the Democrats in New York and approaching them in other states. It seemed to have a future.

The Free-Soil movement, however, revealed some uncomfortable truths to abolitionists. It revealed that Northerners were unmoved by abolitionist arguments and exhortations. Northerners didn't care (to say the least) for people who favored the sudden and total emancipation of the slaves, and as proof of their sincerity shamelessly befriended blacks and demanded equality between the races. *What did move multitudes of Northerners were the actions of the South and the federal government.* These actions, not abolitionist words, mobilized Northern public opinion. Free-Soilism was antiabolitionist for the same reason that it was antislavocrat: fear of blacks invading the territories (virgin white, preserved for whites, no miscegenation there) and perhaps the Free States as well. Whether blacks left their plantations as slaves or freemen didn't matter to these concerned whites. The point was to make sure they didn't leave at all. And so while Free-Soilers regarded slavery as the immediate threat and abolition only a distant one, they declared a pox on both houses and announced loudly enough for all America to hear their attachment to the ideology of white supremacy and de facto apartheid.

A lesson was to be learned here: The white Northern masses, being racist, couldn't be moved out of sympathy for the plight of blacks, but they could be moved by Southern aggression, and when moved could be driven to resist. Some learned that lesson, and they tried to fuse abolitionism and Free-Soilism. Which brings us to Samuel Gridley Howe, George Luther Stearns, Theodore Parker, and Thomas Wentworth Higginson (and later F. B. Sanborn). They realized that abolitionist means couldn't lead to abolitionist ends and that Free-Soil means could. Their task was to spur Free-Soilism to greater militancy in hopes of eliciting a like response from the South, to bring about an extreme situation presided over by "extremists" in both sections.

(Such a strategy had its own corollary: a willingness to exploit or utilize or at the very least tolerate racist phobias because they heightened resentment of the South. But they also heightened resentment of Northern blacks. That's why Gerrit Smith and the old Libertymen were so uncompromisingly opposed to those ex-abolitionists who came to terms with the Free-Soil party, betraying—so he claimed—their principles for short-run tactical advantages. [For Garrison of course this wasn't even an issue. It was, he maintained, the likes of Smith who'd done the betraying when they first attempted to politicize abolitionism, to adulterate its moral truths with worldly power and rewards; they were hoist by their own petard.])

The best assumption, the soundest hypothesis, is that John Brown also learned the lesson of Free-Soilism. He wasn't the man to separate moral belief from possibilities of action. The events of 1845–46 certainly persuaded him—if he hadn't been persuaded earlier—that the slavocracy was openly, defiantly asserting the primacy of Satan. The last stage of the Manichean struggle was beginning. Slavery no longer had to mask its intent; it was nakedly striving for conquest, and it would succeed unless struck down on the fields of Armageddon. He would serve God in that struggle. He surrendered to his calling. He would be a Christian in the tradition of the prophets, saints, martyrs.

Now, anyone who embarks on an extraordinary course of action, a pilgrimage, must feel the hand of destiny. And no doubt a fine line separates that sense of oneself from true madness, fanaticism, etc. To that extent there's some madness in every man who transcends his destiny in seeking to serve it; his madness is perhaps the residue of his greatness, the quantum of difference be-

tween himself and others. As for those people who are only mad
—history has no record of them. John Brown chose his true vocation, and it's of no little moment that he framed his choice in the
Calvinist biblical language by which he lived, by which most of his
contemporaries lived. He'd fight Satan to the death. And how to
fight Satan was the lesson of the Free-Soil party. Not by impugn-
ing slavery and defending blacks (words, words, words), but by
inciting further Southern aggression against the North; by turning
the antiblack North against the slavocrat South; by avoiding the
cul-de-sac of racism. Guerrilla warfare calculated to provoke a
crisis worse than the one that had opened in 1845—this was the
action he contemplated, nourished in his bones.

How do we know that's what he contemplated? Apart from the
logical answer that he had to contemplate some violent plan of action at some time in his life (unless one accepts the view of Southern historians that he was nothing more than a horse thief or typical man on the make whose only interest in principles and ideals
was whether they could help him get rich, etc.), there's Frederick
Douglass's description of his 1847 meeting with Brown in which
he, Brown, lengthily discussed his general scheme to mount an assault on "Egypt" from easily defended strongholds in the southern
Appalachians. And that assault force, as Douglass explains it,
would operate as an extension of the Underground Railroad, seizing slaves, arming the best of them, and running others across the
Appalachian network into Pennsylvania and New York, thence to
Canada. An assault force, then, that would invite the South to follow in hot pursuit. Provocation of conflict, not emancipation of
slaves, least of all slave insurrection, was to be its purpose.

That scheme, vague and ill defined, was for the future. We have
an excellent measure of Brown's thinking at the time in his relations with free blacks, especially those in and around Springfield.

He tried to get blacks to build a community of their own, independent of whites, based on an unyielding ethic of self-help and
mutual assistance. We have some idea of the difficulties he must
have encountered from his unsparing criticism of their weakness
of character—their love of worldy pleasures, their susceptibility to
false promises, their contempt of themselves and each other, their
divisiveness. (Hence his sarcastic essay "Sambo's Mistakes," published by the *Ram's Horn,* a black abolitionist journal, early in

1849.) Brown then tried to organize the blacks to engage in physical resistance. That was in 1851, in the wake of the Fugitive Slave Act. Here was Southern aggression with a vengeance, Congress having granted slave catchers the power to enter any Northern community and without due process seize alleged runaways for immediate extradition. Attempts to enforce the act alienated a large segment of Northern public opinion; whites resented the intrusion of slave catchers more than they did the runaways. It was the lesson of the Free-Soil experience all over again.

With that fact in mind I reread Brown's "Words of Advice" to the League of Gileadites, the black self-defense outfit he helped set up, and for the first time appreciated its full significance. The Gileadites, he said, must learn to use their white friends, must learn, that is, the art of (urban) guerrilla warfare. "Nothing charms the American people as personal bravery. . . . *No jury can be found in the Northern states that would convict a man for defending his rights to the last extremity. . . .* Colored people have ten times the number of fast friends among the whites than they suppose, and would have ten times the number they now have were they half as much in earnest to secure their dearest rights as they are to ape the follies and extravagances of their white neighbors, and to indulge in idle show, in ease and in luxury." Gathering together at a second's notice to protect any black who might be taken, and displaying as much solidarity, bravery, audacity, and cool-headedness as circumstances required, the Gileadites must—and Brown underlined this whole passage—*"go into the houses of your most prominent and influential white friends with your wives; and that will effectually fasten upon them the suspicion of being connected with you, and will compel them to make a common cause with you, whether they would otherwise live up to their professions or not. This would leave them no choice in the matter."* Moreover: "Your enemies will be slow to attack you after you have done up the work nicely; and if they should, they will have to encounter your white friends as well as you; for you may safely calculate on a division of the whites, and may by that means get to an honorable parley."

In other words, blacks could best defend themselves by widening the conflict to include as many whites as possible, polarizing differences between whites, forcing them—particularly those inclined to resist Southern aggression—to act on their convictions.

Brown's "Advice" to his black comrades convinced me I was on the right track. The Fugitive Slave Act gave him a fresh, God-sent opportunity to divert Northern whites from their obsessive dislike of blacks and concentrate their animus on the real enemy. Proof again (to him) that under suitable conditions of extremity or crisis abolitionist ends might be advanced by antiabolitionist or Free-Soil means, that white supremacism was no insuperable obstacle to such a strategy. The pot had to be kept boiling.

And this too, as I'd concluded in my researches on them, was exactly what the Six (or five) believed. They furnished quite a spectacle, these pillars of the community, some of them famous throughout the land (and the world), plotting like thieves, organizing and leading mobs, battling the authorities in their attempts to rescue the poor miserable runaways who were about to be returned to bondage. Behind the spectacle lay another purpose—to bring in and so radicalize the sympathetic white population at large; more generally, to deepen the mood of insurgency and contempt for the law. Their rescues, fascinating in themselves (and too often the sport of their biographers), must be seen as integral to their *political* objectives. Their turning to violence in a popular cause was consistent with their wager (not Gerrit Smith's) that the Free-Soil movement could, if properly directed as the instrument of protracted conflict, become a movement *for* emancipation. The wager began to pay off when the Massachusetts legislature in 1851 elected Charles Sumner to the Senate where he joined other radical Free-Soilers, Chase of Ohio and Hale of New Hampshire. Their presence in the Senate (pretty much dominated by proslavery Democrats) disturbed the South more than all the agitation by all the abolitionists since Garrison launched the crusade in 1831. (Which isn't intended as criticism of Garrison and the other uncompromising abolitionists. Furthest from it. The strategy of uniting Free-Soilism and abolitionism became viable only because more "extreme" variants of abolitionism also existed. Any insurgent movement, if it's to get anywhere, will travel along several paths simultaneously.)

For a while, though, it seemed the wager would be lost. The 1850 Compromise, which included the Fugitive Slave Act, was working. It satisfied a need. Sectional differences quickly relaxed (despite occasional forays North by slave catchers). The country returned to the state of normality preceding Texas annexation. A normality that rested on tremendous prosperity, the triumph of business enterprise, as the United States—that is, the North— approached the "take-off" point of full-scale industrialization. And again we meet the tragic dimension of that prosperity, that hope of an illimitable future. For it was cotton more than any other single commodity that took off in the late 1840s (more and more going to Northern factories); hence the corresponding re- production of slaves. By 1850 there were over three million slaves, (becoming concentrated now in the vast plantations of the Gulf and Mississippi states), and if any institution appeared likely to endure it was American slavery. It must have been hard to be an abolitionist and a realist at the same time.

So direct actionists like Brown and the Brahmin radicals witnessed a retrogression. Worse: defeat. The Free-Soil party, whose career looked so promising in 1848, rapidly shrunk and in the 1852 election received only half its previous vote. More ominously, the Whig party, unable to accommodate itself to sec- tional conflict, went under, leaving the field to the pro-Southern Democratic party. By 1852 the Democratic party presided over the nation's destiny like a colossus. The slavocracy had a strangle hold over the whole federal apparatus—the courts, the adminis- tration and bureaucracy from the President on down, the city of Washington. The slavocracy seemed omnipotent.

The lesson to be learned from this amazing decline of the anti- slavery opposition was the same lesson imparted by the Free-Soil experience during its brief efflorescence—namely that the white North was content with the status quo and could live amicably with the South provided the slavocracy in its turn accepted the status quo and embarked on no further provocations. And the South after 1850 was apparently willing to live with that proviso. Its "extremists" or advocates of secession fared poorly. Why, after all, should the slaveholders oppose the Union? It was serving their interests too well.

(Permanent servitude in the South, apartheid and immiseriza- tion in the North—that was the lot of American blacks under the status quo. The despair of many black and some white abolitionists was an important refrain of the early 1850s, the bleakest of times, the darkest of futures.)

It was appropriate that John Brown should have spent those years cultivating his own garden, working off his debt to Simon Perkins, that he should have occupied himself with domestic and theological concerns (e.g., those interminable arguments over the literal truths of Scripture). We can assume that he never stopped thinking in those fallow years about his great design, his Heaven-appointed mission. But he had to wait for God to intervene, to bring about a fresh crisis. And when would that be?

Unmistakably clear now (October 20) that General Thieu, our puppet in Saigon, was playing a part in the election campaign. His position: The bombing of North Vietnam must continue until the Communists capitulate to him, that is, no longer demand a place in the South Vietnamese government. Since that was what the war was about, Thieu's position—should the United States acquiesce—amounted to an indefinite commitment to go on fighting for him. "We and our allies," he said, "cannot afford to compromise if there is no reciprocation from the enemy. We cannot compromise if we do not want to surrender. All peace loving countries will understand this."

6. TRANSITIONS, 1854–55

From the standpoint of those abolitionists who favored direct action against the slavocracy the Kansas-Nebraska Act of 1854 was a miraculous evocation of God's will. Overnight the North was transformed. The antislavery movement, which had been moribund, fractious, demoralized, came to life. Free-Soilers had their issue again, carried now to more extreme lengths. The slavocrats were on the march, coveting not newly acquired territory, as in 1846, but segments of old sacrosanct territory that had been explicitly declared off limits to them. After Kansas-Nebraska was the rest of Louisiana to be theirs? Why not, since the Missouri Compromise, which had set those limits, was now null and void. And after Louisiana would the Free States also be served up to them? Slavocrat rapacity was insatiable. What's more, by sponsoring this outrage, this coup, the Northern Democracy, especially its peerless leader, the architect of the scheme, Stephen Douglas of Illinois ("the Little Giant"), stood unmasked, exposed as the servitor of the slave empire. So that well before the act was passed on May 30 an anti-Nebraska or Free-Soil movement was sprouting everywhere in the North. By summer it was a rich harvest, and a new party had formed to gather it up. By year's end the Republican party, as it styled itself (Jefferson being its patron saint, the Declaration of Independence its canonical text), had become the second party in the land, the first in the North, and was girding itself to take possession of the federal government and shape national policy to its liking. A revolution was taking place.

Who could have predicted such a change—so swift, so enormous in its implications—during the period of Democratic hegemony only a few months before, when all seemed so hopeless, so desperate? John Brown, however, must have been the least astonished of men. He never doubted that Providence would show its hand, and precisely when least expected, when the slavocrats and their dough-faced allies were at the height of their euphoria.

Brown might have seen in the crisis brought on by the Kansas-Nebraska Act God's specific sign to him. The moment was ripening for resumption of his plan. Now he could map out the details of its execution, bringing violence to bear on the conflict, driving the sections further and further apart. We can infer from the evidence that around this time—1854 or so—he settled on Harpers Ferry, gateway to the Southern heartland and surrounded by Appalachian fastnesses, as the place from which to inaugurate guerrilla war. Certainly guerrilla war in "Africa" was on his mind at this time—guerrilla war, it should be emphasized, conducted against the background of, and in conjunction with, the burgeoning crisis of the sections. It was to be strategy of provoking the provokers.

(Documentary proof is to be found in one of Brown's memorandum books already noted, an entry recorded, Villard guesses, early in 1855: "Guerrilla warfare see Life of Lord Wellington [Joachim Hayward Stocqueler's two-volume *Life of Field Marshal the Duke of Wellington,* published in 1852] page 70 to Page 75 (Mina) [leader of the Spanish guerrillas]. See also Page 102 some *valuable hints* in same book. *See also* Page 196 some most important instructions to officers. *See also* same Book Page 235 these

words Deep and narrow defile where 300 men would suffice to
check an *army*."

(It was opposite this passage that Brown strung a line of cities
in an arc extending from Pennsylvania to the Deep South and
back again. If Harpers Ferry led South, Pennsylvania led back
North.)

But like every American, Brown turned his attention to the
Kansas Territory, testing ground of the Kansas-Nebraska Act. If,
as Stephen Douglas and the Democrats prayed, the issue could be
decided peaceably one way or the other, the settlers themselves
voting slavery up or down, sectional tensions would subside and
Republicans and other worse "extremists" would disappear. But
if, as antislavery radicals prayed, Kansas itself became the scene
of conflict, those tensions were bound to grow along with the
number of "extremists" who battened on them.

Kansas was opened to settlement on July 1, 1854. The first emigrants, naturally enough, came from nearby Missouri and were
proslave. So it wasn't surprising when five months later they voted
to send a proslave delegate to Congress. What was surprising—
and shocking to the North—was the extent of the fraud, the number of votes cast by outsiders brought in for the purpose—as
though the proslave advocates were determined to so overwhelm
the Free Staters that the issue simply wouldn't be contested. The
second important territorial election, held on March 30, 1855, this
one for members of the legislature, was even more shocking, and
though the proslave settlers probably still had a majority, they—
or those who represented them, the Missouri "Border Ruffians"
who entered and left at will—went much further than before in
committing fraud of every description (stuffing ballot boxes, in-
timidating opponents or anyone who took offense at their
methods, among them the governor). No one would believe that
the proslave party fairly won all thirty-nine legislative seats, each
by enormous majorities. Now, Free Staters hadn't thrown up any
resistance as yet. But they were entering in larger numbers, many
of them sent by such antislavery organizations as the New England Emigrant Aid Society, which also supplied leadership,
money, arms.

Following the Kansas events closely, five of Brown's sons and a
son-in-law pulled up their stakes and in the spring of 1855 headed

out there themselves. They were abolitionists, but they were also excited by the stories of fertile land and decent climate coming out of the Territory. They planted their colony in Osawatomie in the southeast part of Kansas, not far from Missouri and cheek by jowl with many proslave settlers.

By the time they got there it was clear to John Brown that Kansas was where he should be too, that it was becoming a situation made to order for him. It was the focus of national publicity. As a potential theater of violence and provocation, the effects of which would ramify across the land, Kansas surpassed "Africa" itself, at least for now. It might also prove a valuable training area for his African expedition, the polestar of his life. In June 1855 he received a letter from his son John: "I tell you the truth, when I say that while the interest of despotism has secured to its cause hundreds and thousands of the meanest and most desperate of men, armed to the teeth with Revolvers, Bowie Knives, Rifle & Cannon, —while they are not only thoroughly organized, but under pay from the Slave-holders—the friends of freedom are *not one fourth* of those *half armed,* and as to *Military Organization* among them it *nowhere exists in this territory* unless they have recently done something in Lawrence. The result of this is that the people here exhibit the most abject and cowardly spirit, when their dearest rights are invaded and trampled down by the lawless bands of Miscreants which Missouri has ready at a moment's call to pour down on them. . . . Now, the remedy we propose is, that the Anti-slavery portion of the inhabitants should *immediately, thoroughly arm* and *organize themselves* in *military companies.* In order to effect this, some persons must begin and lead in the matter. Here are 5 men of us who are not only anxious to fully prepare, but are thoroughly determined to fight. . . . Now we want you to get for us these arms. We need them more than we do bread. Would not Gerrit Smith or someone, furnish the money and loan it to us for one, two or three years, for the purpose, until we can raise enough to refund it from the *Free* soil of Kansas?"

This was all the urging John Brown needed. He departed for Kansas as soon as he cleaned up his business affairs, saw that his wife and children were settled in at his North Elba farm, and raised some money for arms (by speaking at abolitionist meetings). He arrived at Osawatomie in early October 1855.

7. RESISTANCE AND REBELLION, 1856

Free State resistance had begun to crystallize by then. Free Staters had no choice but resistance. The political machinery of the Territory—the governor, the legislature, the judiciary, the militia—was completely controlled by rabid proslavers and their Missouri accomplices (as witness the extraordinary body of laws they enacted prescribing long jail sentences for anyone who espoused antislavery opinions and death for anyone who sided with slaves, excluding from office anyone who didn't swear fealty to the proslave constitution, etc., etc.) So the Free Staters, their numbers swelling by the day, went about establishing *their* territorial government. In late October–early November 1855, at Topeka, they drew up their own antislavery constitution which the people (on December 15) adopted and under which (on January 15) they elected their own governor and legislature. Two governments, two armies, existed side by side in a state of imminent war.

A discussion of the internal dynamics of the Free State forces is important here. For we have in Kansas a paradigm of the North at large.

What should the opponents of the proslave party do? What means should they employ? To what end? Such questions always come down to conflicts between factions and tendencies, conservative to radical, "moderate" to "extremist." As Malin (my cicerone in much of this discussion) points out, a sizable percentage of the Free State settlers had come from the border or slave states and were rather soft toward the proslavers. They didn't feel all that strongly about the abstract issues of slavery and freedom: After all, hardly any slaves were coming in; there were no planters around; there wasn't anything to get upset about. (Moderate proslavers felt the same way and were soft toward the Free State interest.) Then there were the Kansas Republicans,* all of whom wanted slavery forbidden. Liberal Republicans favored restraint, patience, and argued that time was on their side (soon the federal government would be) and that fence-sitting conservatives and

---

* The first Republican party convention of Kansas wasn't held until the spring of 1859. But the Free State forces were heavily Republican right from the start.

moderates must not be antagonized and certainly not driven into the enemy camp. The more radical Republicans held that aggressive measures, including armed defense, must be taken against the proslavery forces, that the federal government, being doughfaced, couldn't be counted on and might have to be resisted too, the only hope coming from a Republican victory in the national elections.

Now, it should be emphasized that none of these Republicans were opposing slavery as such; they had no quarrel with the way their Missouri neighbors lived; they only wanted to be left alone. This meant that they wanted Kansas to be void of blacks, period. The Free State constitution specifically prohibited free blacks from entering the Territory, and those free blacks who happened to be there were denied civil rights. On the subject of free blacks Kansas was the mirror image of the nation.

John Brown, his family and cohorts represented the minuscule "extremist" group. They went beyond the limited ends—the simple nonextension of slavery—embodied in Republicanism. To these "extremists" in fact the realization of such limited ends, the success of Republicanism, constituted a great danger because the crisis would then be over, with nothing resolved. For Brown and the Kansas abolitionists Kansas itself was only a means in the larger unrelenting struggle against the slavocracy. As a matter of short-run tactics, however, they often worked in and through the radical Republicans, or developed ad hoc partnerships with them as occasion dictated. And for their part, the radical Republicans, antiabolitionist as they were, stood to benefit too from the whilom partnership. When the fighting broke out it was John Brown et al. who carried the war to the enemy, took the most parlous risks, such warfare having the salutary effect of radicalizing the liberal Republicans and Republicanizing the conservative Free Staters.

(It will be noted, then, that his tactics were proportioned to his goal, and that goal—emancipation—was as legitimate under the circumstances as any other. He was as "extreme" as the crisis itself, his view being that there was only one way to end it: by destroying Satan. He was therefore no more extreme than the other professed abolitionists, but unlike the apostles of nonviolence who looked to the moral regeneration of the North he tried to demonstrate the possibility of acting, the feasibility of working with men who were racists and didn't care a damn what happened in the South so long as they could lead their own lives in peace. The main thing was that for precisely those selfish reasons they despised the slavocracy and might be willing to take it on.)

By the same token the North was the macrocosm of Kansas. The same factional controversies, on a much vaster scale, agitated the national Republican party. Conservative to moderate Republicans feared that a policy of armed confrontation would alienate ex-Democrats, those still soft on the South, and give the party over to abolitionist or "nigger-loving" fanatics, effectively nipping its chances in the bud; they supported a policy of compromise and accommodation. More radically minded Republicans (Sumner, Chase, Stevens) favored conflict—within governable limits— precisely because it would bring into the party's ranks multitudes of people who'd been neutral or out of sympathy with it, but whose aversion to the slavocracy overrode their phobia of blacks. For the persistence of the conflict would definitively prove that the Kansas-Nebraska Act, on which the Democratic claim to national leadership rested—the claim that the Democratic party alone, as sponsor of the principle of popular sovereignty, could guarantee sectional amity and preserve the Union—was unworkable, a desperate failure in conception and execution, assuring Republican victory in the all-decisive presidential election. Brown's counterpart among Republicans was the group to which Howe, Stearns, Parker, Higginson, and Sanborn belonged. They valued the party only as a means to abolitionist ends. They hoped to see—and labored to bring about—further sectional discord, eventually "disunion" or "revolution." From their "extremist" angle of vision the worst thing that could happen was an accommodation with the South *on Republican lines, with the status quo ante restored, the sections coexisting peacefully.* They regarded Kansas as only the beginning. Their wish was to Kansify the nation.

(A word on the deeply tinged racist character of the Republican party. It was so vehemently antislavocrat largely because it was the party of white supremacy. Republicans affirmed unbreakable limits, lines of demarcation, between freedom and servitude, white and black. They stood for the confinement, the restriction, the coarctation of slaves and blacks both, slaves to be kept where they were for the indefinite future, Northern blacks to be kept seg-

regated and disfranchised. The Democrats were an easy mark for
Republican propagandists. Democrats were trespassers of limits,
defilers of purity, avatars of racial promiscuity, miscegenationists.
It's understandable, therefore, why radical and abolitionist Republicans had to keep their own counsel on the race issue, bite their
lips, stand by and observe it being exploited by their compatriots
for antislavery, anti-Democratic purposes.)

John Brown's activities in 1856 must be perceived against this
background of national politics. The election was everything. If
the Republicans were to win the presidency, would the slavocrats
make their threat of severing the South from the Union? And then
what?

That Brown kept a keen weather eye on national affairs is fairly
well demonstrated in a letter he wrote early in 1856 to Congressman Joshua Giddings, a radical Republican representing
Brown's old Western Reserve district. Shortly before, President
Pierce had sent a special message to Congress declaring the Free
State government in rebellion and then had followed up the message with an order placing federal law enforcement officials on the
side of the proslave government. Brown wrote: ". . . a number of
United States soldiers are quartered in this vicinity for the ostensi-
ble purpose of removing *intruders* from certain dubious Lands. It
is, however, *believed* . . . that the real object is to have these men
in readiness to act in the enforcement of those *Hellish enactments*
of the (so called) Kansas Legislature; absolutely abominated by a
great majority of the inhabitants of the Territory; and spurned by
them up to this time. I confidently believe that the next movement
of the Administration and its Proslavery masters will be to drive
the people either to submit to those Infernal enactments or to assume what will be termed *treasonable grounds* by shooting down
the poor soldiers of the country with whom they have no quarrel
whatever. I ask in the name of Almighty God; I ask in the name
of our venerated fore-fathers; I ask in the name of all that good or
true men ever held dear; will Congress suffer us to be driven to
such 'dire extremities'? *Will anything be done?* . . ."

Giddings replied: ". . . you need have no fear of the troops.
The President will never *dare* employ the troops of the United
States to shoot the citizens of Kansas. The death of the first man

by the troops will involve every free State in your fate. It will light up the fires of civil war throughout the North, and we shall stand or fall with you. Such an act will also bring the President so deep in infamy that the hand of political resurrection will never reach him. . . ."

That, of course, was what Brown wanted to hear. Nothing would have gratified him more than an incident that would "light up the fires of civil war throughout the North." To foment just such an incident was his abiding hope. As he phrased it in a letter of April 7 to his family (my emphasis added for obvious reasons): *"For me, I have no desire (all things considered) to have the slave power cease from its acts of aggression. 'Their foot shall slide in due time.'"* The story of John Brown's sojourn in Kansas could be summed up in those words. He was altogether aware of the national significance of his actions.

We have the explanation we need, then, for his incredible exploits in the spring and summer of 1856 when Kansas bled so profusely.

His strategy, very briefly, was to take advantage of the burgeoning tension between proslavers and Free Staters, the gathering of arms and men, the increasing episodes of violence, and encourage open and sustained warfare between the two sides. His savage murders at Pottawatomie (the accounts of which disgusted me anew) succeeded in accomplishing just this. Earlier I'd called them ideological murders. That's exactly what they were. The five victims were slain not for what they did (they owned no slaves, committed no palpable wrongs), nor even for what they advocated. They were slain because their deaths—and the particularly gruesome way they were dispatched—were certain to cause reprisals and counterreprisals. More than any single deed Pottawatomie was responsible for what followed: the pitched battles, murders, atrocities, pillage, the general and pervasive terror. The country of course hung on every word coming out of the combat zone, each section blaming the other for the crimes of "Bleeding Kansas."

(John Brown was in his element. It was as though all his years of hardship and toil, all his varied experiences, had prepared him specifically for the life of a guerrilla warrior. His powers of endurance were matchless; men half his age and less couldn't keep up with him. He was astonishingly quick, adept, supple in the art of self-reliance, and never more than when under fire, when lives were at stake and judgments had to be unerring. Now, physical reasons don't account for his prowess in the field, as a leader of men. What made the difference was his calling, his mission, the freedom he possessed in knowing that he was God's vicegerent, in having vaulted over the Stygian chasm of death. Hence his dauntless courage, his tactic of impudently assaulting an enemy whose forces were much larger than his, his ability to improvise on the spot. His was a dreadful presence in Kansas. Above all others he was the terror of the proslave community [everyone knew or supposed that "Old Brown" had done the Pottawatomie massacre]; he was believed capable of anything; he was invested with the omnipotence of fable and legend.)

The war he was instrumental in launching thus had its predictable effect on national politics. Congress couldn't decide which of the Kansas governments to recognize as legitimate. Dividing along ideological lines, it reached a deadlock; the House favored the Free State or Topeka constitution, the Senate the proslave or Shawnee constitution. Neither got recognized. So the Republicans had their winning issue. And when in June they met to select a presidential candidate (John C. Frémont, the explorer), they of course made the Free State cause their own, serving notice that it would be the centerpiece of their campaign. The Democrats found themselves in an untenable position. Bleeding Kansas might lose them every Northern state, and to lose every Northern state was to lose the election. So they had to neutralize Kansas, relax their proslave animus, appear impartial and evenhanded. In their presidential convention (held in early June) they accordingly rejected both the incumbent President and Stephen Douglas as candidates because they were too closely identified in the public mind with the Kansas debacle, and instead settled on James Buchanan of Pennsylvania, whom the South regarded as safe as any "doughface" and who in due time, when the election was over, could be counted on to resume the federal government's unabashedly proslave Kansas policy.

And the Democrats were lucky. Suddenly, as autumn arrived, the war quieted down. The recently appointed governor, James

W. Geary, brought a semblance of order, he and the army having
by then built up an apparatus sufficient to mediate or serve as a
buffer between the two sides. If John Brown and the other Free
State guerrillas couldn't operate so easily, neither could the thousands of Missourians on whose intercession all proslave hopes
rested. Nor were the Free State forces averse to a halt in the
fighting. Time, manifestly, was on their side. In numbers they already overwhelmed the proslavers; they were winning the battle
of popular sovereignty; they required an interval of tranquillity to
mobilize their *political* power, their conquest of the Territory.
And the Kansas Republicans had pretty much established their
primacy and had no necessary interest in armed conflict; what
they wanted was an authority capable of maintaining the peace
until the Free State majority, which they now de facto represented, took over the Kansas government.

This was, as noted above, a defeat for John Brown. Had he
risked his life only to help a Republican regime that would keep
out blacks, slave and free alike, nothing else? No doubt the Free
Staters appreciated what he'd done for them, above all for the savage retribution he'd visited on the enemy. (*Vide*, the celebrated
letter by Kansas Republican leader, later governor, Charles Robinson, thanking Brown for his "prompt, efficient and timely action against the invaders of our rights and the murderers of our
citizens," etc.) But they definitely weren't interested in his abolitionism. Certainly not that. So, it transpired, he'd been used for
their purpose, not they his. And should tranquillity prevail in
Kansas the unexampled opportunity for provocation and coun-
terprovocation would go by the boards. Whether it would prevail
for good remained to be seen. At all events there was little more
he could do in Kansas, and he left for the East (artfully eluding
capture along the way) in pursuit of his cynosure.

His Kansas experience had convinced him of several things.
First, that under the right conditions the most timorous, defiantly
racist opponents of slavery—men who sought merely its restriction—could be aroused to battle. Second, that a cadre of guerrillas, tried and tempered in military struggle, could be recruited
for more ambitious undertakings. Third, that a policy of provocation—that is guerrilla war—could best succeed when waged
against the slavocracy itself, not against its agents and sympa-

thizers and yea-sayers in a far-off, sparsely populated territory, important as that conflict was symbolically, politically. Fourth, that only a conflict emanating directly from "Africa" would carry the North beyond the limited, antiabolitionist aims of Republicanism. And fifth, that his plan was more imperative than ever.

Again the Democrats were lucky. The defusing of Kansas as an issue made their victory possible on November 4, 1856. Buchanan managed to win five Northern states (by the skin of his teeth), these constituting the entire margin of difference between his 174 electoral votes and Frémont's 114.

The North, then, wasn't Republican enough, despite the Kansas-Nebraska Act, despite Bleeding Kansas, despite the avowedly proslave federal government and Democratic party. And should peace and serenity settle over the land in the years to come, the North might become even less Republican, or, more likely, produce a Republicanism hardly distinguishable from Democracy, such being the normal status of the American two-party system. Radical Republicans, it followed, were bound to be most seriously hurt by the election and what it portended. The absence of crisis would strengthen the party conservatives and moderates who argued for accommodation with the South on the most generous terms possible within the limits of its principles, flexibly applied. If the South, led by her conservatives and moderates, were amenable to those terms, the status quo just might prevail. Another hope would be squandered.

Hence the attempt by Howe, Stearns, Parker, Higginson, and Sanborn to revive Kansas in 1857—anything to keep the crisis going, anything to engender disunion and revolt (Higginson irrepressibly in the lead). Hence their embrace of John Brown, a kindred soul, a mythic presence, a godsend.

Even we who were kindly disposed toward Hubert Humphrey were losing our patience with him. Signs were appearing that he might have a chance, mirabile dictu, *that Nixon's ratings were falling, that the kind of campaign Nixon was waging—modeled on Tom Dewey's in '48—might enable him also to snatch defeat from the jaws of victory. Why, then, wasn't Humphrey making his*

*move on Vietnam? Was he so cullioned and beaten down that he
couldn't bring himself into conflict with LBJ? We feared so.*

(A new Broadway musical, Maggie Flynn, *with Shirley Jones
and Jack Cassidy, opened on the night of October 23. It was
based—imagine!—on the 1863 New York draft riot in which
hundreds and hundreds of blacks were massacred by Irish mobs.
The* Times *review was a massacre in turn. The lengths to which
show biz would go to discover relevance.)*

*October 24 was also the day George Wallace came to town,
Babylon, enemy country, home of Wall Street, radicals, intellectuals, Harlem—all he'd been demagoguing against since '64
(and with increasing success). Now he was here to beard us in
our very sink of iniquity.*

*His followers arrived by the busload for the monster rally at
Madison Square Garden. A reception committee of demon-
strators, thousands of them, were waiting outside the Garden. A
poor protest, stupid and misplaced. The pathetic souls who came
to whoop it up for their deliverer received the full-brunt elitist,
college-bred insults, most of them personal, a performance that
left a sour taste in my mouth.*

*I imagined a similar demonstration taking place during the
1860 campaign, consisting of radicals on the one hand and
conservatives on the other, "black" Republicans versus dough-
faced Democrats, right here in New York City, where pro-
Southern sentiment was very strong (where in fact the Democratic
mayor later advocated secession from the Union). Wallace's
followers could be likened to the doughfaces of yore.*

8. PREPARATIONS I, 1857

A cameo shot of John Brown striding bumptiously on a Boston
street, heading for the Stearnses' place or Judge Russell's. He's as
dauntless and self-confident in the drawing rooms of these famous
men as he was recently on the battlefields of Kansas. His ego has
nothing to do with it. The opposite: the absence of ego, the absence of a self separate from the universe. He now belongs to
God; his destiny's no longer something dreamed of, prayed for,
awaited, anticipated; it's experienced in every breath and instant,
all temporal distinctions that otherwise define mortality effaced in

the eternality of the chosen. As the instrument of Providence he's master of every occasion. So that this ex-farmer, tanner, shepherd, and entrepreneur who spent years in rural poverty, who until he was fifty-five knew nothing but anonymity, and who now has nothing in the way of worldly possessions or prospects, meets and visits the Brahmin elect of New England, the premier intellectuals of the time, men of commanding wealth, power, standing as equals, as people who can help him carry out his mission. Beyond that they mean nothing to him; the mission is all.

No need to expatiate on what they saw in him, this aged hero bred of their stock, embodying for them the lost New England, the New England that had distributed its seed across the northern tier of America and exhausted itself in the process (the home now of hundreds of thousands of Irish immigrants, a further mark of decline in their eyes). One could easily romanticize the encounter between John Brown and them because the elements of romance were certainly present and counted for something in their prospering relation. But it would be an error to make too much of it (as so many writers do). The relation cut deeper. It must be judged by the seriousness of the enterprise in which they were all engaged: the destruction of the slave empire.

Brown came East seeking financial help to—so he claimed, so it was universally assumed—continue his Kansas operations. If he had the resources, the war would go on and on, with no letup in the bleeding. Free Staters might back down, compromise, welcome a surcease in the fighting; he'd remain the same unflinching Osawatomie Brown of legend—if his eastern friends would only provide the arms and equipment. They had a stake in the struggle and if they couldn't go to the front themselves they could at least give generously to those who did. Brown plucked every sentimental string, recounting tales of horror and woe and derring-do, the suffering of defenseless women and children, the sacrifices of his own family, etc.—whatever moved his audiences most, whatever might induce them to contribute to his war chest.

(A legitimate tactic, this appeal to sentiment. It's part of every radical insurgent movement, especially those involving violence by or against a hated enemy. Fund raising never changes, and sentiment, often maudlin, self-pitying, and exploitative, is its nutriment.)

The "extreme" radicals—those who most feared that a protracted peace would lead to sectional accommodation—gathered under Brown's standard. Enter here the Six—their lives, attainments, social standing, reputations. They all agreed that a policy or tactic of violent provocation was the only one that would work, that is, lead to emancipation. Like an angel of deliverance Brown was exactly the man they sought. His proposals for action corresponded to their beliefs. They formed a Brownian cabal, still perfectly legal and aboveboard (they weren't yet the *Secret* Six), the radical plectrum of the antislavery movement.

Brown of course was deceiving them, too. He was collecting money not for Kansas but for his plan. And such money as he did collect—as much of it as possible—he used to organize his own army, drawn from other veterans of the Kansas campaign, and begin laying in arms (among them thousands of pikes or spears ordered from a Connecticut blacksmith), and hire an "expert" in guerrilla warfare (Hugh Forbes). The Six knew nothing of these preparations. Kansas was a metaphor to Brown; reality lay in Virginia.

Meanwhile, the crisis was heating up again; it needed no "extremist" agitators. To the delight of Republicans it was taking place within the regnant Democratic party.

The crisis could be likened to a Greek tragedy, each political event contributing to the pattern of inexorability. In early March 1857 the Supreme Court handed down its bombshell decision (Dred Scott) on slavery in the territories, declaring that popular sovereignty was null and void since *any* restriction on property rights (those a territorial legislature might impose), hence on the ownership of slaves, violated the Constitution's Fifth Amendment, and that, by implication, the federal government was obliged to *protect* slavery there, as it was obliged to protect all the rights of American citizens in the territories. The Supreme Court in other words, was saying that the Free State position contradicted the law of the land and that the proslave position conformed to it. That was how the South interpreted the Dred Scott decision. And that was how the Buchanan administration interpreted it. But that wasn't how Stephen Douglas and the Northern Democrats he spoke for interpreted it. They maintained that property rights weren't unrestricted *in concreto:* Territorial legislatures could and did outlaw liquor, prostitution, and other such "rights" injurious to community health and safety, and they could similarly outlaw slavery. Popular sovereignty, the argument ran, was the recognition of historical reality, of the Constitution in practice, as lived and applied by the people for whom it was written. The true test of interpretation, however, would come over the political disposition of Kansas.

There the situation was fast coming to a head. By the end of 1857, according to measurable, objective criteria—that is, the election returns—the proslave forces were out of the running, and by a tremendous distance, minimally three to one. What's more, all the administration-appointed governors (no friends of the Free Staters) validated the results. The proslavers then tried a desperate political grab; no pretense, no dissembling. They produced their own (Lecompton) constitution for the whole Territory. This the Free Staters of course rejected by a thunderously large vote. So large that Douglas himself, true to his popular sovereignty principles, now sided with the Free Staters. But President Buchanan went ahead and sponsored the Lecompton constitution, recommending that Congress admit Kansas into the Union as a slave state. Open, implacable warfare broke out between Douglas and Southern (plus administration) Democrats in the winter of 1857–58. The party was effectively cleaved in two.

Douglas's courage might have saved the Northern Democracy from extinction, from being incorporated whole into the Republican party. In any case nothing now could prevent the Republicans from capturing the presidency in 1860.

9. PREPARATIONS II, 1858

The winter of 1857–58. After a perfunctory stay in Kansas John Brown came East again. It was time to put his plan into effect. Piecing everything together in the course of a year and half's research and reflection (and despite the destruction of documents and John Brown's iron reticence), I'd worked out to my satisfaction—I could now place it in its historical context, fuse it with the politics of the times—a usable hypothesis or "explanatory model" of what the plan was supposed to accomplish.

a. The raid on "Africa" ("Egypt," "Israel," etc.) was to be, like Lexington, a dramatic event, a shattering announcement of war. It was to be directed, therefore, against both the slavocracy and the administration and its military command. It was to be a *political* act, attuned to the emerging conflict of the sections.

b. Harpers Ferry was an intelligent choice for making the announcement. A federal arsenal was located there. It was the gateway to the Southern interior. Flanked by mountains, it was situated beautifully for the kind of guerrilla warfare Brown had in mind.

c. After holding Harpers Ferry for a while, during which time nearby slaves were to be taken and their owners held as hostages (and treated with the respect and civility due prisoners of war), the attack force was to proceed to the mountains and find a defensible bastion.

d. A biracial republic, complete with constitution and other formal paraphernalia of government, was to be established in the mountains as soon as feasible. It was to be a moving republic as it were—moving back and forth from the Southland to the North, picking up slaves and prisoners and recruits, growing ever larger as it harassed the slavocracy and conveyed more and more slaves to freedom via the mountain network.

e. The existence of the guerrilla republic would aid the cause of Northern and Southern disunionists both, encouraging them, however, not to go their separate ways but to engage each other in violent conflict. The slaves and hostages and guerrilla bands were to provide the insurance of such conflict. Southerners couldn't allow their peculiar institution to be traduced by abolitionists enjoying sanctuary in the North. Northerners couldn't countenance the invasion of their states by Southerners and federal soldiers in hot pursuit of runaways and marauders. More people would join the guerrilla republic. Both North and South would be committed to the struggle.

Between late February and early March 1858 Brown let the Six in on his plan. He couldn't conceal it any longer. Forbes had already informed them of it. Also how could he justify the amount of money and general support he was asking of them for a Kansas operation that was just about defunct? Day after day he patiently explained it to them, some at Gerrit Smith's place, others in Boston. With surprisingly few reservations, with a burst even of enthusiasm, they agreed to become his coconspirators, the sponsors of his essay in treason. And treason was what it was: They knew Brown was going to take on the federal government—it's perhaps what made the plan so attractive to them. (I discovered in John Weiss's *Life of Parker* something I missed in an earlier reading: Brown's interesting letter to Parker, master wordsmith, asking that he compose a statement addressed "to the officers and soldiers of the United States Army" to be sent out broadcast when the time came. "In the first place it must be short, or it will not be generally read. It must be in the simplest or plainest language; without the least affectation of the scholar about it, and yet be worded with great clearness and power. The anonymous writer must (in the language of the Paddy) be 'after others,' and not 'after himself, at all, at all.' . . . The address should be appropriate, and particularly adapted to the peculiar circumstances we anticipate, and should look to the actual change of service from that of Satan to the service of God. It should be, in short, a most earnest and powerful appeal to men's sense of right and to their feelings of humanity." Parker, content like the others to remain in the shadows of treason, would put his name to nothing that might implicate him in it. What Brown didn't realize was that he could have written a much better appeal of the sort he was requesting than could Parker.) The Six in fact came to know everything but the precise time and location of the attack, for them the least important feature of the plan. The Secret Six, cabalists without precedent in American history.

(The destruction of the incriminating evidence has left a hole in the record which the Six, their survivors and assigns, tried to fill with their memoirs and apologias—so many attempts, years after the awful event, to play down the brutal, outlawish, hardheaded nature of the project and exalt the romantically idealistic motives behind it. That's how they wished posterity to remember them.)

Now, they were responsible, intelligent, prudent men of affairs; they were all *political* men. It's nonsense to assume, as some of the critical biographies of them do, that they suddenly went off the deep end, that they were seduced by John Brown or became temporarily deranged or imagined themselves participants in a Walter Scott novel about Cavaliers and Roundheads (they were the Roundheads), and so forth. No, their decision to sponsor the plan was consistent with their long-professed ideological commitments; in a word, with their brand of political abolitionism.

The Republican party was an irresistible force; by the end of 1858 it held all but a few Northern states. But was it, or would it be, a *revolutionary* force? That was the question before antislavery radicals, among them the Six. Extraordinary shifts were taking place within and between parties—shifts which Republican moderates and conservatives and apparatchiks (a growing army) welcomed and radicals distrusted. For entering the party in massive numbers were people who'd recently been Democrats or Whigs or apostles of the Know-Nothing creed, people who'd hoped the slavery issue would disappear and some other transsectional issue take its place. In 1856 there were well over a million such voters and now, two years later, many of them (how many it would be impossible to estimate) were Republicans.† But they were more demonstrably antiblack and antiabolitionist than other Republicans, more inclined to give the South the benefit of the doubt (if only the South would let them), certainly more favorable to the idea of a modus vivendi, a policy of accommodation (if only the South would co-operate). Radicals, then, had reason to feel apprehensive. As the party advanced to power it ran the risk of losing its revolutionary soul. That's why for them the tempo of crisis had to be stepped up, why the new accessions to the party had to be radicalized, forced to confront the same extreme choices —accommodation on slavocrat terms or resistance—that the first generation of Republicans confronted, why the moderate-conservative faction must not dictate policy and strategy, or at least not be in the position to restrain events, quiet passions, and work toward a reconciliation with *their* Southern counterparts.

Those apprehensions make the conspiracy more intelligible. The Secret Six hoped John Brown's plan would call forth Southern ret-

† In 1856 Buchanan received about a million votes in the North, and Millard Fillmore, the Know-Nothing candidate, about half a million.

ribution, Kansifying the nation (now that Kansas was *hors de combat*), causing the Republican party, despite its conservatism, to become what it always had it in itself to be: the mass army of the revolution. The Secret Six, like Brown, fit the plan into the overarching frame of national politics.

Aside from money Brown's chief problem was getting recruits. Not mere fighting men but true believers. And where better to find them than among free blacks, many of whom by now had heard of him and knew they could trust him. (See W. E. B. Du Bois's biography of Brown, the only study to do justice to the subject of Brown's relation to blacks—to see it from the black standpoint.) So in the spring of 1858 he visited several of the sizable black communities in Brooklyn, Philadelphia, Rochester, Canada, to whose leaders J. N. Gloucester, J. W. Loguen, Henry H. Garnett, William Still, Harriet Tubman, Martin Delany, and of course his old friend Frederick Douglass, he freely confided his plan in general, omitting the details (and breathing not a word about his collaborators).

It was then he held his convention for blacks in Chatham, Canada, where he presented the Constitution on his biracial republic. This Constitution hasn't fared well in the John Brown literature, even from the friendliest of biographers. But the Chatham convention liked it. Brown's men liked it. I saw nothing particularly wrong with it. In the context of the period it was hardly remarkable. Everybody was writing constitutions. Every city, county, state in the country was holding conventions and drawing up constitutions. Every café in Europe must have produced at least one revolutionary constitution. So why reproach poor old John Brown for writing his own, as the earnest of his promise to blacks and others that a new age of freedom was imminent or possible? And there's no doubt that such a republic, if it could have been established, however small and beleaguered, would have caused the United States to take sharp notice of it. Very little, a handful of soldiers, came of the strenuous recruiting campaign. Blacks might admire John Brown and think well of his scheme, too. They weren't going to jeopardize everything—not only for themselves but for their people as well—in behalf of a project so remote, so dangerous, so contingent on large-scale white support. It was for them a pig in the poke.

Meanwhile, unstable Hugh Forbes was letting it all out, writing to Republican politicians that the Six were involved in treasonous conspiracy. A few of the Six panicked and were inclined to withdraw. Some issued disclaimers, prevaricating as necessary. (Dr. Howe's explanation to Senator Henry Wilson: "No countenance has been given to Brown for any operation outside of Kansas by the Kansas Committee." And: "Prompt measures have been taken and will resolutely be followed up to prevent any such monstrous perversion of a trust as would the application of means raised for the defense of Kansas to a purpose which the subscribers of the fund would disapprove and vehemently condemn.") So the plan, over Brown's and Higginson's and for that matter Howe's objections, was laid aside, Brown (now the bearded patriarch Shubel Morgan) and his men beating a hasty retreat back to Kansas.

(It would be interesting to speculate on what might have happened had he raided Harpers Ferry on schedule, say in the fall of 1858.)

He marked time in Kansas, taking part in several inconsequential military engagements. As a national issue Kansas was dead: Its inhabitants were waiting for the 1860 election, after which, presumably, a Republican President and Congress would ease its admission into the Union as a free state.

In the receding days of 1858 he and his guerrilla band conducted their famous incursion into Missouri to liberate slaves. (They had nothing else to do; they were bored.) Then followed the astonishing eleven-hundred-mile, two-month trek northward from lower Kansas to Canada, mostly on foot and wagon—he and his men and the eleven slaves (one of them born en route and named after him)—during which he dared the various posses to go after him and compelled the settlers along the way (I recalled his "Advice to the League of Gileadites," the classic tactic in guerrilla warfare) to choose between his motley outfit and his pursuers acting in the name of law and order. He was also gaining fresh notoriety throughout the land (and a huge price on his head). It was a grave matter, this running off of slaves, this threat to renew the

Kansas bloodletting, a threat felt above all by the Free Staters, who were now satisfied with the status quo and had no appetite to fight a war for liberated slaves. For them it was good riddance to John Brown.

On October 26 Nixon delivered an important foreign policy speech, his most important of the campaign. It carried dangerous implications, signaling to us (so we read them) what we could expect of him as President. Anticipating the possibility that Humphrey might make a spectacular pronouncement on the war—an acceptance perhaps of Communist negotiating terms— Nixon said he resolutely opposed a coalition government in Saigon as "thinly disguised surrender." "To the Communist side, a coalition government is not an exercise in cooperation but a sanctuary for subversion. Far from ending the war it would ensure its resumption under conditions that would guarantee Communist victory." Depressing words, for here undoubtedly was the next President speaking. What he was saying was that they, the Communists, would have to surrender, for a coalition was their minimal objective, one they couldn't abandon without abandoning everything.

And what made the speech so mischievous right now was the encouragement it gave General Thieu to resist the administration in the event the administration made a peace overture to the Communists. Thieu would procrastinate until Nixon took over. Then he'd have his way, and five hundred or more American boys would die every week in perpetuity.

I liked Wallace's remarks to a cheering West Texas audience (as reported in the October 29 Times). *Nixon, he said, is "one of those Eastern moneyed boys that looks down his nose at every Southerner and every Alabamian and calls us rednecks, woolhats, penpickers, and peckerwoods."*

10. THE RAID, 1859

Little need be said here beyond the technical details meticulously recorded in my notes of last year: the creation of a black and white army, twenty-two strong; a description of the men—an

unusual lot, the best of their generation, the first of their generation to give their lives for the abolition of slavery in America; the
renting of the Kennedy Farm in July; the storing there of arms
and pikes; the anonymous letter to Secretary of War John B.
Floyd telling everything, including the exact plan of the assault,
Floyd paying no heed to it; Frederick Douglass's decision not to
join; life on the farm day after day, week after week, surreptitiously moving about, preparing, training for the great event
(abundant, fascinating data on all of this); John Brown's com-
portment; the solemn departure for Harpers Ferry on October 16.

They could be likened to a group going out on a difficult and
hazardous military mission. There's nothing to indicate that they
went in order to sacrifice their lives for an ideal (the standard interpretation), though of course they were ready to do that, too.
Their objective—to become a guerrilla force operating out of the
mountains, exacerbating sectional tensions, radicalizing Northern
public opinion—was clearly defined for them, even if the raid itself wasn't.

As for the raid, some perspective might be in order. That it
should be subjected to microscopically critical analysis is understandable and right; such analysis is the price of (or chief punishment for) any failure. But on further review I thought my earlier
observation correct—that Brown made only one serious error of
execution, and that quite innocently. Yes, he temporized too long;
he should have taken to the mountains at once. And if he did let
the train go through, it was to inform the world; it was one of his
main reasons for being there. The innocent error was to allow Dr.
Starry to slip away and sound the tocsin of alarm. Hence, the sudden appearance of the civil guard which occupied the bridge, trap-
ping Brown and the others. The point is that the raid came close
to succeeding.

And why should Brown have had a blueprint to tell him precisely where the army, the hostages, and the slaves should go and
how they should set up the republic in the mountains? The best
tactic, perhaps, was to do as he did: play it by ear, improvise on
the spot, move about freely, without attachment to any particular
locale; a tactic which would have made it that much harder for the
authorities to track him down.

(I remarked on the contrast between Brown's humane treatment of these hostages and the mob's cannibalistic treatment of his men. I saw borne out again here the thesis that when he did commit heinously inhumane deeds—that is, Pottawatomie—it was for purely ideological or political reasons, not because of an insensate desire for revenge, a theological need to exact an eye for an eye, tooth for a tooth, and other such nonsense ascribed by critics to a weird, fanatical character called John Brown. After all, faced with certain death in the enginehouse, why didn't he kill his slaveholding hostages?)

The battle of the enginehouse: the presence of Robert E. Lee and Jeb Stuart; the horrible death of Brown's sons; his own incredible good luck in surviving the onslaught, Providence interposing for him at that miraculous instant, for Lieutenant Green intended to run him through. (Tolstoy would have appreciated how this ostensibly trivial fact—the size and weight of Green's sword, worn because he didn't happen to have his regulation sword—affected the course of history, mocking men's vanities and pretensions.) And Brown's reprieve—the final irony—which enabled him as a captive in a slavocrat prison to do what he couldn't have done as a guerrilla-provocateur: complete his mission.

On October 29, six days before the election, Eugene McCarthy grudgingly gave his support to Humphrey and advised his followers to do likewise. Was it too late to do any good? Yes, but let it be said that Humphrey could have earned McCarthy's favor sooner and more enthusiastically had he demonstrated more pluck on the war.

It was as though McCarthy had anticipated the next day's news. (Had he been told?) LBJ was ordering a halt to all bombing of North Vietnam. It was a huge concession because North Vietnam promised nothing in return except (what was already known) to negotiate "in an atmosphere that is conducive to progress." In other words, the possibility of negotiating an end to the war was raised for the first time since the United States began it in 1964. For we assumed (the telephone wires burned that night along the Upper West Side) that such negotiations would occur with or without the Thieu regime's acquiescence. How could Thieu refuse? How could he sabotage the proceedings? There was one way. By getting Nixon's support, Nixon the President-to-be. And

Nixon might have an interest in checking the peace move. We'd know soon enough.

11. TRANSFIGURATION AND DEATH, 1859

No abolitionist, not even John Brown himself, could have written the scenario so masterfully. It's as though another plan, invisibly superimposed on John Brown's, was guiding it to fulfillment while appearing to abort it.

The Southern response to the raid was everything Brown and his sponsors and Northern radicals in general could have hoped for. Southern moderates and conservatives had to abandon any possibility of reaching an accommodation with Republicans of a like temper. After Harpers Ferry how could Republican leaders be approached, much less dealt with? For it was well established by documents found on John Brown's person and at the Kennedy Farm that he was part of a conspiratorial network embracing prominent Northerners (none more prominent), members in good standing of the Republican party. These conspirators were extreme radical Republicans, but they were Republicans nonetheless and close to people in high places. Few Southerners were about to draw nice ideological distinctions between, say, Dr. Samuel Gridley Howe at one end of the spectrum and Thurlow Weed at the other, not to mention the subtler shades in between. Once upon a time Southern moderates (the likes of Benjamin H. Percy, Alexander H. Stephens, Sam Houston, Herschel V. Johnson) could have exploited such distinctions to their advantage, against the radicals in their own ranks. No longer. They'd lost their chance of controlling the destiny of the South.

If there was any question that the South and not the North would be cast in the "extremist" role preparatory to the 1860 election, Harpers Ferry settled it definitively. Southern firebrands of the William L. Yancey and Robert Barnwell Rhett persuasion had all along argued that there was no difference between Republicans except in appearance, that those who seemed most conciliatory to the South were the most dangerous because most mendacious, calculating, deceptive. That argument was now vindicated. John Brown represented authentic Republicanism (for which, therefore, he deserved the thanks of every honest Amerian), Republicanism stripped of its lies and hypocrisies. He gave the South (for which again he was to be thanked) a foretaste of what she should expect under a "Black Republican" President. For what Republicans really sought was not the containment of slavery but its abolition, and this by inciting a slave insurrection, race warfare to the death, followed by conquest and domination. Republicans cared not a fig about the blacks (only their white masters did). Republicans simply wanted to subjugate the South totally, irrevocably, reducing her to a colonial appanage of Northern bankers, manufacturers, and other capitalists.

Here, manifestly, was an argument the Southern moderates couldn't counter. They had to admit that the Republican party, conservatives no less than radicals, was as responsible for Harpers Ferry as the perpetrators themselves. By denouncing slavery as evil, by advocating its circumscription and ultimate extinction, the party encouraged, nay sanctioned, the outrages of abolitionist fanatics and other adventurers. It was its policy that prevented it from taking a sufficiently strong stand against the extremists in its rank (the Six, for example), much less disciplining them. To this extent, then, the secessionist firebrands were correct: John Brown was no aberration; he sprang from the loins of the antislavery movement; and Republicans couldn't now declare him an orphan. The Republican party had proved its inability to be a vehicle of accommodation, and should the Union collapse after the 1860 election the party must bear the entire obloquy for it.

(Now, it could be said—and it has been by historians of the period—that the South, having grown more and more paranoid, was ready to follow the lead of her "extremists"; it didn't require a heavy blow; Harpers Ferry was enough. Obviously that's true— but again, retrospectively. Nothing was inevitable at the time. Southern moderates and conservatives thought they had a chance in a sustained period of quiescence or diminishing tensions. Harpers Ferry shattered that chance. Would something else have shattered it if Harpers Ferry hadn't occurred? Perhaps. But if it hadn't, a split might have developed between the militants of the Deep South and the moderates in such states as Tennessee, Virginia, North Carolina, Arkansas, Texas, and Georgia, states where unionist sentiment was strongest. What we do know, at any rate, is

that the raid disarmed the moderates and provided the secession-
ists their lever of invincibility.)

Northern Democrats agreed with the Southern view that
Harpers Ferry could or should be linked to the Republican party,
that treason was implicit in the Republican position on slavery. To
neutralize that charge, which could damage the party's prospects,
each Republican faction in its own way repudiated Harpers
Ferry. Conservatives and moderates (like Lincoln) condemned it
for playing into the hands of the Democrats at the last minute, a
year before the election. Radicals adopted a more complicated attitude toward John Brown. Privately they welcomed the effect
Harpers Ferry was having on the South—it was grand provocation
if nothing else—but like the conservatives they didn't want to rock
the boat in their own section: Nothing could be allowed to interfere with the Republican triumph in 1860, especially since the
Deep South wasn't going to accept it and might make good the
threat to secede. It was, in short, a situation made to order for the
radicals. So, while they criticized Brown's deed they hailed the
man and his soldiers for their heroic idealism, their willingness,
their intention, to die as martyrs for a great cause. *Northern radicals depoliticized John Brown* (Southerners and Northern Democrats of course politicized him for all it was worth) and depicted
him as a saint who must be judged by transcendental rather than
worldly standards of justice, by the higher law of God, which he
served and so must be admired, pitied, prayed for.

Thus arose the myth of John Brown—the myth that he and his
compatriots stood outside the political pale. That Brown might
have had a rational plan of action, as rational—given the dimension of the political conflict—as any of the other strategies offered
by any of the other antislavery groups, was a possibility radical
Republicans preferred not to raise in public. The mythification of
John Brown furnished a useful cover for his political sympathizers: It was the ideal solution: to value him while casting him
into political exile.

(I'd noted several times how the Secret Six became, or made
themselves, part of that myth, and how their biographers have
propagated it further. The Six were moral men pure and simple,
innocent of politics, selflessly concerned to do right, etc., etc.)

Placing John Brown in this context of political myth-making, we can better appreciate his stupendous performance in court and in jail. He *was* a martyr. He seized on the chance to be one, no doubt of it. And what a chance! The whole world was his audience. (Victor Hugo was among his champions.) But to *perform* as one also happened to serve the purposes of the antislavery movement. Eschewing any mention of politics, any suggestion of a wide-ranging plan, keeping a stony silence about the conspiracy, never letting on that his mission was to provoke discord and revolt (not a slave revolt—so much he was eager to allow), John Brown comfortably occupied the ground cleared for him by his mythifiers. His patriarchial appearance, his brave conduct throughout the ordeal of battle and incarceration, the pathos of his life history, the travails of his family, his religiosity, his courtroom statement and jailhouse letters, biblical in their eloquence and power of righteousness (masterpieces of their genre) had their impact on the North. By the time he was executed on December 2 the myth had swept everything before it. He stood alone. The Republican party was safe.

(The myth, incidentally, passed through another stage before coming to rest. When the Civil War began a year and half after his death, Northerners appropriated it, embodied it in themselves: They too were enlisting in the moral crusade [for the Union if not against slavery]; they too were preparing themselves for martyrdom and sanctification. He had preceded them and his soul was marching with them.)

12. THE FACES OF PROPHECY

Sympathetic biographers and historians cite John Brown's last words to demonstrate his propheticism. He failed, his plan failed, everything came to nought, but the cause for which he sacrificed his life (and three of his children's lives) triumphed, and it triumphed just as he predicted it would, by fire and sword, by purging the sinful land in blood. This view of John Brown, it will be seen, is of a piece with his mythification—that is, his spiritualization and depoliticalization.

The emphasis, has been misplaced. John Brown's true propheticism lay not in his life as prisoner, handing down righteous judgments, warnings of retributions, bloody purges, and the like, but in his strategy of action, his approach to abolition, his plan. *His plan, not his words (moving, powerful as they were), anticipated the Civil War.* That plan was to bring about armed conflict between North and South as the necessary condition for emancipating the slaves. He recognized that the overwhelming mass of Northerners would never fight to free blacks—apart from everything else they were too racist ever to contemplate the possibility (hence the bankruptcy of the abolitionist movement, the impotence of Garrison et al.)—except incidentally, in the course of fighting for their own freedom, their own society. Brown's plan envisaged tying one to the other: black emancipation to white freedom. And because that is what happened in the fury of war we can call John Brown an American prophet.

November 7. Nixon's winning at least kept the election from the House. And though Wallace scored better than any previous third-party candidate (13.5 per cent of the vote) he didn't do anywhere near as well as everyone had expected. For that alone we were thankful. Would this mark his demise? I thought so. He had no state and local infrastructure to speak of, no grass-roots organization. (How different, in other words, from the Republican party of the 1850s which issued up from below on the strength of a principle, without relying on charismatic leaders.) And poor Humphrey! To have come so close to the Promised Land, to be denied it by seven tenths of one per cent! Pisgah.

And now that he'd at last be President would we witness yet another Richard Nixon, one corresponding to the political rebirth which he experienced? For those of us who feared the worst in him this was no light question. We searched for clues, portents, signs, sibylline utterances, hoping (against our wiser instincts) that here in fact was a metamorphosed Nixon who'd bring peace —the implied premise of his campaign, the reason he ran, the reason he won—and a modicum of good will and generosity to American politics. We'd settle for another Eisenhower.

We found solace in his victory statement. Frankly, I couldn't recall him ever saying anything better. To quote the Times: *"I saw many signs in this campaign. Some of them were not friendly and some were very friendly. But the one that touched me the most was the one that I saw in Deshler, Ohio, at the end of a long day*

of whistle-stopping, a little town I suppose five times the popula-
tion was there in the dark, almost impossible to see—but a teen-
ager held up a sign, 'Bring Us Together.'

"And that will be the great theme of this Administration at the
outset, to bring the American people together. This will be an
open Administration, open to new ideas, open to men and women
of both parties, open to critics as well as those who support us.

"We want to bridge the generation gap. We want to bridge the
gap between the races. We want to bring America together."

Our fears were somewhat assuaged.

3

By the end of November 1968 my outline of the John Brown
book was done. I had another canvas before me now, roughly
sketched in to be sure, but intelligible. Though he stood out in
bold relief, John Brown was assimilated in the whole picture, and
it remained for me only to paint it in—to determine whether the
picture I'd labored to produce coincided with the truth, whether
the documentary evidence—John Brown's papers, those of the Six
—falsified my hypothetical conclusions. I was confident they'd
bear me out; nothing in Sanborn or Villard or Malin (not to mention the countless others) led me to assume otherwise.

Once again I collected my notes, by now Himalayan in bulk and
disordered beyond reckoning, and stuffed them in a deep drawer
of my desk. With luck I'd return to them the following fall and,
the luck holding out, finish the manuscript for Doubleday by the
summer of 1970. That was my schedule.

As I put John Brown away I realized how far I'd come since
that July day the year before, the Detroit riot having just ended,
when the two black youths, in a conversation I couldn't help
overhearing, caused me to embark on this voyage of inquiry. I
now knew a great deal about Brown and the antislavery movement, and much of that I learned, especially about Northern
racism and what it meant to that movement, astonished me, giving
credence to the hypothesis or explanation of John Brown's plan
that I early on had formulated. I also realized, however, that I'd
returned, *corso e recorso,* to my earliest insight, one that came to

me on the very day I discovered Ruchames's *John Brown Reader* on my table and read it through from cover to cover. For then it occurred to me that he, John Brown, as an "extremist," was an organic part, an expression, of the crisis that took the country to war, that if the crisis itself was extreme, if the contest between slavery and freedom was extreme, so necessarily was every response to it, Abraham Lincoln's (representing moderation and prudence) no less than John Brown's, that the allegation of his fanaticism or monomania or madness, even if true, meant little since one's psyche, or pathology, interesting as that is in seeking out the reasons behind one's motives, intentions, purposes, etc.— the presumed springs of action—is inseparable from the historical dimension of that action (and, as I immediately perceived, historians who make so much of Brown's psyche were really informing me of their predilections, their judgment of the historical event, their identification with the moderates and opposition to the "extremists"). All my subsequent work on John Brown and his accomplices confirmed and deepened that insight.

It was an insight I mightn't have had but for the convulsive moment we were passing through. A moment of extremity, apocalypse, much like the 1850s. John Brown became as credible to me as his counterparts on the left were in 1967. Direct action in the name of conscience, righteousness, higher laws, physical resistance to habits or policies deemed intolerable, was something we were learning to take in stride, too. A witness to the life of my times, I was able during that year and a half to compose the picture of John Brown (setting him against the backdrop of *his* times) now fixed in my mind's eye.

Chapter Seven
Apologia Pro Vita Sua

In 1970 I took a full-time teaching job at Sarah Lawrence College, replacing at a stroke the harsh thralldom of a free-lancer's vocation with the pleasant one of a teacher's; the steady income, the time off, the prospect of lifelong tenure—these weren't unattractive. So I said adieu to Grub Street.

I went on marching and protesting against the war and on occasion ended up in jail (always with fifty dollars on hand to pay bond). I traveled to Washington and back like a commuter, by Metroliner at that—no more buses or cars if I could help it—a delightful three-hour respite. (One trip was notable. Arriving in Washington late in the morning, I hopped a cab to the Pentagon, joined a line of resisters who were attempting to push their way into the building past a cordon of giant black policemen, was arrested [with my friend Sol Resnik], and removed by bus to an internment camp. This set a record of economy of routine.)

The last of my antiwar visits to Washington was also the most dispiriting. I participated in the January 20, 1973, "counter-inaugural," hoping enough people would show up at it to disrupt the inaugural itself, the bright promise of President Nixon's next four years. It was a beastly cold wet day, and we were too few and our demoralization was too deep to pull anything off. (The police easily took care of random unorganized incidents.) We all knew in our chilled bones that we'd lost and Nixon had won, that the truce just worked out with Hanoi would keep the Thieu regime in power indefinitely, or at least until the next round of warfare broke out. After a few desultory speeches and songs we sadly made our way home.

Politically, there was hardly anything left to do. The various radical factions and sects held little interest for me, and I'd stopped writing for *New Politics,* my last active connection with the independent left.

My John Brown project receded into the distance, too. I lost touch with it in the hurly-burly of change, fresh beginnings, other projects. I'd often think about it and discuss it with friends. When I did, it was usually to defend Brown from invidious association with the murderous terrorist groups of recent years (e.g., Baader-Meinhof, Black September, the Japanese Revolutionary Army, the Symbionese Liberation Army, and so on). Their particular stock in trade is to draw world attention to their grievances by inflicting reprisals on innocent people (to them no one's innocent), often as not women, children, bystanders, anyone in the way. John Brown by contrast—the point needn't be labored *here*—was inseparably a part of a mass political movement which arose in response to a profound national crisis, embraced numerous and diverse strategies and ends, and was directed against a powerful, clearly defined, and supremely iniquitous opponent. But I noticed that it was becoming harder to gain a favorable ear for these distinctions, so great was the revulsion against terrorism as such.

Meanwhile, I was managing to keep up with the literature on John Brown. A proliferating literature: five major studies since 1970—Stephen B. Oates, *To Purge This Land with Blood;* Jules Abel, *Man on Fire;* Truman Nelson, *The Old Man: John Brown at Harper's Ferry;* Richard O. Boyer, *The Legend of John Brown;* and Benjamin Quarles, *Allies for Freedom*—each of them sympathetic to Brown without fawning on him. And through him they provide a further reassessment of ante-bellum America, honoring abolitionists precisely for their "extremism," and placing the burden of guilt and pathology on a society that nurtured or tolerated slavery only to extinguish it in a ferocious civil war. But I found nothing *new* in these studies: neither in their interpretations nor analyses nor presentations of evidence; and while their research is exhaustive (I refer here to Oates and Boyer, models of scholarship) they traverse the same ground—more accurately, more finely to be sure—covered by Sanborn and Villard and their epigones. Which isn't at all to diminish their value. I wasn't reading them from the general public's standpoint but with the tightly focused, bloodshot eye of the specialist who has a hypothesis lying dormant somewhere in the back of his mind.

And I was pleased that so many books and articles were now emphasizing the importance of white supremacism in shaping American history. Several struck me as quite fine: Leonard L. Richards, *"Gentlemen of Property and Standing"; Anti-Abolitionist Mobs in Jacksonian America;* Eric Foner, *Free Soil, Free Labor, Free Men**; George M. Fredrickson, *The Black Image in the White Mind;* Joel Kovel, *White Racism, a Psychohistory;* David Brion Davis, *The Problem of Slavery in the Age of Revolution;* and of course Winthrop Jordon's tour de force, *White over Black* (which I'd read all too hurriedly when it came out in 1968). But the works don't answer, to my satisfaction anyway, the questions I put to myself on discovering that white supremacism and democracy went hand in hand in the North, that the simultaneous rise of both might have been more than coincidental or merely concomitant—the question, namely, of what they owed each other, what common ethos they both sprang from. The answer awaits someone who will look fearlessly and clear-visioned into the cloacal depths of early formative American democracy.

I didn't forget the book *I'd* contracted to write. But I couldn't flog myself to undertake it. Least of all did I want to do a biography or study of John Brown along conventional lines, however unconventional its views or explanations. On more than one occasion, especially after receiving delicate inquiries from my editor, Loretta Barrett, I was tempted to throw up the project and return the advance. But I stopped short every time.

One day in the spring of 1974, I argued at length about John Brown with a colleague whose intelligence, knowledge, and moral sensitivity I respected. He wanted proof that Brown wasn't just another bloodthirsty ideologue and omelet-maker like the Palestinian terrorists who'd killed the Israeli athletes at the Munich

* Foner's book, which expands on his several articles published in the sixties, also points out that some Republicans publicly defended blacks and even went out of their way to help them; indeed whole communities did (e.g., the Western Reserve district of Ohio). But we come away from the book more convinced than ever that Republican antiracists were a small, ineffectual group indeed.

Olympics (this being his specific example). I went back to my drawerful of notes and papers; it was the first time in five years. What I beheld astonished me. A vast archive containing a record of daily events (mainly New York *Times* clippings) along with marginal comments on those events, plus other detritus—scraps and pieces of information, political, personal, familial, and other —gathered during those heated years 1967–68, plus (of course) the tons of material on Brown, his accomplices, his contemporaries, his epoch, plus an elaborate chapter-by-chapter outline or rather summing-up of the projected work.

Staring in wonder at this archaeological deposit, I remembered the whole experience, the time and suffering that went into producing it. And in that very instant I realized I now had my book: What else but the history of that whole experience, that encounter with John Brown, that exigent moment in my own life? I'd present the massif, properly reduced and ordered, pretty much as I'd accumulated it, doing justice to the sense of curiosity and discovery that had drawn me deeper and deeper, often against my better judgment, into his life and times, his *Erlebnis*. I resolved to leave it provisional, tentative, hypothetical, and keep the varied styles, the redundancies, asides, divagations, excursuses, making such changes as I had to for the sake of clarity and coherence. I'd be my own editor-amanuensis, furbishing the story of my journey through two disparate worlds.

And so I informed Loretta Barrett that I was working on the John Brown book after all and would one day, soon I hoped, have it on her desk. I should have added that it might not be the book she expected to get, that it would be about John Brown and me and our strange friendship, how and why it happened and what became of it.

Bibliography

In a sense the book itself is a bibliographical essay; another one here would be redundant. Below I specify the works I used roughly according to the order in which they are cited or figure even indirectly in the text. (For exhaustive surveys of the John Brown literature the interested reader should consult Oswald Garrison Villard, *John Brown* [to 1910], and Stephen B. Oates, *To Purge This Land with Blood* [to 1970].)

CHAPTER I

Louis Ruchames, *A John Brown Reader*. New York, 1959.

Allan Nevins, *Ordeal of the Union*. 2 vols. New York, 1947. Vol. 2.

Allan Nevins, *The Emergence of Lincoln*. 2 vols. New York, 1950. Vol. 2.

C. Vann Woodward, "John Brown's Private War," in Daniel Aaron, ed., *America in Crisis*. New York, 1952.

Charles Berg, *Clinical Psychology*. London, 1948.

Edward H. Williams, *The Doctor in Court*. Baltimore, 1929.

CHAPTER II

Richard B. Morris, ed., *Encyclopedia of American History*. New York, 1965.

Frederick Douglass, *Life and Times of Frederick Douglass*. Hartford, 1881.

Richard B. Morris, *Fair Trial*. New York, 1952.

CHAPTER III

James Redpath, *The Public Life of John Brown*. Boston, 1860.

James Redpath, *The Roving Editor*. New York, 1857.

Osborn P. Anderson, *A Voice from Harper's Ferry*. Boston, 1861.

Hermann E. von Holst, *John Brown*. Boston, 1888.

Joseph E. Chamberlin, *John Brown*. London, 1899.

Jonathan W. Winkley, *John Brown, the Hero*. Boston, 1905.

F. B. Sanborn, ed., *The Life and Letters of John Brown*. Boston, 1885.

F. B. Sanborn, *Reminiscences*. 2 vols. Boston, 1909.

Richard J. Hinton, *John Brown and His Men*. New York, 1894.

W. E. B. Du Bois, *The Souls of Black Folk*. Greenwich, 1965.

W. E. B. Du Bois, *The Negro Artisan*. Atlanta, 1902.

W. E. B. Du Bois, *Black Reconstruction*. Philadelphia, 1935.

W. E. B. Du Bois, *John Brown*. Philadelphia, 1909.

Oswald Garrison Villard, *Fighting Years, Memoirs of a Liberal Editor*. New York, 1939.

Michael Wreszin, *Oswald Garrison Villard, Pacifist at War*. Bloomington, 1965.

Oswald Garrison Villard, *John Brown*. New York, 1910.

Hill Peebles Wilson, *John Brown, Soldier of Fortune*. Lawrence, 1913.

Stanley J. Kunitz and Howard Haycraft, *Twentieth Century Authors*. New York, 1942.

Robert E. Spiller et al., eds., *Literary History of the United States*. New York, 3rd. ed., 1963.

Louis Rubin, ed., *I'll Take My Stand*. New York, 1962.

Robert Penn Warren, *Who Speaks for the Negro?* New York, 1965.

Robert Penn Warren, *John Brown, the Making of a Martyr*. New York, 1929.

James C. Malin, *John Brown and the Legend of Fifty-six*. Philadelphia, 1942.

CHAPTER IV

Octavius B. Frothingham, *Gerrit Smith, A Biography*. New York, 1909.

Ralph Volney Harlow, *Gerrit Smith, Philanthropist and Reformer*. New York, 1939.

Calendar of the Gerrit Smith Papers in the Syracuse University Library. Albany, 1941–42.

Samuel Gridley Howe, *An Historical Sketch of the Greek Revolution*, edited by George G. Arnakis. Austin, 1966.

Laura E. Richards, ed., *Letters and Journals of Samuel Gridley Howe*. Boston, 1906.

Laura E. Richards, *Samuel Gridley Howe*. New York, 1935.

Julia Ward Howe, *Memoir of Samuel Gridley Howe*. Boston, 1876.

F. B. Sanborn, *Dr. S. G. Howe, the Philanthropist*. New York, 1891.

Harold Schwartz, *Samuel Gridley Howe, Social Reformer 1801–1876*. Cambridge, 1956.

Theodore Parker, *Works*. 15 vols. Boston, 1907–13.

John Weiss, ed., *Life and Correspondence of Theodore Parker*. 2 vols. Boston, 1864.

Theodore Parker, *The Rights of Man in America*, edited by F. B. Sanborn. New York, 1911.

The Trial of Theodore Parker. Boston 1855.

Henry Steele Commager, *Theodore Parker*. Boston, 1960.

John W. Chadwick, *Theodore Parker: Preacher and Reformer*. Boston, 1900.

Octavius B. Frothingham, *Theodore Parker*. New York, 1880.

Thomas Wentworth Higginson, *Army Life in a Black Regiment*. New York, 1962.

Thomas Wentworth Higginson, *Cheerful Yesterdays*. Boston, 1898.

Thomas Wentworth Higginson, *Contemporaries*. Boston, 1899.

Mary Thacher Higginson, ed., *Letters and Journals of Thomas Wentworth Higginson*. Boston, 1921.

Thomas Wentworth Higginson, *The New Revolution*. Boston, 1857.

Thomas Wentworth Higginson, *A Ride Through Kanzas*. New York, 1856.

Thomas Wentworth Higginson, *Travelers and Outlaws*. Boston, 1889.

Tilden G. Edelstein, *Strange Enthusiasm*. New Haven, 1968.

Frank Preston Stearns, *The Life and Public Services of George Luther Stearns*. New York, 1907.

Ralph Waldo Emerson, *Remarks on the Character of George Luther Stearns*. Boston, 1872.

J. C. Furnas, *The Road to Harper's Ferry*. New York, 1959.

CHAPTER V

Chaplain Morrison, *Democratic Politics and Sectionalism*. Chapel Hill, 1967.

Charles Buxton Going, *David Wilmot, Free Soiler*. New York, 1924.

Eric Foner, "Racial Attitudes of the New York Free Soilers," *New York History*, Vol. 46.

Eric Foner, "Politics and Prejudice: The Free Soil Party and the Negro, 1849–1852," *Journal of Negro History*, Vol. 50.

Wendell Phillips Garrison and Francis Jackson Garrison, *William Lloyd Garrison, the Story of His Life*. 4 vols. New York, 1885–89.

William Lloyd Garrison, *Selections from Writings and Speeches*. Boston, 1852.

The Liberator. Boston, 1831–59.

Aileen Kraditor, *Means and Ends in American Abolitionism.* New York, 1967.

John L. Thomas, *The Liberator.* Boston, 1963.

Walter M. Merrill, *Against Wind and Tide.* Cambridge, 1963.

Martin F. Duberman, ed., *The Anti-Slavery Vanguard.* Princeton, 1965.

Benjamin P. Thomas, *Theodore Weld, Crusader for Freedom.* New Brunswick, 1950.

Lorman Ratner, *Powder Keg; Northern Opposition to the Antislavery Movement.* New York, 1968.

James Bach McMaster, *A History of the People of the United States.* 8 vols. New York, 1893–1911. Vol. 6.

Joel T. Headley, *The Great Riots of New York.* New York, 1873.

Joel T. Headley, *Pen and Pencil Sketches of the Great Riots.* New York, 1882.

Leon Litwack, *North of Slavery.* Chicago, 1961.

Dan King, *The Life and Times of Thomas Wilson Dorr.* Boston, 1859.

Martin R. Delany, *The Condition, Elevation, Emigration and Destiny of the Colored People.* Philadelphia, 1852.

Edgar J. McManus, *A History of Negro Slavery in New York.* Syracuse, 1966.

W. E. B. Du Bois, *The Philadelphia Negro.* Philadelphia, 1899.

Sterling B. Spero and Abram L. Harris, *The Black Workers: The Negro and the Labor Movement.* New York, 1931.

Charles H. Wesley, *Negro Labor in the United States, 1850–1925.* New York, 1927.

Phillip M. Foner, ed., *The Life and Writings of Frederick Douglass.* 4 vols. New York, 1950–55.

Ohio Anti-Slavery Convention of 1835. Cincinnati, 1835.

The National Trades' Union. New York, 1834–37.

Proceedings of the Colored National Convention of 1855. Philadelphia, 1855.

John R. Commons et al., eds., *Documentary History of American Industrial Society.* 10 vols. Cleveland, 1909–11. Vols. 5–8.

Bernard Bandel, *Labor: Free and Slave.* New York, 1955.

Herman Schlüter, *Lincoln, Labor and Slavery.* New York, 1965.

Joseph G. Rayback, *A History of American Labor.* New York, 1967.

Williston H. Lofton, "Abolition and Labor," *Journal of Negro History,* Vol. 33.

George E. McNeil, ed., *The Labor Movement.* New York, 1886.

The Colored American. New York, 1837–42.

Roy P. Basler, ed., *Abraham Lincoln, the Collected Works.* 8 vols. New Brunswick, 1953. Vols. 3–7.

Albert Fried and Gerald E. Stearn, eds., *The Essential Lincoln.* New York, 1962.

Andrew W. Crandell, *The Early History of the Republican Party 1854–56.* Boston, 1930.

David M. Potter, *Lincoln and His Party in the Secession Crisis.* New Haven, 1942.

Kenneth Stampp, *And the War Came.* Baton Rouge, 1950.

Charles H. Wesley, "Lincoln's Plan for Colonizing the Emancipated Negroes," *Journal of Negro History,* Vol. 4.

Eugene H. Berwanger, *The Frontier Against Slavery.* Urbana, 1967.

V. Jacques Voegeli, *Free But Not Equal.* Chicago, 1967.

James S. Pike, *The Prostrate State: South Carolina Under Negro Government,* New York, 1874.

Robert F. Durden, *James S. Pike: Republicanism and the American Negro 1850–1882.* Durham, 1957.

James M. McPherson, *The Struggle for Equality.* Princeton, 1964.

Che Guevara, *The Diary of Che in Bolivia.* Calcutta, 1968.

CHAPTER VI

Winthrop Jordon, *White over Black.* Chapel Hill, 1968.

Paul Ricoeur, *The Symbolism of Evil.* Boston, 1967.

Alexis de Tocqueville, *Democracy in America.* 2 vols. New York, 1954.

Marvin Meyers, *The Jacksonian Persuasion.* New York, 1960.

Frederick Grimké, *The Nature and Tendency of Free Institutions.* Cambridge, 1968.

Moisei I. Ostrogorski, *Democracy and the Party System in the United States.* New York, 1910.

John W. Ward, *Andrew Jackson, Symbol for an Age.* New York, 1955.

CHAPTER VII

Stephen B. Oates, *To Purge This Land with Blood.* New York, 1970.

Jules Abel, *Man on Fire.* New York, 1971.

Truman Nelson, *The Old Man: John Brown at Harper's Ferry.* New York, 1973.

Richard O. Boyer, *The Legend of John Brown.* New York, 1973.

Benjamin Quarles, *Allies for Freedom.* New York, 1974.

Leonard L. Richards, *"Gentlemen of Property and Standing"; Anti-Abolition Mobs in Jacksonian America.* New York, 1970.

Eric Foner, *Free Soil, Free Labor, Free Men*. New York, 1970.

George M. Fredrickson, *The Black Image in the White Mind*. New York, 1971.

Joel Kovel, *White Racism, a Psychohistory*. New York, 1971.

David Brion Davis, *The Problem of Slavery in the Age of Revolution*. Ithaca, 1975.

INDEX